D0223851

AGGRESSION

This title is part of the PSYCHOANALYTIC **ideas** series, which brings together the best of Public Lectures and other writings given by analysts of the British Psychoanalytical Society on important psychoanalytic subjects.

Series Editors: Inge Wise and Paul Williams

Other titles in the Psychoanalytic ideas Series:

AGGRESSION

From Fantasy to Action

Edited by

Paul Williams

Psychoanalytic Ideas Series

KARNAC

First published in 2011 by
Karnac Books Ltd
118 Finchley Road, London NW3 5HT

Copyright © 2011 to Paul Williams for the edited collection, and to the
individual authors for their contributions.

The rights of the contributors to be identified as the authors of this work
has been asserted in accordance with §§ 77 and 78 of the Copyright
Design and Patents Act 1988.

All rights reserved. No part of this publication may be reproduced,
stored in a retrieval system, or transmitted, in any form or by any means,
electronic, mechanical, photocopying, recording, or otherwise, without
the prior written permission of the publisher.

British Library Cataloguing in Publication Data

A C.I.P. for this book is available from the British Library

  ISBN 978 1 85575 891 9

Edited, designed and produced by The Studio Publishing Services Ltd
www.publishingservicesuk.co.uk
e-mail: studio@publishingservicesuk.co.uk

www.karnacbooks.com

CONTENTS

ABOUT THE EDITOR AND CONTRIBUTORS

John, Lord Alderdice, FRCPsych, was appointed Ireland's first Consultant Psychiatrist in Psychotherapy in 1988, retiring in 2010 both from the Centre for Psychotherapy he had established in Belfast and as Visiting Professor at the University of Virginia. He applied his psychological ideas on political conflict resolution in various parts of the world, but especially in Northern Ireland as Alliance Party Leader (1989–1998), a negotiator of the 1998 Belfast Agreement, Speaker of the Northern Ireland Assembly (1998–2004), and later an international commissioner on terrorist violence (2004–2011). He was the President of Liberal International, the world-wide federation of liberal political parties (2005–2009) and is currently Chairman of the Liberal Democrat Party in the House of Lords and Chairman of the World Federation of Scientists Permanent Monitoring Panel on Motivations for Terrorism.

Anne Alvarez, PhD, MACP, is a consultant child and adolescent psychotherapist (and retired Co-Convener of the Autism Service, Child and Family Department, Tavistock Clinic, London). She is author of *Live Company: Psychotherapy with Autistic, Borderline, Deprived and Abused Children*, and has edited, with Susan Reid,

Autism and Personality: Findings from the Tavistock Autism Workshop. A book in her honour, edited by Judith Edwards, entitled *Being Alive: Building on the Work of Anne Alvarez* was published in 2002. She was Visiting Professor at the San Francisco Psychoanalytic Society in November 2005, and is completing a book on levels of psychotherapeutic technique with severely disturbed and developmentally delayed children.

Donald Campbell is a training analyst and past President of the British Psychoanalytical Society, former Secretary General of the International Psychoanalytical Society, and previously served as Chairman of the Portman Clinic, an out-patient NHS facility in London that offers psychoanalytic psychotherapy to violent and delinquent patients and those suffering from a perversion. He has written on the subjects of violence, aggression, suicide, child sexual abuse, perversion, and adolescence.

Paola Capozzi is a psychiatrist and psychoanalyst of the Italian Psychoanalytical Society, and works in private practice in Milan. She has published papers on dreams and psychosis and on sexuality. She has edited the Quaderni del Centro Milanese di Psicoanalisi, including the *Herbert Rosenfeld. Italian Seminars,* and *Eric Brenman. Clinical and Theoretical Work.*

Franco De Masi is a Training Analyst of the Italian Psychoanalytical Society and former President of the Centro Milanese di Psicoanalisi and Secretary of the Training Institute of Milan. His main interests have been focused on the theoretical and technical psychoanalytical issues related to severely ill or psychotic patients. His books include: *Sadomasochistic Perversion: The Object and Theories* (Karnac, 2003); *Making Death Thinkable: A Psychoanalytical Contribution to the Problem of the Transience of Life* (Free Association Books, 2004); *Vulnerabilty to Psychosis* (Karnac, 2006); *The Enigma of Suicide Terrorism* (Karnac, 2011). He edited the book: *Herbert Rosenfeld at Work. Italian Seminars* (Karnac, 2001). In Italian: *Karl Abraham: alle origini della teoria analitica.* (Karl Abraham: At the Roots of Psychoanalytical Theory) (Armando Roma, 2002).

James Gilligan, MD, is a clinical professor of psychiatry in the School of Medicine and Adjunct Professor in the School of Law,

New York University. From 1966 to 2000 he was on the faculty of the Harvard Medical School, where he was responsible for providing mental health and violence prevention services to the Massachusetts prison system. He was President of the International Association for Forensic Psychotherapy, 1999–2001. He has served as a consultant to, or been appointed to, advisory commissions by the World Court, the World Health Organization, the World Economic Forum, the Secretary General of the United Nations, President Clinton, Tony Blair, MP, and the Law Lords of the House of Lords on matters relating to the causes and prevention of violence. He is the author of *Violence: Reflections on Our Deadliest Epidemic*, and *Preventing Violence*.

Richard Ingram is a Consultant Psychiatrist working in the Belfast Health and Social Care Trust, where he provides services in Forensic Psychotherapy and Psychosexual Medicine. He is a Fellow of the Royal College of Psychiatrists and a Member of the Institute of Psychoanalysis. From 2004 he has been Chair of the Northern Ireland Association for Psychoanalysis, a training organisation for psychoanalytic psychotherapy in Northern Ireland.

Philip McGarry is Chair of the Royal College of Psychiatrists in Northern Ireland. He is a consultant psychiatrist who leads the Home Treatment Team in the Belfast Trust. He has a major interest in policy development and public education in mental health. He has had a long-standing interest in suicide, publishing a paper on this topic in 1988, and he is currently a member of the Northern Ireland Suicide Strategy Implementation Board. As a trainee psychiatrist, Dr McGarry worked with the late Dr Tom Freeman. He is a supervisor in interpersonal psychotherapy and has worked with the Belfast Trust to develop an IPT service.

Carine Minne is Consultant Psychiatrist in Forensic Psychotherapy at the Portman Clinic (Tavistock & Portman NHS Foundation Trust) and Broadmoor Hospital (West London Mental Health NHS Trust). She is also a psychoanalyst with the British Psychoanalytical Society. She was the first psychiatrist to be dually trained in forensic psychiatry and psychotherapy, working in NHS forensic psychiatry settings where she also applied her psychoanalytic training. Her special interest is the provision of long-term continuity of psychotherapy with same therapist for some patients treated in high security who eventually move through medium security, low security, and back to the community, where their treatment continues. She is the Training Programme Director for the North West London junior psychiatrists' training in forensic psychotherapy and chairs the Royal College of Psychiatrists' special interest group in that speciality.

Maria O'Kane is a consultant psychiatrist in psychotherapy in the Belfast HSC Trust. Her interests are in working with patients with severe disturbance who are deemed as 'risky' to themselves or others, namely patients who self harm and those who present with significant personality disorder.

Marianne Parsons is a psychoanalyst working with children, adolescents and adults. Formerly Head of Clinical Training at the Anna Freud Centre and editor of the *Journal of Child Psychotherapy*, she has contributed several papers to books and journals. For nearly twenty years she was Consultant Child and Adolescent Psychotherapist at the Portman Clinic, London, where she was a member of the Violence Research Group led by Mervin Glasser and developed a special interest in children and adolescents who act violently. She was also Course Director of the Portman Clinic Diploma in Forensic Psychotherapeutic Studies. She now works in private practice. She teaches and supervises for a number of training schools, and is a visiting lecturer for psychoanalytic trainings in Finland and Florida.

Paul Williams is a training and supervising analyst with The British Psychoanalytical Society and a member of the Royal Anthropological Institute. He was a consultant psychotherapist in the British National Health Service, retiring in 2010. From 2001–2007 he was Joint Editor-in-Chief, with Glen O. Gabbard, of the *International Journal of Psychoanalysis*. He has published widely on the subject of severe disturbance. He lives and practises in Hampshire, UK.

Marie Zaphirou Woods, F.Inst.Psychoanal., is a psychoanalyst working with children, adolescents, and adults. She is currently the clinical lead for the Child Psychotherapy Service at the Anna Freud

Centre, having previously managed the Anna Freud Centre Nursery and the Parent–Toddler Service. She works privately with children, adolescents, and adults, and teaches and supervises for a number of training schools. She is a training analyst and supervisor for the British Association of Psychotherapists. She has published a number of articles and book chapters, and co-edited, with Inge Pretorius, *Parents and Toddlers in Groups: A Psychoanalytic Developmental Approach* (Routledge, 2011).

Paul Williams

This two day conference—the second International Psychoanalytic Conference to take place in Belfast, Northern Ireland—convened in extraordinary circumstances. During and prior to the period of the conference, the region experienced the effects of the volcanic eruption in Iceland that sent volcanic ash high into the atmosphere, affecting air travel throughout Europe. In the days prior to the conference many airports were closed completely, including those in Northern Ireland. Speakers and delegates had their flights cancelled, some many times over, and for a brief period the conference seemed to be in jeopardy when it appeared as though the ash might cripple most of the air traffic into Northern Ireland during the two days of the event. News arrived of the enormous efforts delegates and speakers were making to attend: switching of routes, opting for trains and ships, taking to cars, and so on. An emergency format was arranged so that speakers unable to travel could give their lectures via audio link to the delegates who could make it. In the event, three speakers were unable to attend in person—Rosine Perelberg, Anne Alvarez and Don Campbell—as they were stranded in London, unable to fly due to the ash. The rest, by dint of perseverance, ingenuity, and breaks in the weather, were able to make it, sometimes with only minutes to spare. The same situation applied to delegates, who came from all quarters of the globe and who negotiated the troubles of European air space to take their seats in the Hilton Hotel, Belfast, where, amazingly, there turned out to be almost a full house. What follows is a transcription of the papers that were delivered to the conference, together with edited summaries of discussions from the floor that followed each paper. There are a small number of omissions from this book: Rosine Perelberg spoke from notes, so her paper is not available, and portions of discussions from the floor of workshops were, unfortunately, not recorded due to technical difficulties.

The standard of the papers given was extremely high. What was noticeable from the outset of the conference was the intensity of focus on understanding the origins of aggression and violence from a psychoanalytic perspective. This intensity persisted throughout the two days, leading to a number of fascinating discussions. A debt of gratitude is owed to everyone who organized and participated in the conference to make it such a success, under uniquely adverse circumstances. Special thanks are due to The Royal College of Psychiatrists in Northern Ireland, to Nora McNairney, who organized the conference, and to Lisa Losty and Liz Main for their invaluable help in helping to make the conference a reality.

Introduction

Philip McGarry, Chair, Royal College of Psychiatrists in Northern Ireland

Welcome, everybody, to the conference. Am I glad to see you all here! They say in Northern Ireland that we have lots of weather and normally we are hoping it will not be raining or terribly windy or cloudy all day; however, I was delighted this morning to hear that there were winds blowing the volcanic ash away from Ireland, and that the airports were open. Thank you all for coming. Some delegates will be coming a little late and also some of our speakers will not be able to be here in person as a result of the ash, but they will be here via audio link, including two of our speakers this morning.

This Conference, the second International Psychoanalytic Conference organized in Belfast, is sponsored by five key organizations: The Royal College of Psychiatrists, The Centre for Psychotherapy, the Belfast Trust, the Northern Ireland Association for the Study of Psychoanalysis, the Northern Ireland Institute of Human Relations, and the British Psychoanalytic Society. I would like to thank all these partners for the tremendous work they have put in over the past eighteen months organizing the conference. We are also very grateful for support from a number of organizations, including the Department of Health, Belfast City Council, The Northern Ireland

Assembly, and Pfizer for their support. Thank you very much for all the help you have given to this conference.

Today's topic—aggression, including violence—is a very important one and, of course, a challenging and potentially controversial one. It is always slightly concerning that, in the middle of a general election campaign, as we are now, when the debate moves on to crime, the quality of the intellectual debate goes down and we invariably hear simplistic statements about good and evil. Part of the point of a conference such as this is to look at this challenging and difficult topic in an intelligent way, and I know that this will happen over the next two days. We are delighted that we have such a distinguished panel of speakers to talk to us on these topics. We are pleased, in Northern Ireland psychiatry, to have a very good working relationship with the Department of Health and we know that the Department of Health has tried to prioritize mental health at a time when resources are very limited, and we are delighted that the Department of Health has been working over the past two years to put together a strategy for psychological therapies. This brought together the professional groups, the users, the patients, the carers, and it is a tremendous strategy in that it gives priority to psychotherapy. Clearly, in this current financial situation, it is vitally important that we are able to generate the funds to make sure this strategy is implemented. We are very pleased today that Dr Michael McBride is going to open our conference. Dr McBride is the Chief Medical Officer for Northern Ireland and he has an incredibly busy schedule, a man who has to deal with whatever the world throws at him. It could be the H1N1 virus, otherwise known as "swine flu". It can be the reorganization of the Health Service in Northern Ireland, which is a challenging task, and, of course, dealing with the challenges of managing our local politicians who take an interest in health and who sometimes can be constructive and informed and sometimes are not quite so constructive and informed. I know that Dr McBride has an interest in mental health and, indeed, I recall that a number of years ago I had a patient who was a patient of Michael's. My clinic was on the ninth floor of the Royal Victoria Hospital and Michael was working on the third floor and we were dealing with a patient who was known to both of us and was clearly very unwell. The man was, in fact, manic, and we tried every which way to intervene, but it was inevitably going to be admission to hospital. Michael stayed until well into the evening waiting for the approved social worker and other people to come along, and we had a useful discussion during that time about mental illness. I was deeply impressed that Michael showed an understanding of mental health in a way that not all physicians do. We very much appreciate his coming to speak to us today.

One or two brief housekeeping rules: we will be taking a few photographs purely for internal use. Also, inside your pack, in the programme you will find a change to this morning's events. The second session this morning, which would have been Dr Anne Alvarez, will be this afternoon at half past two, and Professor Perelberg's session will come this morning after coffee. There are feedback forms in your pack, so please fill these in as they are incredibly useful. Our fist presentation this morning will be via audio link from Donald Campbell. Dr Richard Ingram will chair the session in place of Dr Siobhan O'Connor. Dr O'Connor is on her way via cars, boats, and trains, and will be here shortly, but she probably will not have slept overnight and Dr Ingram has kindly stepped in. After Dr Campbell speaks, there will be chance for a discussion. Someone will go round with a roving microphone to take questions. Thank you again for coming, and thank you Dr McBride, Chief Medical Officer, for giving up your time to speak to us this morning. Dr Michael McBride.

Michael McBride, Chief Medical Officer, Northern Ireland

Thanks for those kind words of introduction, Philip, and good morning, ladies and gentlemen. Could I add my warm welcome to Northern Ireland and to Belfast. First, can I say that after all the recent travel problems it is a delight to see that so many of you have been able to make it here. I am sure each of you have stories to tell of some of the many challenges you have faced coming here. I do, as Philip said, get up-to-date information on a range of things. I deal with many issues, and one thing I get is three-hourly updates on where this volcanic ash is heading and some of the health and travel implications, so, if you have time over coffee, I will look at my Blackberry and let you have the latest updates I get. I am also conscious that many of you have travelled from all around the world, and I am particularly delighted that Northern Ireland has been chosen for this, the second conference, and, one hopes, not just because of our sometimes troubled and violent past. Interestingly, Northern Ireland has increasingly become a tourist destination and has attracted more and more visitors over the past few years. I am aware that you are having your conference dinner this evening in one of our finest old buildings, Belfast's City Hall. I would also recommend, if you have time, that you take one of our many city tour buses, which will educate you in our more recent troubles, including through the colour murals, which are a highly visual expression of people in those communities, and you can see the transition in terms of the manifestations of these murals in recent times. I think they are a reflection, windows into communities in terms of how we have managed to move on both politically and also as a society. Having done my bit to promote the local tourist economy, I must move on and note your choice of the challenging and emotive topic of "Aggression" for your conference.

As you explore your understanding of aggression and violence, I see that you are going to hear about and discuss these topics in a variety of settings, including the social and political aspects with which we are very familiar here in Northern Ireland, given our recent past. I believe there is a key message here for the public, and also for our politicians and all of us in public life, in that aggression and violence has to be viewed within a societal context. We must continue to promote the fact that within society the contribution to violence of mental illness is low, and thus avoid adding to the stigma already faced by people with mental health problems by enforcing often misguided public opinion. As you will all know, despite the occasional high profile case that increases public fear of mentally ill people and is often accompanied by outcry for more restrictive practices within our services, the vast majority of violence is not perpetrated by people with a mental illness. This is especially true in cases of stranger homicide, which attracts particular public interest. Instead, our focus needs to be on promoting the work of experts in the field like each and every one of you in this room, who are seeking to understand the complex associated factors and causes of violence in order to truly reduce long-term risk throughout society. While not claiming any psychotherapeutic expertise, I would like to use a couple of quotes some of you may be familiar with to illustrate what I feel is the importance of psychotherapy. Both are, appropriately, by Plato, who first said "if we are ever to have pure knowledge of anything we must get rid of the body and contemplate things by themselves with the soul by itself". And it is not just having knowledge or understanding that is important; Plato, when talking about intervention, also said this, "and therefore if the head and body are to be well you must begin by curing the soul, that is the first thing and the cure, my dear youth, has to be effected by use of certain charms and these charms are fair words". So, Plato endorsed talking therapies some time ago, but is ancient wisdom enough now in a world of cost effectiveness and evidence base? As Phil has said, we face very challenging times economically, and our services will come under increasing pressure. At such times of economic uncertainty within many health services, events like this conference are so important in ensuring that psychotherapy, particularly, is recognized as effective in the management of our most complex cases. Equally, as we move towards the goal of increasing the choice available to those who use our mental health services through what is often called a more personalized approach, it is events like this conference, through media coverage, that can raise the public profile and benefits of psychotherapy, and I congratulate the organizers for providing such an attractive and stimulating programme.

As Dr McGarry has already referred to, in Northern Ireland we have had an independent review to modernize our mental health policy legislation and services. It was named the Bamford Review, after its late chair, Professor David Bamford. This review recommended that psychological services be developed, and the government response, published last year, was an action plan that included the development of a strategy to improve access to psychological therapies. This psychological therapies strategy is reaching its final stages prior to publication, and, as some of the audience who have been involved will know, it stresses the need to develop psychological therapies as a core component of all mental health services. I know that this strategy has been long awaited and will provide the framework for future service development over the coming years.

Finally, one particularly striking aspect for me, from a public health perspective, in your programme is the emphasis on children and their early acting out of violence. I thought of my own experience, while I was in P1 at school, and I could think back to certain children in P1 who had problems that I recognized, aged five years of age, at six years of age, and at seven years of age. They were children whom I avoided in the playground. Some of my classmates who ended up either at Her Majesty's pleasure in certain institutions, or who got caught up in the violence here in Northern Ireland, and others who grew up in various parts of Belfast during the times of the troubles, will have similar stories to tell. I think it is important that we concentrate on children and, in particular, on the early years increasingly in terms of public health. We know that the early interventions are the particularly important ones. I do not need to mention recent cases widely covered in the media that demonstrate the potential for young people towards violence, but the real message for me is that it is only by addressing the associated factors and causes of morbidity at an early stage within people's lives that we are likely to achieve the greatest benefit for society as a whole. I do not wish to hold up the proceedings any longer: you have a very busy day ahead of you. I would once again congratulate all the organizers and sponsors, and wish you well over the next two days in tackling these difficult issues. I hope you enjoy your visit to Belfast, and look forward to receiving colleagues' feedback from the conference. Thank you very much for the invitation to speak to you this morning, and I hope to be able to stay and speak to some of you over coffee. Thank you very much.

CHAPTER ONE

The nature and function of aggression

Donald Campbell

Dr Richard Ingram introduces Mr Donald Campbell

"Well, it is an unexpected pleasure for me, in the absence of Siobhan O'Connor, to introduce our keynote speaker, Don Campbell. For those of you who do not know about Don's career, it is a very distinguished psychoanalytic career. Don has been a past president of the British Psychoanalytic Society, Secretary General of the International Psychoanalytic Association and has worked for over thirty years in the National Health Service at the Portman Clinic in London. Within the British Society, he is a training analyst, and he has published widely on a range of topics, including violence, suicide, perversion, and adolescence. It is with great pleasure that I pass over to Don to speak to us today."

Donald Campbell: "Good morning everyone. I hope you can all hear me and get used to this way of communicating with each other. When I thought about having to present my paper to you over the phone, I thought back to my days as a child listening to the radio, and I hope this will be a bit like listening to a good radio programme. I want to thank the organizers for inviting me to present this keynote address to what I think is an unusually well organized conference. By that I mean it has brought together people who have had clinical experience with violent and aggressive patients and this is true, I think, of everyone who is presenting. I am very impressed with the way this conference has been organized. I want to thank Nora McNairney and Lisa Losty for their really stalwart efforts to pull things together when the volcanic ash curtailed our flights to Belfast and to give you my apologies for not being with you today. I have not only had my flight cancelled, but I have been extremely anxious about being able to get back from Belfast, even if I had got to see you there, in order to get back for my son's wedding, which is this weekend. So it has been a fraught time on many fronts."

Introduction

Mr Davis was one of the first violent patients that I saw at the Portman, thirty-seven years ago. His father had left home in his first year. As a youngster, Mr Davis's antisocial behaviour was too much to manage for his depressed mother and the local school. He was sent to a boarding school when he was nine years old. There were hints that he had been sexually abused by one of the teachers. Mr Davis was a loner who occasionally worked on building sites. He was referred to the Portman because he was habitually getting into pub fights after bouts of drinking. When I brought my early sessions with Mr Davis to a peer supervision group, I was made aware that I was defending against the anxieties I felt about his potential for violence towards me to such an extent that I was out of touch with Mr Davis's potential for violence in the consulting room. I was asked if I thought it was safe to have a glass ashtray on my desk within easy reach of Mr Davis. (You can tell how long ago this was by the fact that smoking was still allowed in NHS establishments.) I was embarrassed and alarmed that I had not thought about it. I removed the ashtray immediately.

As he sat down for the start of the next session, Mr Davis said, with a barely disguised sense of triumph, "I noticed you removed the ashtray." I cannot remember whether I said anything in reply or kept silent. But to this day I remember feeling that I had been caught out and I felt ashamed that my fear of Mr Davis's violence had been publicly exposed.

Aggression is, by definition, hostile and destructive. I do not have to remind the citizens of Northern Ireland that aggression, particularly its physical expression in violence, is, in reality, dangerous. It can hurt. It can wound. It can kill. So, when we are with someone who has been violent, it is not the probability of violence, but the possibility, the chance of it occurring, that eats away at our minds. That is the rock bottom reason why we mental health professionals unconsciously and consciously defend ourselves against the violent individuals we are working with. We can try to put that fear out of our mind, or we can use the "small dull smears of meditative panic", as the writer Don DeLillo put it in *Point Omega*, to sharpen our attention in the here and now. The peer supervision group and I first thought of ourselves as potential victims and acted in a self-protective way, initially by denial, on my part, and by recommending action on the group's part. In addition, I had felt shamed by my exposure in the peer supervision group. These responses undermined my thinking about the perpetrator and led to action. I would not be surprised if we all struggle against these reactions during the conference.

For many mental health professionals, the word "unthinkable" starts us thinking. So, when I thought further about this incident, I could see that I reacted to the group's projection of their anxiety about Mr Davis's violence. Neither the group nor I were able to use our anxiety to think about what was going on between Mr Davis and me. Instead, I relied upon action to protect myself. It is not uncommon for the victim to defend him or herself by identifying with the aggressor. To the extent that I acted by removing the ashtray, I was unconsciously identifying with the aggressor, Mr Davis. I think this is a common mistake, which often occurs unconsciously. As you can see, there were consequences for my therapeutic work with Mr Davis.

First, I had failed to appreciate how dangerous I was as a transference figure for Mr Davis and the importance of a weapon for ensuring Mr Davis's safety. He had often used broken glass beer bottles in his pub fights. Removing the glass ashtray, an act that was intended to help me feel safe, had effectively disarmed Mr Davis, increased his feelings of defencelessness, and put me more at risk. Second, Mr Davis now knew that beneath my professional exterior and neutral façade I was personally anxious about his violence. And this made Mr Davis more anxious. I knew that behind his triumphant tone, Mr Davis was anxious that my fear of his violence obscured my view of him as a whole person, and diminished my capacity to help him. I knew enough about Mr Davis to know that he resorted to violence when he felt his paranoid projections were confirmed. In subsequent sessions, it emerged that by acting as I did, I confirmed his expectation that I was like him, that I also dealt with my fears by resorting to action. In addition, I confirmed Mr Davis's fear that I, like all the authorities he had faced before, could not and would not think about his violence with him, but that I would have to do something about it. I wanted to begin this presentation the way I will end it, with a reference to what it is like working with violent individuals. As you can see, if I had thought more about the transference, and, especially, been more sensitive to my countertransference, I could have been more helpful to Mr Davis.

Hale (2008) maintains that the defining characteristic of the psychopath is the capacity to bring out the worst in the individual clinician and the institution to which he or she belongs. That was my experience of Mr Davis. But we should not feel too bad about this. It is inevitable, especially when we are inexperienced, because we are working with individuals who are dependent upon projection to get rid of a devastating sense of their badness. It is the patient's reliance upon projection that makes our countertransference such an essential diagnostic and therapeutic tool, whether we are working in an outpatient clinic, a prison, or a secure hospital.

Hale (2008) describes a vicious cycle that most of you are familiar with, which, in over-simplified terms, goes something like this: chronic and intense projections generate an active paranoid state, which is itself a prodromal psychotic state. The individual acts violently to subdue the now life-threatening objects of his projections. This leads to confinement in prison, which drastically reduces the prisoner's opportunities to defend against psychotic anxieties with violence. This, in turn, leads to a shift from chronic to acute psychosis and a transfer to a secure hospital with a diagnosis of schizophrenia and the prescription of neuroleptic drugs, which often bring about a rapid decrease in violent behaviour. However, as the psychosis recedes and the psychopathic state predominates again, the nursing staff, who bear the brunt of the patient's intimidations, question the previous diagnosis of schizophrenia. The point Hale makes is that the nurses and psychiatrists are both right and that a dual diagnosis of an underlying psychosis and a defence against its emergence by psychopathy, which presents as a kind of pseudo normality. From the point of view of our conference theme, the psychopathic orientation to the outside world, underpinned by violence, is the preferred state of mind because it is far less frightening than the paranoia of psychosis.

After lunch, Dr Carine Minne will talk about her psychotherapeutic work with the kind of patient I have been referring to, patients at Broadmoor who have murdered. You will see that their inability to use violence to project intolerable internal states leads them to murder their memories and their reflective selves. Dr Minne will describe how she helped her patients move from a personality disordered or a psychotic presentation to a post traumatic stress disorder that leaves them feeling worse, but helps them recover a capacity to think about who they are and what they have done to others and to themselves.

I will consider violent acts, that is, aggression that breaks the body boundary, from the individual perpetrator's point of view. Bearing in mind the impact that violence has on the victim and witness, it is easy to think of the perpetrator as merely a violent person, but our aim should be to consider the perpetrator as a whole person. That is why we need to remind ourselves that there are broader social and political factors that contribute to violent acts. But I will leave the presentation of these issues to John Alderdice, that rare psychiatrist who is also a respected and effective politician. In fact, this conference on "Aggression: from fantasy to action" mirrors John's multi-dimensionality by bringing together a refreshing variety of perspectives from esteemed psychoanalysts who write from their clinical experience with violent child, adolescent, and adult patients and adult prisoners. I have read the papers and I am impressed by the links they have to each other while also making distinct contributions, which I will refer to during my Keynote Address.

The self-preservative function of the ego

I view aggression as an instinct that is available to the ego in the pursuit of its primary function—the preservation of the self. This view of aggression and its relation to the ego is based on Freud's remarks in 1915 in "Instincts and their vicissitudes": when considering hate, he wrote,

> the relation to unpleasure seems to be the sole decisive one. The ego hates, abhors and pursues with intent to destroy all objects, which are the source of unpleasurable feeling for it, without taking into account whether they mean a frustration of sexual satisfaction or of the satisfaction of self-preservative needs. Indeed, it may be asserted that the true prototypes of the relation of hate are derived . . . from the ego's struggle to preserve and maintain itself. [Freud, 1915c, p. 138]

We share this primary aim with all living creatures. Modern Darwinism has confirmed that within all species a constitutional predisposition to replicate one's genes is the primary motive for the individual's aggressive and reproductive behaviour.

Returning now to homo sapiens, when I view the ego's primary function as the preservation of the self, I am referring to anything that constitutes a threat to physical or psychological homeostasis. This includes, narcissistic equilibrium, that is, good enough feelings about oneself, appropriate self-esteem, and psychological integrity. The aim is to maintain a dynamic balance; a steady state of physical health and psychological well-being at optimum levels. You can consider this as the psychoanalytic equivalent of James Lovelock's ecological hypothesis, the Gaia principle, which views the biosphere and the physical components of the Earth as a complex interacting system that maintains itself in a preferred homeostasis. By 1920, Freud suggested that there was a self-destructive "daemonic force" (Freud, 1920g, p. 35) that opposed the pleasure principle and worked, instead, to return the living organism to its previous, inorganic state. Freud referred to this search for quiescence as the "Nirvana principle", which led to his concept of the death instinct (*ibid.*). Then, in 1930, Freud maintained that "aggressive instinct is the derivative and the main representative of the death instinct" (Freud, 1930a, p. 122)

As you can see, I do not have a place in my theory for the death instinct. Many psychoanalysts ignore the concept, as Anna Freud did, or consider it to have been a detour in Freud's thinking, as Black (2001) does. Winnicott said,

> I have never been in love with the death instinct and it would give me happiness if I could relieve Freud of the burden of carrying it forever on his atlas shoulders . . . while he knew all we know about human psychology . . . he did not know what borderline cases and schizophrenics were going to teach us in the three decades after his death. [Winnicott, 1969, p. 242]

In my clinical experience, I have never had to turn to the death instinct to make sense of a violent act, however destructive and apparently random and "evil" it appeared to be. In the broader perspective, the death instinct seems to me to contradict the modern Darwinian view that the aim of every individual animal is to reproduce its gene pool, not to destroy itself.

The ego's task is to solve problems that threaten to destabilize us. Therefore, the "best" solution negotiated by the ego is that which creates and maintains a feeling of physical safety and psychological well-being. A violent act, a neurotic or psychotic state, a symptom, or a character trait, a defence mechanism or a perversion, however maladapted in the outside world, may be the "best" solution the ego can negotiate given the external circumstances and the ego's internal resources (Sandler & Sandler, 1992). Sexuality and aggression, with their accompanying fantasies and enactments, are our most fundamental resources for the resolution of our problems.

In psychoanalysis, we can see that current fantasies, developed as solutions to conflicts in the present, are permeated to a greater or lesser extent by primitive fantasies representing solutions to earlier developmental conflicts. For instance, paranoid fantasies in response to no real threat are likely to be based on earlier anxieties about safety. These archaic fantasies define our character, aims, and behaviour, including violent behaviour.

Ruthless aggression

Following Glasser (1998), I distinguish between two types of aggression: first, ruthless aggression, which is primary, and, second, sadistic aggression, which is derived by modifying ruthless aggression. Bio-physiologists such as Cannon (1939) have shown that the body has an elaborate reflexive reaction pattern that prepares it for fight or flight in the presence of danger. This reflexive fight/flight mechanism, which we share with all living organisms, is our most primitive defence and serves the ego's self-preservative instincts. The fight mechanism is a primary aggression, which I will refer to as ruthless aggression. In the psychic sphere, all aggression is self-preservative. All of us as infants and adults are capable of self-preservative aggression. When ruthless aggression is enacted in relation to an object, it becomes ruthless violence.

Ruthless violence is a fundamental, immediate, and substantial response to any threat to the self with the aim of negating this source of danger. Here is an example: if you suddenly found yourself being stalked by a lion in the African bush and unable to run, you would normally react with self-preservative aggression with the aim of getting rid of the lion. Self-preservative aggression has a single-minded, narrow-vision quality, like a laser beam, which focuses on the dangerousness of the object rather than the object itself. If the victim's look is experienced as threatening through accusation, it is the eyes that are attacked; if what is being said is intolerable, the mouth is punched, and so on (Glasser, 1998, p. 888). In infants, or in extreme situations, the laser beam quality is lost and violence is directed indiscriminately.

Meloy (1992) makes a distinction between predatory aggression and affective aggression. He views *predatory aggression* as planned, purposeful, focused, unemotional, ego syntonic, and in response to no apparent threat from the object. We would encounter this type of violence in the psychopath, the prime example of the ruthlessly violent individual. *Affective aggression*, according to Meloy, is in response to a specific threat. However, in my view, when we move from an understanding of aggression based on behaviour to its aim, we will find a threat that is real, or the result of the perpetrator's projections, in predatory aggression as well as in affective aggression.

Returning to the lion, his violence may be motivated by: (1) the presence of an object that is perceived as intrusive and dangerous, such as another lion who is intent on driving a rival out of the pride. In this scenario, the lion does not hate the rival *per se*, but will hate it when it poses a threat to its place in the pride. Or, (2) by the presence of a prey that might escape, that is, by the threat that that which will satisfy his hunger might get away. As Lantos (1958) observes,

> the animal hunting its prey is driven by hunger. Hunger makes it angry, but his anger is not directed against the prey. On the contrary he is pleased when it comes his way. The point I want to make is that the lion does not feel hatred of the prey while chasing, catching, tearing, biting and swallowing it. [p. 118]

Later today, Dr Anne Alvarez will discuss Meloy's "predatory violence" further. She will also bring many clinical examples of the complexity of psychopathology, the consequences of projections on to children, leading to identification with the aggressor, and the technical issues that arise from the transference and countertransference.

During a moment of self-preservative aggression or violence, the object holds no personal significance other than his/her dangerousness: an attack is carried out in the interest of self-preservation and any other considerations are not relevant. The response of the object in any other respect is of no interest (Glasser, 1998, p. 891).

With this view of the self-preservative nature and function of ruthless aggression in mind, I will turn now to the mother and her infant. Winnicott (1945) recognizes a "primitive ruthless self" in the normal play of the young infant, during which the infant actually hurts the mother and wears her out. The child's capacity to exercise ruthless aggression and the mother's ability to tolerate it is critical to the child integrating its aggression, and owning it as part of itself. When the mother fails to contain her child's ruthless aggression, "the child can only hide his ruthless self and give it life in a state of dissociation" (Winnicott, 1945, p. 154).

However, ruthless aggression in young children can also be observed outside play. Threats to the infant's psyche and/or physical survival (the infant cannot not be expected to know the difference between them) normally mobilize ruthless aggression directed towards the object, which is perceived as dangerous. The threat may be experienced as a direct assault, engulfment, smothering, or abandonment to starve. As I had explained earlier, the aim of ruthless aggression is to negate the threat.

However, when the object that is perceived as threatening the child's survival is the same object upon which it depends for its survival (the mother), the exercise of ruthless aggression poses a dilemma for the child. How is the child to survive if it cannot afford to get rid of its mother? Some children fashion an ingenious solution by "borrowing" from a familiar, mildly teasing way of relating to its mother. This is an early use of sadomasochism, which all mothers and babies employ to deal with anxieties about loss and separation. The games of peek-a-boo or hide and seek are common examples of this. In teasing the mother, the child fuses their aggression with their love for her. In this way, the child changes the aim of its ruthless aggression from eliminating mother to controlling her in a libidinally gratifying way. Ruthless aggression is, thereby, converted into sadism, where gratification is derived from inflicting anxiety, fear, discomfort, or pain upon another. As you can see, sadism, like the primary, ruthless aggression it is based on, is motivated by self-preservation.

The role of sadism

In a ruthless attack where the aim is, by fight or flight, to eliminate the threat to one's survival, the impact upon the object is irrelevant beyond the achievement of this aim. However, *in a sadistic attack, the relationship to the object must be preserved, not eliminated. By radically altering the relationship to the threatening object to ensure that both self and object survive, sadism now offers the child a second line of defence.*

Subtly modulated, mild sadomasochism emerges now as a libidinal component of the good enough bond between mother and child. However, when the mother's sadism is not tempered by reparation, or extends beyond the child's capacity to recover a nurturing image, or when mother's narcissism makes it impossible for her to be aware of her infant's needs and respond appropriately, the child may rely on more frequent and more intense sadomasochistic exchanges to control a not good enough mother.

When the line of development from self-preservative aggression to the libidinization of aggression progresses to the intensification of sadism, the psychic groundwork is laid for the use of sadism as a solution to neurotic or psychotic conflicts. When the mother's sadism fails to defend her against what she experiences as her child's persecution, she is at risk of relying upon ruthless aggression or its psychic equivalent. The child's well-being is then no longer relevant to the mother. The mother's only concern is negating or eliminating any aspect of the child that poses a threat to *her* survival. At this point, the child's self-development is at greatest risk.

Initially, the child responds to what is experienced as an accelerating risk to *its* survival by intensifying its sadistic control of any increasingly dangerous parent. But what recourse does the child have available if its sadism fails to satisfactorily control a frightening parent? In such cases, the child, and later the adolescent and adult, is likely to abandon its sadomasochistic relationship with the object and regress to reliance upon ruthless aggression with the aim of eliminating a too painful reality by psychotic withdrawal or destruction of the object.

During Workshop 1 tomorrow, Mrs Marie Zaphiriou Woods and Mrs Marianne Parsons will take a developmental perspective to consider the parent–child role in the transformation of a child's aggression from infancy to latency and through adolescence. Woods will present clinical material from the analysis of an aggressive seven-year-old boy to show how the lack of parental empathy and excessive use of negative maternal projections led to his enacting violent intercourse fantasies. Parsons will present session material from her work with a seventeen-year-old Portman patient to look at how the mother's failure to help her child establish a permeable psychological membrane leads to the child developing a rigid protective internal barrier, which does not mitigate annihilation anxieties and increases the adolescent's reliance upon an indiscriminate aggression as a defence.

I have found that when the child, persistently over time, has to rely upon sadomasochism to defend against anxieties associated with engulfment and abandonment, sadomasochism permeates fantasies, masturbation fantasies, and the way their body is used in relationships, the foundations are laid for perverse sexual development, and/or the eroticism of aggression and, in some cases, the repetition of violence to generate sexual gratification.

Dr Capozzi and Dr De Masi, in Workshop 3, will distinguish between aggression as an expression of hatred and violence mobilized as a defence against threats to survival. They make the point that destructivity is always aimed at the roots of life.

Violence rarely occurs in pure form as simply ruthless or sadistic attacks. More often, the violence is mixed, or begins as a sadistic exchange that breaks down and, thereby, increases the perpetrator's anxiety and his or her reliance upon ruthless violence.

An account of a violent assault

I would like to illustrate my views about the ruthless and sadistic nature of aggression by telling you about Mr Giles' account of an assault on his girlfriend, Sylvia, which he described as follows: He and his girlfriend Sylvia were having dinner with an "older woman" at her flat. He found himself being irritated by the older woman, who said "ridiculous things". Mr Giles took Sylvia back to his flat and made sure that there were no neighbours around because he "didn't want the police alerted". He then tried to force Sylvia to admit that the woman had said ridiculous things, but Sylvia denied that this was so. He escalated his threats and attacks from slapping to punching as Sylvia repeatedly refused to agree. Eventually, he found himself kneeling over Sylvia on the bed with his fingers in her eyes trying to gouge them out. At this point, he suddenly realized what he was doing and backed away. Afterwards, he felt shame and guilt about having made Sylvia feel "so worthless". Sylvia, who was, in fact, badly bruised around the head and eyes, left him. This was not the first time he had been violent, but I think it was the first time he caught himself about to inflict permanent damage on his victim, and this is what alarmed him.

In my work with Mr Giles, he acknowledged that he felt humiliated and ashamed in front of his girlfriend Sylvia by the older woman who said ridiculous things. The older woman reminded him of his mother and her intrusiveness. She had a way of getting into him and making him feel small, especially in relation to his violent father.

The shame shield

We feel shame when we are completely exposed, conscious of being looked at, and not ready to be visible. Robert De Niro's improvised remark in the film *Taxi Driver* (1976), "Are you lookin' at me? Are you *lookin'* at me?" is so enduring because it captures the paranoid reaction to the other's stare. The reaction to the projection conveyed by the other's look is expressed as, "Don't look at me like *that*." Shame arises when we believe that an other sees some shameful aspect of ourselves. There is always a witness to shame, either an internal object or an external one.

Internally, shame develops as an affect with a signal function, which triggers a withdrawal to protect physical and mental attributes that have been, or are in the process of being, integrated into a sense of the self. Hiding prevents further exposure of weakness and/or lack of control and restores the self to a safe, private, hidden place where it can be reconstituted. In this sense, shame functions as a psychic shield. I refer to this aspect of the defensive function of shame as a shame shield (Campbell, 2008).

> The protective function of shame as an external signal depends for its success upon the object perceiving the external manifestations of shame as a shield between self and object, which the object recognizes as a signal of failure and respects enough to react sympathetically to the self. [*ibid.*, p. 78]

Erikson (1977) views shame as the result of inhibited aggression; a passive ego is overwhelmed and unable to actively fight off an external threat. Aggression is turned from the object to disgust of the self.

Ordinarily, a strong sense of shame could deter an individual from acting in a delinquent or violent way. However, early and persistent breakdown of the shame shield increases the child's reliance upon its earliest reflexive reaction of fight or flight. If flight is not possible (except into psychosis), fight, of the most primitive and ruthless kind, is the only other option.

In Workshop 1 tomorrow morning, Professor Gilligan's paper will extend and deepen my brief examination of the nature of shame and its role in triggering violence. Interestingly, both Mr Giles and Ross L, who is the subject of Professor Gilligan's study, attacked their victim's eyes.

Later, Professor Rosine Perelberg will discuss this failure to control violent impulses in men who have not been able to shift from the unconscious fantasy of a father who is being beaten—

murdered—that is still within an anal-sadistic structure and the origin of so many psychopathologies from violence to psychoses and perversion, to the fantasy of a dead father. Enabling these fantasies to emerge in an analysis is an important achievement for some men as an expression of their sexual choice and masculine identification. The shift from the murdered to the dead father represents a shift from the real to the symbolic, an attempt to regulate desire, and the institution of the incest taboo.

Conclusion

I am approaching this breakthrough of violence in Mr Giles as the result of a shame shield that has been breached and left unrepaired. When this occurs, shame is projected and is not available as a deterrent to enacting conscious or unconscious sadistic fantasies. This is what happened with Mr Giles and Sylvia, who had witnessed Mr Giles being shamed.

I have used this assault to illustrate the nature and function of sadistic and ruthless aggression. In an effort to reverse his experience of feeling "put down" by the older woman's ridiculous remarks, Mr Giles attacked Sylvia sadistically in order to bring her under his control. This was premeditated. He checked to be sure the neighbours were not around so the police would not be called. He hurt Sylvia in order to get her to agree with him. His sadistic violence escalated from slapping to punching as Sylvia resisted his attempts to control her, until his sadism broke down and he resorted to a ruthless attack on her eyes. He gave up trying to control Sylvia and tried to get rid of her eyes, the eyes that had seen him being shamed.

References

Black, D. (2001). Mapping a detour: why did Freud speak of a death drive? *British Journal of Pschotherapy, 18*: 185–198.

Campbell, D. (2008). The shame shield in child sexual abuse. In: *Shame and Sexuality: Psychoanalysis and Visual Culture* (pp. 75–91). London: Routledge.

Cannon, W. B. (1939). *The Wisdom of the Body*. London: Kegan Paul, Trench, Trubner.

DeLillo, D. (2010). *Point Omega*. New York: Picador.

Erikson, E. (1977). *Childhood and Society* (2nd edn). St. Albans: Triad / Paladin.

Freud, S. (1915c). Instincts and their vicissitudes. *S.E.*, *14*: 117–140. London: Hogarth.

Freud, S. (1920g). *Beyond the Pleasure Principle. S.E.*, *18*: 7–64. London: Hogarth.

Freud, S. (1930a). *Civilization and Its Discontents. S.E.*, *21*: 59–145. London: Hogarth.

Glasser, M. (1998). On violence: a preliminary communication. *International Journal of Psychoanalysis, 79*: 887–902.

Hale, R. (2008). Flying a kite: observation on dual (and triple) diagnosis. *Criminal Behaviour & Mental Health, 18*: 145–152.

Lantos, B. (1958). The two genetic derivation of aggression with reference to sublimation and neutralisation. *International Journal of Psychoanalysis, 39*: 116–120.

Meloy, J. R. (1992). *Violent Attachments*. London: Jason Aronson.

Sandler, J., & Sandler, A.-M. (1992). Psychoanalytic technique and the theory of psychic change. *Bulletin of the Anna Freud Centre, 15*: 35–51.

Taxi Driver (1976). Film, directed by Martin Scorsese.

Winnicott, D. W. (1945). Primitive emotional development. In: *Collected Papers: Through Paediatrics to Psycho-Analysis* (pp. 145–156). London: Tavistock, 1958.

Winnicott, D. W. (1969). The use of an object in the context of Moses and Monotheism. In: C. Winnicott, R. Shepherd, & M. Davis (Eds.), *Psycho-Analytic Explorations* (pp. 240–246). Cambridge, MA: Harvard University Press, 1989.

Discussion of Donald Campbell's paper

*R*ichard Ingram: "Thank you very much indeed, Don. We now have about fifteen minutes for questions. There is a roving mike, so if you'd like to put your hand up, stand up and introduce yourself, we'll get the mike over to you. While we're waiting for questions, I was wondering, Don, about your initial comment about your reaction to the patient, where you removed the ashtray from the room? I was wondering—are there some necessary adaptations to the clinical setting that need to be thought about in dealing with potentially violent patients, or do you think this is something that could be quite destructive or negative in the process?"

Don Campbell: "Yes, I think there definitely are some limitations that need some technical and very practical considerations to be made: in fact, Carine can tell you about some of her experiences at Broadmoor in this respect, with the use of panic buttons and so forth. In an outpatient setting, and I think this probably says more about the type of patients we see at the Portman Clinic than necessarily the setting itself, we often debate whether we should have a panic button in the room in case the patient becomes violent. What is interesting is that, and I hope, Richard, that I am answering your question by going in this direction, because I couldn't quite hear it. Is that what you had in mind?"

Richard Ingram: "Yes, thank you."

Don Campbell: "I've worked at the Portman for over thirty years, and during that time we had only four acts of violence during sessions, and interestingly, three of them were perpetrated by women. In each case they occurred with an inexperienced staff member. I thought that was a pretty good record, and what occurs when we discuss these incidents in our supervision groups and staff meetings is that it takes us back to the breakdown in our analytical orientation to the patient. What triggered that breakdown? And it is usually the breakdown in the analytic orientation to the patient which makes the patient more anxious, which then leads to an outburst of some kind. In these rare cases, a shoving match, or a bit of what you in a hospital setting would think of as very mild violence. So, we've tended not to introduce any kind of practical controls into the consulting room, more really for the clinicians' sake, to ensure that they don't rely on that kind of protection for themselves when they should be continuing to try to think about, say, the transference or the countertransference. In the Portman setting, it seems to have been effective over the years, but I certainly would not recommend it with Broadmoor patients, with more severely psychotic patients."

Richard Ingram: "Thank you very much Don, we have a question from Siobhan O'Connor."

Siobhan O'Connor: "Hello, Don, sorry I'm late."

Don Campbell: "I'm glad you made it."

Siobhan O'Connor: "Richard brought up a point that I was thinking about, and it's great to participate from this point rather than as the Chair, because I can perhaps bring it out a bit more in terms of general psychiatry, because when you described that incident I thought it was really fascinating to see where you were at, and even the fact that it was an ashtray and you were talking about how long ago it was and how much development there has been in the area of countertransference. I think even in psychoanalysis we're becoming much more attuned and aware of it in all spheres, and if I look at that in the general psychiatric setting, I think an important message you're giving is about countertransference awareness of violence and feeling comfortable and safe and being able to contain the experience. From my previous work in a psychiatric intensive care unit, and now in crisis teams, I think the crucial thing I do with my teams is to make them feel safe but also aware of the violence and of being able to differentiate the act of violence from the person. I think what happens in the face of violence is that people get confused and into the denial that you are describing. What you also described, I think, is it being picked up in the countertransference on reflection with your colleagues. That's what I focus on in the general psychiatric setting: to try to introduce a practice of risk assessment that does not rely on the individual. I am trying to encourage all risk assessments to be brought to, and reflected upon, in a group. That's the sort of thing that was triggered in my mind with regard to the general psychiatric setting."

Don Campbell: "Thanks very much, I know you have done a lot of work in this area, and perhaps through the conference it would be useful for you to bring in some examples of this work. I don't want to mislead people when we think about this dynamic relationship between the therapist and the perpetrator that you are only thinking about the perpetrator, you're thinking about the perpetrator through your countertransference. In other words, I think the point you are making is that you can use countertransference to alert yourself to, say, increases in tension in the room, or increases in anxiety in a room, when you feel yourself threatened. I didn't make this point in the paper, but it is probably obvious that clinicians who are working with patients who rely primarily on sadistic violence are safer than those who are working with patients who rely primarily on ruthless violence. The aim of a ruthless attack is mainly just to get rid of the object, just to get rid of the therapist, to eliminate the threat. Whereas, if you are dealing with someone who relies upon sadism, they need the object to remain alive in order to torture them, in order to make them suffer, in order to control them, and although it's more uncomfortable working with a sadistic patient, it's important to get the distinctions right because it's a way of gauging when the therapist is more at risk; when there is that shift from sadistic aggression to more ruthless aggression, the clinician is going to be more at risk. Understanding violence in these two respects is particularly helpful to the clinician in the consulting room. I thought that what I didn't do with Mr Davies was use my countertransference to see how I needed to rely so much upon action when I was anxious. That would have helped me to identify with him, I think, and to understand his need for action, his need for a weapon, instead of disarming him in the way I did."

Richard Ingram: "Thank you very much, we have a question from Professor Gilligan."

James Gilligan: "Donald, I wanted to say that I really enjoyed your paper and I agree strongly with your notion that preservation of the self is the intention of violent behaviour. I just wanted to add a footnote to that and ask if that corresponds to your own experience. It seems to me that most of us, in ordinary conversation, when we speak of so-called instinctive self preservation, we take it for granted that this includes preservation of the body for our physical survival. What I have observed in several decades of working with violent patients in the Massachusetts equivalent of Broadmoor is that the most violent patients that I work with had lost an integration of the body with the soul and were aiming at preserving the self, or saving the self, even at the price of their own physical death, and now that we live in the age of the suicide bomber, I think we see in the headlines of the newspapers every day examples of people who are quite willing to sacrifice their bodies if they feel that it is the only means they can imagine by which to save their souls. So, I wondered whether that fits with your notion of self preservation—that for the violent person self literally means the psychological construct that we speak of in psychoanalytic terms as constituting the self as dissociated from the body?"

Don Campbell: "Yes, thank you for your comments, James. I agree with you in this respect and I found this was confirmed over and over again in working with suicidal patients, where such a split is created that the body is actually seen as a threat to the survival of the self. We are talking about psychotic processes at play here, but this very much confirms your view about the loss of the integration of the self and the body, and the split is created. There is, in prisons, a high level of vulnerability to—and rate of—suicide among murderers. I think it is because the psychotic process that emerges when they are not able to resort to another's body as a source of projection, so that their own body becomes the one they project on to. A shameful bad self gets projected on to the body, and the body can then be got rid of. The fantasy is that they can then survive in another mention as a self that is not haunted in that way. A lengthy answer to agree with your views."

Richard Ingram: "We have time for one last question from a delegate in the front."

Siobhan Murphy: "As usual, a beautiful paper. What it reminded me of is my difficulty in distinguishing Mervin Glasser's theory from Meloy's theory, and I know when Mervin published his, there was what might be called a sort of snippy exchange in the literature, in which Meloy said there were some similarities between the two theories but that there were also important differences. I always forget what the important differences were and I was hoping you might be able to remember them."

Don Campbell: "The way I understood the difference was that Meloy regarded aggression in two respects—the predatory and affective aggression—and what he said was that affective aggression is in response to a specific threat. Mervin and I view all aggression as in response to a specific threat. Predatory aggression, in Meloy's terms, is the kind of very cold psychopathic response to the object, but he thought it was in response to no threat from the object and my view is that when you look at these apparently psychotic attacks in detail you begin to see the threat that is posed by this (often quite unknown) object. The threat is posed by virtue of the projection, so the distinction Meloy was making between predatory attacks, which he felt seemed to arise out of a purely aggressive response to the object without any danger, was something Mervin disagreed with and I also disagree with."

Richard Ingram: "I'm sorry, we've run out of time. Thank you very much again Don, it was a very successful presentation given the current difficulties. Thank you again".

CHAPTER TWO

Which violence and whose violence? Questions arising in the psychotherapy of aggressive children

Anne Alvarez

Dr Maria O'Kane introduces Dr Anne Alvarez

"Dr Alvarez hoped to come to Belfast today, but unfortunately she has been a victim of the ash, as other people have been, but she has very kindly agreed to do the presentation by audio link from her base in London. I'm sure she is well known to most of you. I think it is very important for those of us who work in adult psychiatry to understand the importance of the development of the child when we are trying to understand the adult, and I think you will agree that Anne Alvarez has helped us enormously in understanding very disturbed mental states and how they extend from childhood into adulthood. You will see from the description she has provided of herself that she is a consultant child and adolescent psychotherapist; she trained as a clinical psychologist in Canada and the USA before training as a child and adolescent psychotherapist in the UK. She is a consultant child and adolescent psychotherapist, and retired co-convener of the autism service, child and family department at the Tavistock Clinic in London. She is also the author of *Live Company*, a book I would recommend, *Psychotherapy with Autistic Borderline Deprived and*

Abused Children, and has edited, with Susan Reid, *Autism and Personality*. A book in her honour was published in 2002, edited by Judith Edwards, and titled *Being Alive: Building on the Work of Anne Alvarez*. She was Visiting Professor at the San Francisco Psychoanalytic Institute in November 2005."

Anne Alvarez: "Thank you, and thank you Professor Williams, Nora, Lisa, and the College for making this happen under these extraordinary conditions. I have my Belfast city guide sitting beside me just to remind me of what I am missing and where I am not. I need to say about this paper that I think it is a pretty pedantic paper. I think something about old age has made me get into making distinctions and classifications and I fear that this may not make for easy listening, but in any case I hope you can bear with me and bear it."

Introduction

I shall try to distinguish three factors contributing to violent behaviour: (1) disturbance or disorder; (2) deficit and neglect; and (3) deviance. I shall also say a little about the need to adjust our technique and our understanding depending on which factor is dominant at any moment—much easier said and written about than done—especially as all three factors may be present in a single child. Two dimensions which seem to run through these categories and to illuminate them a little are, first, the question of which violence—that is, the motivation and emotion which accompany the violence; the second question is whose violence: that is, when we study the inner world of violent children, we discover vast differences in the relationships between the self and the internal objects or representational figures of other people. These two questions will be raised whenever we try to treat these children or adolescents.

Which violence? One distinction

Meloy, a psychologist who has had a long and intensive experience with violent inmates in prisons in the San Diego area in California, has made a very helpful distinction between what he calls "affec-tively evoked aggression"—aggression evoked by the perception of threat—and "predatory aggression"—aggression directed towards the destruction of prey, usually for food-gathering in sub-human species. "It involves minimal autonomic arousal and vocalization." Meloy points out that when a household cat is cornered and threat-ened, the neurochemical set produces a display of affective aggres-sion: hissing, hair standing on end, dilating pupils, active clawing, arching back. "When the same cat is stalking a bird in the back-yard, predatory aggression dominates: quiet stalking of the prey, the absence of ritualistic display, and focussed [sic] attention on the target." He states that predatory aggression is the hallmark of the psychopath (Meloy, 1996, p. 25). (He is careful to distinguish between the severe and the mild end of a continuum of psychopa-thy, and thinks people from the milder end tend to be treatable.) Meloy suggests that the anecdotal descriptions by workers in foren-sic treatment and custody settings of certain patients' or inmates' eyes as "cold, staring, harsh, empty, vacant, and absent of feeling" and the consequent feeling of eerie fear should be taken very seri-ously. He points out that this experience of chilling fear does not seem to arise with even very dangerous explosive combative patients (ibid., p. 70).

Parallel to his distinction between affective aggression and predatory aggression, Meloy made a distinction between aggres-sion in the borderline personality and in the psychopath: in moments of aggression he thought we should study the nature of the internal object (the representation of other people that the aggressor carries around in his internal world. In both types of patients there may be an internalized predatory stranger. Meloy pointed out that in the borderline, the predatory stranger is intro-jected, but not necessarily identified with (Meloy, 1996, p. 46). (Jon Venables, one of the killers of Jamie Bulger, seemed much more frightened of his mother than of the detectives interviewing him (Morrison, 1997).) In the psychopathic patient, however, this preda-tory figure is identified with, the self is no longer afraid because the fear is projected into others, the victims.

It is interesting that the more modern psychiatric classifica-tions tried to avoid what had in part become the pejorative and wastebasket use of the term "psychopath". However, the newer terms—"conduct disorder", "antisocial personality disorder", even "sociopath"—become equally inadequate (American Psychiatric Association, 1994) because their purely descriptive level of meaning does not distinguish between the kind of destructiveness that is motivated by anger, that by bitter hatred, that by outrage, that by sadism, and that by casual brutality. This has been even more true in the field of child psychiatry, although finally this is beginning to change, at least in the research: Viding (2004) has suggested that psychopathy should be seen as a developmental disorder, and Frick and White (2008) have reviewed the research on the importance of callous–unemotional personality traits for a particular sub-group of antisocial and aggressive youth. Unlike the previous textbooks, the research shows that the youths themselves know it is not a simple question of anger. Indeed, they seem more than comfortable with their lack of empathy. The review suggests that making these distinctions is important for treatment, but is not clear as to what treatment they consider might reach such children. One later study does cite some evidence that psychological treatments seem to reduce psychopathic features (Loeber, Burke, & Pandini, 2009).

But to return to the distinctions: certainly, motivated, vengeful, paranoid violence is different from addictive, habitual violence. We need much more study of the trajectory of the development of psychopathic aggression, and the conditions under which the hot aggression turns cold: addictive violence may have *begun* as a defence against some horror, then gradually acquired sadistic and exciting overtones, but eventually, under certain conditions of life-long chronicity, become almost motiveless and certainly casual. The enormity of the act may no longer bear any relation to the amount of feeling left in the perpetrator. An addiction is different from a defence.

I remember my own reaction to the first photographs published in the press of the two ten-year-old boys, Robert Thompson and Jon Venables, the boys who murdered two-year-old James Bulger: I thought Robert looked out at the photographer with bold yet some-how dead eyes, whereas Jon looked animated and ordinary. I thought Robert was the strong one, and Jon the weaker and, as reports emerged, the more openly emotionally disturbed. According to Blake Morrison, in *As If*, his account of the trial, people in court also saw Robert as the leader and initiator of the violence, but, in fact, Morrison pointed out that Jon was also capable of real violence (Morrison, 1997). It is hard, in the aftermath of terrible crimes, not to want simplistic solutions and identifiable scapegoats. The complexity and sheer *spread* of the facts of multiple causation provides a poor outlet for our sense of horror and outrage: it scatters and dilutes it; we need a more concentrated target, a focus for our shock. Morrison was horrified by the fact of the children being tried in an adult court, and also by the fact that the psychiatrists called by both defence and prosecution were not permitted by law to address the complexity of motivation and causation; they could comment only on whether the children knew what they were doing, and whether it was right or wrong. The psychiatrists felt they had to say yes. Because of Robert's history of family violence, and Jon's emotional immaturity and disturbance, Morrison said no. He said no partly because he thought that a ten-year-old child, especially a disturbed and deprived one, could not possibly understand fully that death is death and is final, and he cites evidence from the tapes of the boys' interrogation by detectives.

But a complicating factor, and this may have influenced the psychiatrists (two of whom were also psychoanalysts), is that while some violent acts have a more purely evacuative motive, to get the aggression out on anyone anywhere, others do, I believe, carry a powerful intention to kill. Somewhere in our brains, bones, teeth, and nails, I think we can know, even as children, what it is to want to kill, and to *mean to kill*, finally and forever. And these feelings are not the province only of the psychopaths. What restrains most people in a particular society—except where whole nations have been traumatized by brutal oppression or genocidal massacres—are other elements in their personality which modify and restrain such impulses: a capacity for empathy, fellow-feeling, identification, or at the very least, fear of retribution from society. The latter is not to be dismissed: when a psychopathic child starts to recover, he is unlikely to go straight on to feelings of empathy for others or remorse for his destructiveness. Sometimes all that happens is that he becomes a little less grandiose and a little more concerned for himself and for his own fate—expulsion from school, or from a decent foster family. *And that can be a development.* However, we also need to remember how far we have yet to go with such patients: Melanie Klein has helped us in psychoanalysis to understand the difference between conscience based on love, guilt, and concern, and the more Old Testament "paranoid position" fear of retributive justice from a vengeful superego (Klein, 1935). Both, at different moments, may exert restraint, but liberal thinkers agree that the former signals a more advanced development in character structure and in civilization.

I am going on to make some further distinctions for purposes of clarification of differences in types of violence. I will use case material to illustrate the difficult technical issues for the psychotherapist or care worker. I think we have to know the *nature* of the violence before we can treat it. I shall, therefore, try to distinguish three factors which may need to be identified in acts of violence: disorder, deficit, and deviance. All of these concern the relation between the self and its internal objects in the inner world. I will look at the location or source of the anger in the sense of whether, within the patient's inner world, it is felt to arise from the self or from the inner representational figures.

Factor 1: Disturbance or disorder

Aggression arising in the self as a reaction towards a figure felt to be infuriatingly frustrating or disappointing, or else highly dangerous and terrifying

I am describing here a paranoid reaction where there is considerable persecutory feeling, similar to Meloy's affectively evoked aggression. In some cases of abuse, trauma, or persecution, there may be a profound and lasting sense of outrage and injustice. One child whom I treated had been horribly abused by his mentally ill mother, and, during a long break in treatment when I stopped to have a baby, took to killing small animals in the fields near his home. He had also been attacking anything soft or vulnerable in my playroom. For a long while I interpreted his jealousy of my baby, until my supervisor, Sydney Klein, pointed out that I was persecuting him with my interpretations, and I began to talk about, instead of jealousy, a feeling of betrayal. This more sympathetic understanding turned things around quite quickly and led me— eventually and long afterward—to begin to understand something about the sense of *rightful* needs, such as the need for justice and even for fantasies of revenge (Alvarez, 1997). The novelist Milan Kundera (1982) pointed out that these can lead to necessary "rectifications", and, I would add, these may be a necessary step on the way to healing for victims of torture and huge injustice. If we simply keep telling the patient how angry he is, we may overwhelm him with more of his already intolerable helpless rage: if, on the other hand, we understand that sometimes badness needs to *stay out there*, we can talk about his feeling, not that he wished we hadn't gone off to have a baby, but that he feels we *shouldn't have* done so.

Aggression which is not the patient's own, but erupts because he is possessed by a violent figure which has been internalized unconsciously

Such aggression acts like a "foreign body" (Williams, 1997). He may have witnessed much violence, or received it, and may even be in unconscious identification with the aggressor, but the point is that the identification is unconscious, and the child may not know why he did something or where the impulse came from. (Perhaps when Jon Venables and Robert Thompson each accused the other of throwing the first stone, they meant it.) Many borderline psychotic people do not feel as though it was they themselves carrying out the violent act. They may be right, in a sense, if there was a considerable degree of depersonalization and dissociation. Here, we need to show that we understand that "it is in them to do" but not say things such as, "You were very angry when you . . .". This is because sometimes he was not angry, although someone inhabiting him inside certainly was.

Aggression arising when a child has been very heavily projected into by a care-giver who sees him as violent when in fact he is not

The child begins to identify with the figure's view of him and cannot shake it off. I would like to spend a moment illustrating this factor, where a fairly non-violent child is seen as violent by a possibly quite paranoid care-giver. I have seen this latter situation where the child may begin to act in a violent manner, but the observer may begin to get a sense that when the violence erupts, it is not really the child doing it. One three-year-old boy, Kenneth, was really believed by his very paranoid mother to be evil. She believed he had been out to destroy her peace of mind ever since he was a baby. Although, by the age of four, he often was aggressive, his very sensitive therapist and also a very kind teacher could both get him out of these states by telling him, in their different ways, that they could see that he did not mean it. (This would be a very foolish thing to say to a psychopathic child, who, by the time he has hardened up, has owned it.) The therapist also had to make it clear to Kenneth over and over again that *she* neither expected nor wanted violence from him. Unfortunately, he had to change to less understanding, somewhat more critical and over-reactive teachers, and, in addition, his therapy had to be interrupted for a period. The next therapist who took him on at age six noticed that he had begun to identify with this violent identity: he had begun to own it. He presumably had had to make some sense of what he was being exposed to, and perhaps in a terrible way it stopped him going mad with confusion. This can signal a dangerous progress towards the deviance I shall describe in Factor 3: there are points in development where regularly occurring states of mind become personality traits (Perry, 1995).

Factor 2: Deficits in the development of loving affectionate relations between the self and other people, in self-reflective function, and in capacity for ordinary excitements and pleasures: the issue of neglect

Deficit in the internal representation of good figures and of a good self, and of intelligent figures

This produces hopelessness, despair, and sometimes emptiness and eventual deep cynicism. Many abused and traumatized children are not simply abused and traumatized: they are usually deprived as well of ordinary opportunities for pleasurable interactions, the stimulation of learning and of ordinary interpersonal relations (Music, 2009). They are also usually deprived of a sense of protective figures, and of the sense of a right to such protection. Morrison described the ugliness of the landscape in the area of Liverpool where the boys lived, and asked whether, if you are habituated to the absence of something (goodness, beauty, fineness), you know what you are missing. According to Perry (2002), neglect (note, not abuse) means that certain dendritic growth, migration of cells, and synaptic connections simply do not take place. Such children seem blunted cognitively (I think they are different from the dissociated traumatized children) and they may even get a diagnosis of pervasive developmental disorder, but some of them seem to open almost like flowers when they realize there is a mind out there that assumes they have a mind and feelings, too. It is important to work very slowly with the dissociated and psychopathic patients whose hidden vulnerabilities have not yet been owned (Alvarez, 1995), but we also have a long road ahead with the severely neglected children who have never properly developed. One very violent boy, who was both traumatized and neglected, who had seen much violence and seen his alcoholic mother die in front of him at the age of two, returned from his three-week summer break from therapy and insisted to his therapist that there were no cars in the box of toys he had always used in his sessions with her. She showed him that his usual cars were still there. He replied, "Oh no, those cars were from a long time ago with another lady." This gives an indication of how faint and remote was his memory of his almost year-long intensive treatment with her. The process of building up a mind capable of memory, internal representations of good and reliable objects in patients so fragmented and with such profound ego deficits, is painfully slow.

Another horribly abused boy, after a period in therapy, finally began to have dreams in which terrible things were being done to a child. The beginnings of some degree of symbolization, which signals the process of recovery from trauma, seemed to be under way, but neither the child, as he recounted the dreams, nor any figure in the dreams, seemed to evidence shock or protest over the cruelty. Finally, he had a dream where some adults were looking on "astonished" at what was being done to the child. His internal objects had not yet acquired the capacity to feel outrage, or to try to rescue the child, but his therapist and I felt that astonishment was at least a start, and might lay the ground for eventual appropriate shock and outrage. Sometimes the next stage of recovery involves an identification with the therapist as a caring figure, and this can look as though it is some sort of manic omnipotent defence against the patient's own needs. But it may be a real development if the adolescent, say, has never been able to identify with a caring figure before. We should not analyse such developments away as defensive; instead, we should handle them with great delicacy and from a developmental perspective.

Here, I want to say something about the importance of "stupid" objects. I have seen too often the murderousness of certain children not towards their abusive fathers, who may have been quite lively in between episodes of violence, but towards the depressed or denying mother, seen as weak and unable to, as it were, *get it*. This sometimes evokes more rage than the actual abuses of the tormentor. I think the "stupid object" requires much more study. The image of all adults, or all women, say, as being stupid may not be the result of the ordinary adolescent contemptuous devaluing; it may be the result of never having found a parent interesting or worth listening to or looking up to. Such objects are unvalued, not devalued, and they may evoke huge rage and despair (Alvarez, 2006).

Deficits in the capacity for self-reflection and thoughtfulness, what psychoanalysts term ego deficits, and deficits in symbolization, particularly in the area of self-regulation of excitement and arousal

Most abused children have not been taken out to the park much to play ball with their fathers, or played many pretend tea-parties with their mothers. In the sexually abusive families, the whole family may genuinely not know that excitements other than sexual ones can exist. Often, even when these violent patients give up their most violent or perverse activities and phantasies, they have little idea how to have other forms of adventure. They may be either bored or highly over-stimulated by more ordinary forms of excitement and need much help and sensitivity from therapists and carers in managing their toddler-level turbulences. Therapists have had fifteen-year-old sexual offenders begin to play ordinary peeka-boo games, and this may be an important development (Woods, 2003).

Factor 3: Deviance owned, idealized, and eventually found to be thrilling

Aggression arising where the child has begun to own the identification with the aggressor

In the case of the psychopathic children, the internal object is not seen as dangerous, simply as another piece of prey. These children may be suspicious, but they are not angry and they are not afraid: people are afraid of giants, but only suspicious of pygmies or equals.

Addiction to violence

Violence has become habitual, as any of the above factors combine and lead to secondary developments. A consequence of such addiction is that it may become a solution to much more minor problems and more minor stresses. (However, where there is a reactivity to particular forms of stress, sensitivity on the part of residential workers, therapists, and families to current or recent separations, changes, and losses may help to turn the apparently invisible and seemingly minor triggering stimuli into visible, verbalizable, and thinkable-about issues.) That aspect, however, is sometimes easier to deal with than the casually habitual aggression. I think we can be much firmer with the latter, and I shall illustrate this later.

Perverse excitement accompanying violence

This is a worrying development, particularly as ordinary pubertal sexuality may be blocked because of personality difficulties. Grotstein points out, in the introduction to Meloy's book, that psychopaths experience a characteristic hypo-reactivitiy of their peripheral autonomic nervous system, and pursue exciting aggression to compensate (Grotstein, 1996).

With the deviant children, where there is addiction to violence, or even perverse excitement about it, as therapists, we may need to know when to allow ourselves to feel, not only our outrage, but our boredom with the repetitive nature of the preoccupation. Some very cruel games may start off because the child genuinely needs to project his victimhood into some other figure in the play. But, moments later, the same piece of play may turn into something not needed, indeed damaging to the child's mind. The therapist needs to be alert to these moments and to know when to cool things down.

I have spent some time above trying to distinguish between different types of violence, but it is clear that in most of our patients the motives are mixed. I shall move on to a mixed case.

A five-year-old girl, Susie, had been abandoned at birth and raised in an Eastern European orphanage. She was not adopted until she was eighteen months old, but there was some evidence that at least one of her carers in the orphanage was very fond of her, and in spite of her aggression to her naturally born sister in the adoptive family, and her set hard look, she sometimes had fleeting moments of a slight softening. She was referred because of eruptions of furious jealousy towards her little brother. There were also cruel, calculating acts towards children in her nursery. And yet, sometimes in the sessions there were powerful indications of her yearning for some sort of lap she had had so little of, as she made cosy bed after cosy bed for herself in which to be safe and content.

It did not take long, however, for her to get into extremely cruel games with the dolls and the animal toys in the sessions. The doll that stood for me was called Anne, often a worrying sign that the play is not really pretend and symbolic, but feels more like practice for the real thing, in this case, torture and murder. It was not only that the Anne doll was tortured most days in a variety of ways, but I would be then made to watch helplessly as my mother was tortured and murdered. I sometimes felt this five-year-old child had been trained by a sinister expert in interrogation techniques! In fact, her adoptive parents were warm, loving, yet also capable of being firm when it seemed appropriate.

I should say that sometimes the games were carried out with a sense of desperate revenge, and I went along with them because, at these points, I felt I and the Anne doll had to bear the brunt of these desperate projections. At other times, there was a worryingly perverse sense of excitement about the cruelty and I usually tried to cool things down under those conditions. But there came a point when I began to feel bored by the relentless repetition, and also to notice that sometimes Susie was not desperate, or even sadistically excited, just casually brutal. It was almost as though she did not know what else to do or how to stop, and was probably a bit bored herself sometimes. I began to refuse to collaborate in the games. Also, her parents, with whom I worked closely, were cooling things down at home, and the frequency of the cruelty in the sessions and in real life began to diminish. Real revenge can sometimes exhaust itself, but this was more like addiction.

In a very different session, after some cancellations, when we had finally got back into our usual two times weekly routine, Susie came in and made a lovely field, with the fences surrounding the farm animals, and two tall trees, one of which was damaged. She then made a beautiful farmhouse made of cushions and strong chairs. I was invited to visit and it turned out there was a lovely river there where I could swim. A beautiful white fish kissed me. I think Susie was making some effort here to rewrite her early infantile history.

In the outside world, the eruptive violence continued, but, like the colder cruelty, was also much reduced, and Susie began to seem somewhat happier. I have not had time to mention the fact that I had to do a lot of work on myself to be able to look her in the eye when she was at her most cold and cruel: it was not only a question of bravery in terms of looking evil in the eye—I also needed to keep looking into her eyes trying to find the real child behind the armour-plated veil. Sometimes I managed it, sometimes I did not.

I have tried to give some idea of the importance of distinguishing types of violence and sources of violence within the internal world of object relationships. This may help us to refine and develop our therapeutic instruments, but it is unlikely to mean, as this last case illustrates, that this work with very disturbed patients is ever going to be easy!

Summary and conclusion

I have distinguished disorder from deficit, and both from deviance, and suggested some possible sub-categories in each:

1. Disorder
    - Aggression arising in the self as a reaction towards a figure felt to be infuriatingly frustrating or disappointing, or else highly dangerous and terrifying.
    - Aggression which is not the patient's own, but erupts because he is possessed by a violent figure which has been internalized unconsciously.
    - Aggression arising when a child has been very heavily projected into by a care-giver who sees him as violent when in fact he is not.

2. Deficits in the development of loving affectionate relations between the self and other people, in self-reflective function, and in the capacity for ordinary excitments and pleasure: the issue of neglect.
    - Deficit in the internal representation of good figures and of a good self, and of intelligent figures.
    - Deficits in the capacity for self-reflection and thoughtfulness, what psychoanalysts term ego deficits, and deficits in symbolism, particularly in the area of self regulation of excitement and arousal.

3. Deviance owned, idealized, addictive, and eventually found to be thrilling
    - Aggression arising when the child has begun to own the identification with the aggressor.
    - Addiction to violence.
    - Addition of perverse excitements.

It is important that we know what we are taking on when we agree to treat such patients, and that we know *how they see us*. The aim in the psychoanalytic psychotherapy would be, eventually, to turn action into thought, the concrete into the symbolic, via work in the transference–countertransference relationship. This is likely to be a slow process, where there are few shortcuts, especially where there are borderline psychotic or psychopathic features. The psychotherapist tries to treat the person, not the symptom, but such powerful and disturbing symptomatology is bound to put particular pressures on the transference and countertransference relationship.

The work is very upsetting and it needs to be. Communication within the network of concerned professionals and family is essential with patients whose inner communication system is so concrete and faulty. As with all deeply disturbed patients, such communication needs to be balanced against issues of confidentiality.

Acknowledgements

I am grateful to Lucy Griffin-Beale and Jan Cousins for permission to use clinical material.

References

Alvarez, A. (1997). Projective identification as a communication: its grammar in borderline psychotic children. In: *Psychoanalytic Dialogues*, 7(6): Symposium on Child Analysis, Part I.

Alvarez, A. (2006). Narzissmus und das dumme object- Entwertung oder Missachtung? Mit einer anmerkung zum Suchtigen und zum manifesten Narzissmus. In: O. F. Kernberg & H.-P. Hartmann (Eds.), *Narzismus: grundlagen- Storungsbilder-Therapie* (pp. 211–224). Stuttgart: Schattauer.

American Psychiatric Association (1994). *Diagnostic Criteria from DSM-IV*. Washington, DC: American Psychiatric Association.

Frick, P. J., & White, S. F. (2008). Research review: the importance of callous–unemotional traits for developmental models of aggressive and antisocial behaviour. *Journal of Child and Psychology and Psychiatry*, 49(4): 359–375.

Grotstein, J. (1996). Foreword. In: J. R. Meloy, *The Psychopathic Mind: Origin, Dynamics, Treatment* (pp. ix–xvii). London: Jason Aronson.

Klein, M. (1935). A contribution to the psycho-genesis of manic-depressive states. In: *Love, Guilt and Reparation and Other Works 1921–1945* (pp. 262–289). London: Hogarth, 1975.

Kundera, M. (1982). *The Joke*. Harmondsworth: Penguin.

Loeber, R., Burke, J., & Pandini, D. A. (2009). Perspectives on oppositional-defiant disorder, conduct disorder, and psychopathic features. *Journal of Child Psychology and Psychiatry*, 50(1–2): 133–142.

Meloy, J. R. (1996). *The Psychopathic Mind: Origin, Dynamics, and Treatment*. London: Jason Aronson.

Morrison, B. (1997). *As If*. London: Granta Books.

Music, G. (2009). Neglecting neglect: some thoughts on children who have lacked good input, and are 'undrawn' and 'unenjoyed'. *Journal of Child Psychotherapy, 35*(2): 142–156.

Perry, B. D. (1995). Childhood trauma, the neurobiology of adaptation and 'use-dependent' development of the brain: how 'states' become 'traits'. *Infant Mental Health Journal, 16*: 271–291.

Perry, B. D. (2002). Childhood experience and the expression of genetic potential: what childhood neglect tell us about nature and nurture. *Brain and Mind, 3*: 79–100.

Viding, E. (2004). Annotation: understanding the development of psychopathy. *Journal of Child Psychology and Psychiatry, 45*(8): 1329–1337.

Williams, G. (1997). On introjective processes: the hypothesis of an omega function. In: *Internal Landscapes and Foreign Bodies: Eating Disorders and Other Pathologies* (Chapter 10). London: Duckworth.

Woods, J. (2003). *Boys Who Have Abused: Psychoanalytic Psychotherapy with Victim/Perpetrators of Sexual Abuse*. London: Jessica Kingsley.

Discussion of Anne Alvarez's paper

Maria O'Kane: "Professor Alvarez, thank you very much. You've certainly given us plenty of food for thought. I have been fortunate to have access to the paper before the conference, but what you have done is try to get us to think about which violence and whose violence, essentially sub-categorizing different ways of thinking about violence and then to think about violence in the context of object relationships. You've talked about children and their violent activities towards things and towards other people, but I wondered whether or not you feel the model you are suggesting would work in the context of self harm.

Anne Alvarez: "Yes, I realize I didn't say anything about masochism and self harm and I'm sorry about that, it ought to be there, because you can get all three factors. Once the self harm becomes very addictive, and even sexually exciting, there are some people who say they like to see the blood flow and it can begin as wanting to bring to life a dead object, and a dead self, a depersonalized self, but, of course, it can gather other motivations to it. That's the problem with every symptom: it can start gathering other, secondary motivations and begin to take over the whole personality and I agree with you about that."

Maria O'Kane: "Over the next ten minutes we'll take some questions. Who would like to start? Are there any questions at this point, or do you want to hold until the plenary at the end, would that suit? Yes? All right. What I'm going to suggest is that we take refreshments; during that time we will collect questions for yourself and the other speakers then we'll get back in contact with you to start to think about those and the discussion. Thank you."

Note

For technical reasons it was, regrettably, not possible to record and transcribe the discussion of Anne Alvarez's paper.

CHAPTER THREE

Violence to body and mind: treating patients who have killed

Carine Minne

T he nature and function of aggression, described so elegantly by Don Campbell in his chapter, and the theme of the conference, "Aggression: from fantasy to action", are subjects that have intrigued me for many years and caused so much suffering to the patients I have seen, and to those around them, particularly their victims. In particular, I have wondered what is it that makes a mind that entertains an aggressive fantasy, a common occurrence, transform into a violent muscular action, a much less common occurrence. When violent patients have psychoanalytic psychotherapy as part of their treatment plan, and the prospect of understanding develops, what does one need to indicate has changed in the patient and, indeed, how can one demonstrate any changes that may have arisen which would mean the patient is now less at risk of being violent again? Generally, clinical risk assessments on patients who have been violent tend to focus on the patients' behaviour, combined with a psychiatric mental state examination. This often neglects what, if any, changes may have arisen in the patients' internal worlds, and it is here that a psychoanalytic approach can contribute to clinical risk management, one that emphasizes the fluidity of risk as opposed to presenting a snap-shot.

I will present work with patients suffering from personality disorders who have been fatally violent to others, violent to themselves, and who have a phenomenal capacity to be violent to their own and others' minds. These disturbed and disturbing patients present psychotherapeutic challenges, having less integrated mental structures than would generally be considered able to make use of a psychoanalytic approach. I propose that some can make significant changes with this treatment, in the context of a multidisciplinary team care, within a containing physical environment. This progress can be monitored clinically and recorded (I use the Operationalized Psychodynamic Diagnosis system) and involves manifest changes in their mental states.

A major task of this treatment is to enable an awareness of the mind and its functions to become available to the owner of that mind, the person known to us as the patient. This refers to an awareness of who they are, what they have done, and the impact of this on their minds and on the minds of others. Regardless of their diagnoses, people who have carried out serious violent offences often have limited awareness of themselves and of the seriousness of what they have done. This absence, or avoidance, provided by an arsenal of defences, psychotic and non-psychotic, appears to be necessary for the patient's psychic survival. Indeed, addressing their defences can cause massive anxieties about "cracking up" and can lead to psychotic breakdowns and, perhaps, to suicidality or even suicide. Yet, to leave these defences untouched can leave essential ingredients intact for being violent again. The therapist's task is a delicate and complicated one. First, helping the cultivation of awareness in the person's mind without seeming to commit a violent assault to that mind. Second, clinically judging if and how such awareness is developing and, third, continually gauging in what way that person is using this. These are the mental state changes that we look for in the monitoring of our work. It is also these shifts, or prognostically positive internal world changes, that can provoke particular negative therapeutic responses. In some cases, the careful and limited use of antipsychotic medication can helpfully sedate the more intense psychotic anxieties, making ongoing psychoanalytic treatment possible.

I would like to refer to how these patients are traumatized threefold because this is so relevant to working psychotherapeutically with them. First, they are traumatized by their appalling background histories, second by the offences they committed, and third, by their gradual discovery, during treatment, of having a mental disorder. This can lead to a development and manifestation, during the course of treatment, of a post traumatic stress type of disorder, which should be seen as a positive prognostic indicator. In other words, as awareness and understanding develops, patients begin to suffer from the consequences of this. These are the shifts that can provoke particular negative therapeutic reactions, the aims of which are to return the patient's mind to its previous disturbed but familiar state. One reason for this is that a return to oblivion (and potential action) is more desirable than managing the burden of awareness (and fantasy). I will illustrate some of what I have said with case examples. After that, I will describe the interpersonal and mental structural changes that one monitors in the course of the psychoanalytic part of their treatment as evidence for the revised risk management.

Case 1

Mr A, now twenty-six years old, was admitted to high secure hospital having been convicted of murder. Late one night, he carried out what appeared to be an impulsive unprovoked and fatal attack on a lone woman using a huge knife.

At first, he described his offence as a one-off event, a handbag theft that had gone wrong. However, the extreme violence used was not in keeping with this explanation and it was considered early on that psychically, a different scenario may have been acted out and after several months in treatment, it emerged.

Mr A pleaded to have therapy, but then complained about how little this was compared with what he needed. His mother had left the family home with a lover when his younger sister was born, leaving her husband to look after a three-year-old toddler, Mr A, and a newborn baby. This major loss, perhaps in combination with his particular constitution, may have produced unbearable feelings of rage he had to get rid of. Around the age of four years, he began repeatedly to draw violent pictures of people attacking each other with weapons. He also started to behave aggressively towards children who seemed to have "nice mummies" bringing them to school.

With the onset of puberty, Mr A's unresolved rage became attached to his developing sexual feelings. He began to masturbate to fantasies of rape and strangulation. This evolved into stalking women, and several times he came close to attacking a particular woman he had been following, only to "chicken out" at the last moment, leaving the woman totally unaware of what had nearly happened to her. The victim was not so fortunate. What was presented by him initially to the team as a theft that went wrong could later be seen in quite a different light, an apparently impulsive attack, which was actually one that had been premeditated and rehearsed over several years. There had been an ominous development of escalation in his dangerousness, from fantasy only to practising carrying these out, and, finally, an incomplete enactment of his main fantasy. Here we can see how the capacity to symbolize through the use of fantasies gradually broke down as the severity of psychotic functioning increased, leading to the need to act out. Anxiety became engendered by the very fantasies that were created in order to attempt to alleviate it. This fuelled the escalation until the fantasies no longer sufficed and a deterioration, or spillage, into action occurred.

This is a young man whose early feelings of rage at the loss of his mother may have threatened to overwhelm his psyche. He had to get rid of these in the only way he could, by projecting them violently into a recipient that fulfilled his unconscious criteria. Any woman (or man) could be a potential victim of his, if they were experienced by him to ignore him, and to behave as if there was nothing the matter. His female victim, who in reality turned away from facing him and was, by all accounts, happily on her way home, could be said to represent the mother who turned her back on him, but she was also the object of his envy, since she was free of the disturbance he was full of that moment. Perceiving the woman to be ignoring him and happily going home, he had to defend against the rage and anxiety that his feelings of motherlessness and homelessness provoked in him but which he felt had been provoked by the object. Instead of feeling at the mercy of a cruel and abandoning object, he attempted to control the object by the attack. One could say that it was not her handbag he was trying to steal but her sense of, in his mind, undeserved well-being.

This offence has profound transferential implications. In the early years of his therapy, one way he tried to defend against the perceived attacks on his psyche was by presenting himself to me as knowing exactly what he needed and demanding this. When he experienced the inevitable frustrations of his unmet demands, or when he discovered that he was not in control of his object, me, he could become furious. This could be triggered by, for example, me saying that the session had ended. The loss of omnipotently created control of his object led to a fury, in those early years of treatment, that had no other way of being experienced other than discharging itself violently. I am referring to when the patient actually required treatment in the intensive care unit of the high security hospital, during which time the therapy was able to proceed in a glass-walled room with two nurses sitting outside, seeing but not hearing.

A similar situation could arise when, occasionally, I was not what and how he wanted me to be. He could either respond with fury, when he would shout angrily at me or walk out before "losing it". Alternatively, he experienced being the victim of my psychic assault on his mind.

During these two kinds of moments, Mr A is highly dangerous. In the first situation, that of losing his omnipotent control of his object, his propensity to act violently towards me or somebody else on the ward is massively increased momentarily, or, at least, until that particular state of mind subsides. In the second situation, the risk of dangerousness is greater against him, when he might deliberately harm himself while he feels himself to be my victim. He can be simultaneously identified with both aggressor and victim, as well as expertly projecting these into me. The experience of being his therapist is that one could be made feel very anxious and frightened at those intense moments, and it was important to use those feelings constructively to formulate the best interpretation under the difficult circumstances, speaking to the patient informatively about what he was then doing to me, his object.

At other times, this patient has presented himself as innocent and harmless, as a nice young man. At these moments, the patient is sufficiently disturbed to believe his delusion of being a nice young man who is misunderstood. This presentation can be very convincing as well as alluring, and professionals, including me, have had to work hard not to be taken in. One way of trying to avoid feeling anxious and frightened while being with such a patient is to collude with their delusion of sanity. This is when serious errors of clinical judgement can be made. To reassure the patient at this moment might well function as a sedative for both patient and therapist, but the "reassured" states are temporary and can swiftly shift to a more obvious hostile presentation. For example, the patient was telling me about his feelings for a nurse he had developed an eroto-manic attachment to and, later in the session, spoke excitedly about another patient who hated her and wanted to kill her. I eventually addressed his feeling like killing her before considering addressing this in the transference to me, and he screamed at me in response, "How can you say that? You treat me as if I was a dangerous person!" Another time, he agitatedly paced around the room, furious about having been secluded after threatening to smash up the ward. He shouted at me, "Don't they know yet that I am not a danger!" At these moments, the patient's awareness of who and how he is is not available to him. I, in order to retain a useful psychoanalytic stance, have to be prepared to remind him what he definitely does not want reminded of. This interpretation can be experienced as an attempt by me to kill him, albeit psychically, which he needs to defend himself against. Again, we have a moment of increased risk of dangerousness when he might get rid of his feelings by acting them out. The next immediate interpretation, therefore, needs to be to show the patient how, when he is reminded of who and how he is, he feels traumatized by this. The hope is that when this has been repeated in therapy hundreds of times, each time it may become less necessary for this to be a bodily experience of rage and terror for the patient and more able to be experienced in his mind.

Case 2

The next patient I would like to tell you about is one whose prognosis is much worse. Ms B is a twenty-seven-year-old woman who killed her nine-week-old daughter and, later, seriously wounded a nurse. She comes from a large and highly dysfunctional family where trans-generational incestuous relationships have resulted in no one being sure of who is who in the extended family. Violence between different sets of parents, mother with father and mother with stepfathers was the norm. There was no experience of consistent mothering. This young woman developed a tic disorder around puberty, which was eventually treated with medication. She met a young man when she was nineteen years old, made a conscious decision that he was the man she would marry and have children with, and she and her husband lived with his alcoholic mother following their marriage.

Ms B was soon delighted to discover she was pregnant. However, the stress of this event on such an ill-equipped young couple led to the breakdown of their marriage late in her pregnancy, so she returned home to live with her own mother. Within days of delivering a healthy baby girl, her mother asked her to leave. This was quite typical of this mother, who later, for example, frequently told the patient, her daughter, that she would be better off committing suicide than causing all this trouble. Ms B and her new baby moved in with a family friend.

Ms B developed concerns about her baby soon after the birth. She was convinced that the baby was sick and called her Health Visitor and family doctor regularly but could never accept reassurance. She once stated that the baby had started manifesting facial tics like her own of such severity that the baby's breathing was affected. The mother and baby were admitted to hospital for the baby to be monitored. Initially, the baby was found to be well. but after two days the baby's condition began to deteriorate. No cause for this deterioration could be found. The baby became critically ill, was transferred to intensive care, and died.

Ms B, bereft, went home with her mother. Soon after the baby's death and post mortem, laboratory reports showed toxic levels in the baby's blood of the medication Ms B was on for her tic disorder, which had caused the death. She was arrested and charged with murdering her baby. She denied any wrong-doing until the end of the trial, when she admitted having given the baby her medication, not to kill the baby, but out of concern that the doctors and nurses were not looking after the baby properly. Retrospectively, it could be suggested that she projected her own bad experience of being mothered twice over, once into her own baby, by identifying with her mother, and then again by projective identification with the nurses and doctors, who became the bad parents for not noticing what was going on within the sick baby, herself, as well as the actual sick baby.

Following her conviction, Ms B was admitted to medium security on a hospital order from the court. She was transferred to high security after seriously wounding a nurse who had suggested it was time to take down all the photographs of her baby, in other words, asking her to give up her failed attempts to mourn. She had also become violent towards herself, cutting herself deeply, hanging herself, and making attempts to strangle herself.

Ms B started psychotherapy with me following her transfer to high security. During the early months of treatment, she presented as a distressed patient who spoke about what a dreadful thing she had done, but all of this had a pseudo-feel to it. This way of presenting to me was gradually shown to her and interpreted as one way she had of avoiding feeling traumatized or victimized by her own disturbed state of mind at the time of her offences and now, in the room with me. This led to suicidality and a further increase in her self-harm.

Later, she became more able to speak to me about what she did to her baby, how she crushed her tablets and secretly fed this to the baby, over and over again. At these moments, her real distress was very apparent. She described her preoccupation at the time with her belief that the baby was not being looked after properly by the nurses and doctors. I said to her, at these moments in her sessions, how she wished to be the baby that could be looked after properly. This is a highly ambivalent situation for this patient, where she is faced with the problem that to be looked after properly negates her view of what proper looking after within her family structure means, creating a sense of betraying her family if she followed the trend of her therapy. I had to be kept, therefore, as someone who was bound to harm her in some way and her history and offence were once more re-enacted.

The pathological mother–child dynamic present in this patient's mind could also be seen in her therapy when, unbeknown to anyone, she took an overdose before a session and then came to her session, appearing with glazed eyes and bilateral hand tremor. She denied several times that anything was the matter when her physical state was commented on, before becoming angry and shouting that there was no point in all this, she wanted to be with her baby, another reference to her suicidality. She kept me in a concerned state and, after considering the likelihood of her having taken an overdose, I told her that I thought she wanted me to be a good mother and guess what was the matter. This was followed by a long silence. I said I believed she would be relieved if I guessed. I then told her I thought she wanted me to know she had taken an overdose. If I did not notice this, she could congratulate herself that she was right, no one notices she is serious (about suicide). If I did notice, she would get something from me but it would feel spoilt because of how she got it. In this situation, the patient did finally admit to having taken an overdose, which had to be urgently dealt with, medically. Again, in this session, the offence is repeated: a baby, herself, is harmed, again with medication, but this time the baby is saved. Indeed, the "being saved" actually led to a manic outburst of profuse thanks from the patient, diluting the seriousness of what had just happened and avoiding the experience of guilt that such a saving could provoke.

Late in the fourth year of treatment, Ms B's mental state deteriorated into a more overtly psychotic presentation when she appeared perplexed and had paranoid delusions of being poisoned by staff as well as experiencing hallucinations. She stopped eating and drinking and required transfer to the medical ward, where she seemed relieved and gratified from being tube fed, which she never refused, as though delegating her need to torture herself to those around her, including her therapist. Many sessions were brief and consisted of the patient slowly shuffling into the room, head down, no eye contact, and in a monotonous voice saying she wanted to be with her baby, she could not stand the pain and didn't deserve to live or die. She would eventually ask a nurse to come and liberate her from me. I would try to show her how she mercilessly punished the baby's mother, herself. I would also take up with her how I was felt to be the punitive one, punishing the baby's mother. She was the baby as well, being harmed by me and needing rescuing from me by the nurses.

What emerged following this more psychotic presentation several months later was a patient who appeared depressed and who complained of flashbacks and nightmares, the content of these always being about her daughter's last hours attached to life-saving equipment and then in the morgue with a damaged dead body. There seemed to be a clash in her mind between the part that killed her baby and knew it, colliding with the grieving part that experienced the flashbacks and longed to be an ordinary grieving mother. A main difficulty at this time in the therapy was whether she could face up to knowing who she was and what she had done and therefore be able to change, or whether she needed to go back to a state of not knowing. By staying unaware, she remains a chronic risk to her babies, actual or symbolic. The pathological mother–child dynamic remains intact. If awareness can develop, with the support provided by the clinical team, the risk to these babies diminishes.

In parallel with this conflict, Ms B fluctuated between three main states of being: first, being distressed, withdrawn, experiencing flashbacks and self-harming; second, psychotic with delusions of being poisoned; or third, being manically freed of all problems, hostile towards carers, and stating herself to be "cured".

During these first five years, Ms B had two relationships with male patients at the hospital. The first lasted for one year until he was discharged, subsequently reoffended, was convicted of rape and attempted murder, and incarcerated in prison. This was a particularly difficult time for Ms B as she attempted to address her pathological attachment to this man in his absence and to distance herself from him. Given her history of perceiving herself as betraying her family by behaving differently (decently), exploring this was extremely difficult for her. Her mother further complicated the situation by repeatedly telling her, when she broke off the relationship, that she should "stand by your man". Indeed, her mother began visiting this man in prison, which further confused the patient. Ms B subsequently began another relationship with a man in the high security hospital, whom she married while they were both still in-patients. This occurred during one of her phases of being manically "cured" and any attempts on my part to show her how she was repeating aspects of her troubled family history were to no avail. Indeed, in the context of a system that could be described as colluding with delusions of normality, psychotherapeutic work around this was rendered almost meaningless. He was discharged and they kept in contact. After one year, he informed her by phone that he was seeing another woman. She phoned her mother in a very distressed state to tell her the awful news and, after listening, her mother told her there was something she needed to know—she, the mother, was the other woman! She then phoned her sister even more distraught and her sister complained to her for not wishing her mother happiness. Given this constellation, it is not difficult to see just how strong the impact of Ms B's current situation, as well as that of her history, continues to jeopardize the chances of getting better.

Ms B managed to break off contact with her mother for over two years after learning of this affair and also began divorce proceedings. During this time, a more receptive involvement in her psychotherapy developed and her mental state was more stable. Relationships with nurses improved and it was felt that there was just a glimpse of the beginning of change possible in her way of relating. In particular, there seemed to be the start of giving up the usual sadomasochistic way she had of relating with her "internal" mother, but this was only possible by simultaneously breaking off contact with the actual mother. However, her mother resumed contact with Ms B after the affair ended. She told her daughter, my patient, that she should be grateful to her for having saved her from being with such a terrible man. In an instant, the idealized mother resurfaced in Ms B's mind and her therapist once more became the "bad" person or object. Ms B's progress was halted in its tracks. This was a further indication to me and the team that contact with her mother was truly detrimental to her mental health and if she had been a child, child protection laws could have been invoked to prevent contact with her mother for the sake of the well-being of that child.

Unfortunately, this patient has remained stuck, now somatizing her unbearable mental experiences or risking developing overt psychotic symptoms. Both these positions prevent her from being able to engage in a dialogue about the contents of her mind with her therapist. The team's main countertransference responses are around hopelessness and anxiety, which she cannot afford to feel. It is very likely that this woman will require permanent institutional care.

Discussion

The aim of the therapy, as part of the overall treatment, is to attempt gradually to help the patients develop knowledge of themselves, what they have done, and what kind of mental life they lived before that allowed these awful events. In other words, enabling them to understand the shift from fantasy to action that arose. A second aim is to use the concept of countertransference to help the clinical team members become more aware of their different responses, and bringing these together so the patient is provided with a more consistent therapeutic approach. What is required is a consistent interpreting stance offered over many years and provided in a supportive manner, and where the clinical team is regularly informed by the therapist of mental state changes. The physical security provides the necessary external boundaries before internal boundaries have formed. The communication between therapist and clinical team offers the patient a new model of consistent "parenting" where the "parents" communicate thoughtfully about the patient instead of exposing the patient to frightening and perplexing violent actions. The changes that are seen to arise and which I hope to have illustrated clinically are in several areas, and I will describe these using the OPD interpersonal relations (axis 2), where you will see the transference and countertransference dimensions contained, and mental structure model (axis 4) and compare and contrast the two patients.

Interpersonal relations

For the clinical team involved in Mr A's care, the balance between care and firmness needs to be delicately and regularly negotiated with him. He experiences others as friend or foe, manifested by him trying to control, make demands, or be contemptuously rejecting of them. This leads others to respond caringly towards him but, given that this provokes his need to control and "fuse" with the now idealized person, others then find themselves wanting to cut off or give up, thereby setting up the vicious circle. The professionals involved in his care, to whom this has been fed back, need to discuss these responses from and towards him regularly in order to provide him with a consistent unified response that he does not expect. This will gradually enable him to form less split ways of relating which are more reality based.

Ms B experiences others as idealized or denigrated, neither of these providing her with the possibility of mature reciprocity and leaving her feeling fused or isolated. A less split version of this can arise when the illusory "wonderful" mother diminishes and carers are allowed to become helpful. This, however, can provoke feelings of betraying her mother, which leads to the reinstalment of the idealized–denigrated split version. She then fuses with the ideal-ized person, needing no one, or she feels cruelly abandoned, which can provoke her into being clingy. Others can experience her as extremely dismissive and contemptuously controlling. Her carers also get a sense of wanting to look after her and protect her, but this is often interrupted by a wish to withdraw from her hostile attacks. This then leaves her once more feeling isolated, triggering a repeat of the cycle. This pattern is helpful for the clinical team to be aware of as different members become the recipients for the different aspects at various times and, with awareness, the responses to the patient's provocations, positive and negative, can be moderated and modified and the risk of team splitting reduced. The aim is to expose her repeatedly to an alternative way of relating and responding in the hope that this cycle of idealization–denigration can be interrupted and reduced.

In this way, one could say that the therapist's involvement with the team, or psychoanalytic input in forensic psychiatry settings, is thought to provide the necessary immunization against the conta-gious symptoms of personality disorders.

Axis 4 mental structure

The first necessary change in the damaged mental structures, I believe, arises in the area of attachment, or with the capacity to begin introjecting new objects. The chance to relate differently is fostered by offering a stable, balanced person to relate to over a long period of time, in other words, offering the chance to develop object constancy, which the patients have never had. Further changes in other aspects of structural dimensions then have the opportunity to germinate. First, in self-perception, the patients develop some curiosity about this new situation, and after many attempts over years to get the object to respond in the expected way and, in many instances perceiving this to be the case, they become able to take the risk that the object may be different. Mr A gradually achieved this and has been able to maintain it, but Ms B, who caught a glimpse of this, lost it again once her "old world" resurfaced upon the return of her mother in her life. In the presence of a constant object, albeit one that is still perceived as unpredictable, he or she can gradually develop a capacity for self-reflection. Both patients presented were able to manage this shift, but again, Ms B's ability to do so swiftly evaporated once her mental state regressed, a further indication of just how fragile the shifts were that she had made. Second, after hundreds of occasions identifying the various affects in sessions, patients become aware of these when they arise (externally or internally provoked) and even eventually to differentiate between them. Mr A has maintained his newly and slowly developed capacity to recognize his affects and changes that can arise and what may have caused these. Ms B, sadly, regressed to her previous disintegrated structure, where she experiences strong affects, often of anger and despair, and believes these to be always provoked by those people around her.

Simultaneously, the capacity for object perception can evolve with concomitant subject–object differentiation, awareness of the affects of the other, and, thereby, the beginning of capacity for empathy with, much later on in treatment, consequent guilt and remorse, when suicidality can arise. This is when the constellation of post traumatic stress disorder type symptoms can emerge. With the improved self and object perceptions, attachments gradually become less disordered, communication becomes more reciprocal, and the main defence modes, which relate to these other structural dimensions, can mature. Regulation and tolerance of affects can be more internally located and less reliant on external measures. Mr A has been able to maintain an overall progress in these areas; despite the occasional regressions in his states of mind, he is able to retrieve this progress. Ms B has been unable, unfortunately, to maintain or retrieve her slight progressive shifts.

It is important to note that, at times of stress, when increased demands are placed on the patients, their mental states can regress and this is when a return to previous functioning, albeit in a modified way, is possible. At these times, patients are prone to minor re-enactments, which cause major anxiety in those looking after them. In other words, the mental structure changes remain fragile and can shift back to being less integrated. However, Mr A's capacity to continue making progress and retrieve this when it is lost at times of "stress and regress" is to be contrasted with Ms B's inability to do so. In my view, this makes quite a difference in the risk assessment of these two patients. Both are, of course, prone to minor re-enactments, but Ms B is at much greater risk of major re-enactment than Mr A. This is the opposite picture to what would have been assessed comparing these two patients ten years ago, both of whom presented with relatively disintegrated mental structures. It was only in the course of this long treatment, monitoring changes using the OPD tool, that a more detailed and evidence-based risk assessment could be carried out.

Why such a difference between the two? If, in infancy, excessive hostility and consequent paranoid anxiety is experienced towards the primary object, which is more likely to have been the case for Ms B, the stronger the fixation and the deeper the split between a bad and a highly idealized object. There are, consequently, transferential complexities that arise from treating people whose primary figures, mother and symbols of mother, were abandoning, unreliable, replaced, and frequently violent objects, leading to the employment of omnipotent defence mechanisms characterized by excessive splitting and projection. In the transference, right from the start, the patient's fixation at paranoid levels of development and their defences have to be repeatedly analysed in order eventually to mobilize the patient's capacity for experiencing love, depression, and guilt. After ten years, I can state that Mr A has been able to and Ms B just could not.

The patients presented are both diagnosed as suffering from personality disorders (Mr A, antisocial and narcissistic; Ms B, borderline). Both became unwell during their adolescence and I believe that these were their second breakdowns, the first having also occurred unnoticed when they were small children and which led to the disordered personality development. The presenting symptoms, consistent with the PD diagnoses, are also consistent with those of a prodromal phase of a psychotic illness, the psychosis becoming manifest at the moment of the killing. The evidence for this is available in the histories. In the months leading up to the killings, these patients became periodically withdrawn, egocentric, and grandiose, similar to those young people harbouring a schizophrenic illness. Mr A came close to killing women on several occasions beforehand and managed to retreat from doing so by still having a sane part of his ego which could overcome the demands to kill coming from the psychotic and mad part of his superego, the pull from fantasy to action. When he killed the woman, this is the moment that his psychotic illness triumphed over the personality disorder, which was no longer able to defend him against the propensity for enormous splitting and projection, and led to a spillage out of the mind into action. Ms B became convinced that the doctors and nurses were not looking after the baby properly, had a grandiose delusion that she knew better, and acted on this. She has repeated this over and over during treatment.

After several years of treatment, symptoms reminiscent of post traumatic stress disorder can arise and the evidence for these is: the emergence of flashbacks, nightmares, preoccupation with the awful events that happened to them growing up and those that they later caused, states of mind alternating between being depressed or being manically freed from this, and, eventually, a capacity to experience guilt. Even these, as we can see from Ms B, who experienced them, are not necessarily reliably stable, positive shifts. Due to the structural changes that can arise, the experience of remorse may occur and is often accompanied by a complex mixture of depressed and angry feelings with a psychical longing to return to a state of oblivion. This was once beautifully described by another patient— one who had killed his mother: "It's much worse for me now doctor, all this thinking and analysing—but I could never go back to how I was before you helped me train the muscles of my mind, even though I'd like to sometimes. Before, if I didn't like something, I'd smash it to pieces. Now, if I don't like something, I start thinking, why don't I like that? Oh, it's because of this or that reason. By the time I've worked it all out, I don't even feel like smashing it any more!"

To conclude, the process of treatment appears to require a complicated and lengthy transition period from the patient knowing very little about him or her self to developing awareness and dealing with the profoundly traumatic effects of this, where thoughts and feelings about what happened and their predicament in relation to this could be experienced in mind without the need to get rid of these in the familiar ways of acting them out violently. With consistency over a long period of time, it is possible for some of these patients to make tentative shifts towards the "depressive position" and this is something that needs to be worked through over and over until the negative therapeutic responses, triggered by the positive shifts, or provoked by "getting better", lessen in severity and frequency. Long-term continuity of treatment throughout the patient's moves through different levels of security is necessary to enable this to arise. It is a lot to ask of people who suffer the triple traumas described earlier, as well as being a challenge to those treating them. The chance to develop a mind and life which is reliably different can only be realized within the necessary physical security to start off, the mutual commitment of patient and therapist, collaboration with the clinical team, and regular supervisions for all concerned with these patients.

Note

The two case histories have appeared in other published papers.

Discussion of Carine Minne's paper

Richard Ingram: "Thank you very much indeed, Carine, for a wonderful paper and an insight into working with this level of disturbance in a very high secure setting. I'm sure we have lots of questions we would like to put."

Question from the floor: "Would psychotic transference be an appropriate for Mr A's thinking in the immediate build up to the killing of his victim?"

Carine Minne: "Definitely, yes."

Question from the floor: "Is it a term you would use nowadays?"

Carine Minne: "Yes, it would still be used and I think it makes sense to use it because it's quite clear what it means."

Question from the floor: "It reflects the intensity?"

Carine Minne: "Absolutely, what I was trying to describe was how at that moment, that's when he became overtly psychiatrically psychotic and not just psychoanalytically psychotic."

Brian Martindale: "Thank you very much, Carine, for a wonderful paper, very rich and easy to follow as well this horrendous psychopathology you are working with. My question is about your work with the other staff. I've a feeling we know that in hospitals and in outpatient services there are all kind of complex relationships between our colleagues and I think there is a tendency to idealize them at times and not perhaps come to ground with a range of things that go on. So, what I'd like you to comment on is the nature of your work with the staff who work alongside you with these patients and how you help them look at some of the things that happen in these places between patients and staff."

Carine Minne: "Thanks, Brian. It's a big question in a sense and we have discussed this over and over again with colleagues at the Portman Clinic because the Portman provides consultations to different secure forensic psychiatry settings and on the other hand there are few of us actually employed by Broadmoor, working in Broadmoor. So, there are two kinds of approaches: one is the internal approach, that is, an insider trying to work with the staff, and the alternative is an external consultant going in and providing relational security, as it is now called, by the Department of Health input. I think there are benefits from both kinds. Because my work is directly with the patients I think it's really important for me to communicate with the staff, otherwise it's a little split off thing that happens. I can't even say in a proper consulting room, sometimes it's the telephone kiosk on the ward that we end up using, because it's whatever room might be available and usually the solicitors and dieticians have priority. If the therapist comes along you are third or fourth on the list to get a room; sometimes you don't even get a room. There a different ways of involving the clinical team. I always say to the patients right at the beginning, because of the whole issue of confidentiality, that if any security matters were to arise, the nitty gritty day in-day out stuff of our sessions is between the therapist and the patient but if any security matters arise, which is a very broad term for anything I might get worried about, then we'll discuss it with your primary nurse and/or the RMO. Quite often, with both these patients, at the end of the session where there have been some concerns about maybe self harm or harming someone else, I have invited the primary nurse or the RMO, or, indeed, both, to come in and to enable the patient themselves to say what they think, and if they haven't felt able then at least they hear me saying what I think they were worried about and, indeed, that I'm worried about. So, the patients are exposed to what I was trying to describe earlier about parents discussing them in a more thoughtful way than I think they have ever experienced things before, and I think for the staff it is really important to involve them in the therapy, otherwise you are just a split-off thing, a little notice on the door, "therapy in progress, do not disturb". I think it makes the work for the primary nurse more interesting when they know what is going on, and indeed many of the primary nurses have wanted to take on patients in therapy, under supervision, and so on. I attend ward rounds, I go to case conferences, reports that I write on patients I discuss with the patient, so they know, and if they don't agree, what the work will be for the next year. The other approach to working with the clinical staff is the external consultation approach, which takes more of the staff dynamics into consideration because, if we go back to what Rob Hale described as the psychopath bringing out the worst in you, we know very well that places like Broadmoor, medium secure, they are very sick places. There is high staff turnover, high rates of sickness, great tension between the disciplines, and I think it is really important that the staff do get a chance to discuss these things and relate it to the clinical work that they are doing and how contagious the patients' disorders are. So, I hope I've addressed your point.

Cathal Cassidy: "The last question Professor Perelberg was asked (she presented her paper on male violence), and someone asked her, "What about female violence?" They didn't quite get an answer to that, but you have, in that you have presented a male patient and a female patient. The male we recognize, as in Professor Perelberg's cases, the violence, the physical violence, the killing, but you also then present this female, and isn't that a lot of the answer to that question that was put to Professor Perelberg? The female violence you describe, not only in the patient, but also in the patient's mother. The emotional violence, the psychological violence, the merging, the no boundaries, and even that she kills the child, but she kills the child by dispensing medication, a way of caring for the child. So, you say a little bit about that, about drawing that distinction between male violence and female violence. I don't want to use the word aggression, but I think a lot of us have difficulty in understanding and recognizing female violence and seeing how it is different from male violence and this brings thoughts about Estelle Welldon's book."

Carine Minne: "It's a big question, and in a sense I wish Estelle was in the audience to say some more about it. Interestingly, when Don spoke about violent incidents, when Richard had asked earlier about procedural matters and how rooms are sorted out, panic buttons and so on were mentioned. At the Portman Clinic we don't use panic buttons; what we've generally done is always had the patients sitting close to the door. They are more likely to become paranoid and need to get out quickly, which goes against what we were all taught at the Royal College, which was to sit nearest the door in case you need to make a getaway. He was saying that out of the four violent incidents at the Portman in the last thirty years, three involved women patients. I've only used the emergency button twice in my fifteen years at Broadmoor, and on both occasions it was with that female patient. I'd like to add something else about that. The male patient that I described just now, talking about panic buttons, we generally sit the patient nearest the door, but the panic button is nearest us and as this patient got better, but consequently felt much worse, on one occasion he opened up the session by saying, 'It's really not fair, Dr Minne, you get to sit next to the panic button, what if I feel threatened by you and I want to press the button and get the nurses to rescue me from you.' He was absolutely right, it never occurred to me. After that I started trying to put the panic button in the middle. Then I wrote to the authorities trying to get two panic buttons in each room. Of course, they thought I was completely mad. It hasn't happened, and I think we probably need another 1000 years of civilized society before we get to that. I think there is a generalization about female and male violence, that male violence is more externally directed and female violence is more internally directed, towards the body or towards the products of the body, that is, the babies. I think there is a lot to be said to that and certainly many of the female patients that we would see have been extremely violent and far more violent to themselves or their babies than the kind of male violence where it is frequently others, stranger or mother or whoever, that has been attacked. But you can also see from the presentation that I just gave that there is a huge degree of overlap between the two. Both these patients are completely scarred, up and down, from self-harm. Both patients have attacked members of staff; indeed, the female patient stabbed a nurse. Luckily, it was wintertime and the nurse had many layers of clothing and that protected her somewhat. So, I think there is a great degree of crossover and that's what I hope to have shown today. But I think the general division that Estelle and others have written about does hold."

Deyra Courtney: "There are two things I have been wondering about. The first was from the second to last question, and that was about the impact of your work in Broadmoor and having staff wanting to take on cases in conjunction with the work that you are doing with them, and I was wondering how you see the impact of staff having psychotherapy cases on their way of relating to the patients and on the broader scheme of things in the unit. The second thing I was wondering about, from Dr Cassidy's question, was in terms of the two cases you presented and the male patient's violence being a much more external thing and his internal structure changing. Would you consider that in the case of the female patient, the ongoing aggression or violence is in terms of the internal destruction of what is happening as well, and the continuation of the idealization and the denegration and her actions with regard to what has been achieved in therapy?"

Carine Minne: "You've answered your second question. If I go back to your first question, I'd like to answer it by referring to something that I heard recently from a colleague who has been doing some of these consultations that we were talking about with Brian, in a prison session with an in-reach team. They were struggling and wanted someone to help them think about the prisoner patients they were seeing. What was really interesting was that after a few months of him providing these reflective practice type meetings, two team leaders left, then several other members left, and I think the thinking became too much. They started to get in touch with what was really going on and what they were really exposed to and what the poor people were exposed to in the prison setting and it became too much. And you could say it is a healthy to leave a post that is so difficult and so toxic. That's not what I hope to do in Broadmoor, but I think one of the problems we have in secure settings like that, in order to have the right amount of manpower, a lot of inexperienced, not highly trained people end up working there and they are exposed to extremely difficult patients and I often think of the comparison with a place like the Royal Brompton Hospital, the cancer specializing hospital, and they have highly specialized nurses and we don't get that, we get a few highly specialized nurses and they end up in management, and the really hands-on people are often nursing assistants who are well-meaning but who haven't had the kind of training we have had the privilege of having. I think it's really important to be available to help them process what kinds of things they are exposed to, otherwise the degree of enactments that can happen, or burnout, is extreme."

Richard Ingram: "Time for one last question."

Question from the floor: "I'd like to thank you for that paper. I have two questions: one is I'm curious about the projections that might be placed upon yourself by the staff in this idealized therapeutic environment, although you shattered mine when you described the kiosk (I had illusions of you having a nice comfortable therapy room). The other question is in terms of the therapy you provide in Broadmoor which is highly ordered and structured. Other therapists, such as myself, have gone into prisons on a one-off basis and I have mixed feelings about that in terms of an unstructured way in which a patient can leave the therapy room to go back to the ward. I was wondering if you have done consultancy work with people like what I was doing in terms of working in a very structured way and have you any thoughts on that?"

Carine Minne: "It's extremely difficult, it's kind of luxurious, the kind of work I'm describing to you in Broadmoor, even though it's quite a difficult place to get to, apart from anything else. To get in is ever more difficult: you have to have your fingerprints matched, but working in the prison system is probably the hardest of all of the forensic settings because it's about action, it's all action orientated and it's all about procedure and physical security and the more relational security, that is, thinking about things, it's designed to destroy the possibility of that in a sense. I think it's really important not to give up, to keep trying to do it despite the relentless attacks. No room being available, or it's lock up or lock down, or that patient you've had in treatment for four weeks has now been moved to another prison without you being warned, all those inevitable things, it's important to carry on. More importantly, to speak to the staff who are working there. They are the ones who are with those people twenty-four hours a day and receive all the projections and sometimes don't realize what is happening to them and then end up having knee-jerk punitive responses to what they are exposed to. You asked about the projections on to me? Of course, it makes you feel like giving up all the time, and I think it's supervision that keeps me going, and the patients, but I couldn't do it without having supervision, which I have regularly with Dr Leslie Sohn and have the privilege of having supervision with Don Campbell, whom you heard this morning."

Richard Ingram: "We've run out of time, but I'd like to express our appreciation to Carine."

CHAPTER FOUR

The interpretation of violence

James Gilligan

C *arine Minne*: "It's a huge pleasure for me to introduce James, whom I've known for many years, and we're very privileged to have him here. It's great that he has made it. I think James was the only man who caught the flight from London to Belfast on Wednesday morning. It was the one and only flight that went that day.

"James is a world expert on violence and on the psychoanalytic understanding of violence, and has been in the field working for over forty years and probably seen more people who have killed, more murderers, than anybody else on the planet. James is Clinical Professor of Psychiatry at the School of Medicine, an Adjunct Professor at the School of Law and Collegiate Professor at the School of Arts and Science at New York University, and I won't say all the other things that he has done, but he has published profusely, he is writing all the time, his books are wonderful, his papers are fantastic, and we are going to be thrilled by what he is going to say this morning. I am sure it's going to lead to a very rich discussion afterwards. Over to you, James, and thank you very much."

Professor James Gilligan: "Thank you very much, Carine, it's a great pleasure to be here."

*   *   *

I am very lucky to have been able to get here without nearly the amount of trouble other people have had. I am very grateful to the organizers of this International Psychoanalytic Conference for inviting me here, because the opportunity to talk with you makes it possible for me to speak directly about the psychoanalytic nature of my work. To me, violence and the people who act violently have become a window through which it is possible for us to see into the human psyche, and, more specifically, to observe aspects of psychic functioning that reveal relationships between the mind and the body, and psyche in the culture, that are less clear or even invisible when our gaze is directed elsewhere. In my work over the past forty years, violence has become an entry point for a psychoanalytic enquiry that is at once theoretical and clinical. I have been drawn to the study of violence not only because the problem of human violence has become so overwhelmingly important in this age of genocide and thermonuclear weapons, but also because the study of violence has proved so psychologically revealing. Approaching violence from a psychoanalytic point of view illuminates the psychology of violence; in addition, however, I have come to see the study of violence as contributing in significant ways to what I hope you also will see as the larger psychoanalytic project—that is, to our ability to understand and interpret the human world.

So let me begin by reiterating the most basic of psychoanalytic premises—Freud's discovery of the logic in the apparently senseless or irrational, such as dreams, delusions, myths, and neurotic symptoms, by learning how to interpret or translate them into rational language and show how they relate to people's lives and their unconscious purposes.

I have spent many years struggling to understand and make sense of violent behaviour that often appears to be senseless, self-defeating, and unrelated to any rational purpose. And I have found that I could do so by approaching it psychoanalytically, that is, by making three assumptions. The first is the assumption that all human behaviour is meaningful, whether it is a thought, a symptom, or an action; that it has a logic, a motive, and a meaning; and that to discover that one needs to talk with the person and listen seriously to what he or she says. Twenty-five years of doing this with violent people has convinced me that violent behaviour, even at its most apparently senseless, incomprehensible, or even psychotic, can be understood—that it makes psychological sense.

The second assumption is that the logic of violent behaviour is a symbolic logic that can only be understood by interpreting the symbolism and thus revealing the hidden, or unconscious, meaning and motive of the violent act. The third assumption is that all behaviour has a history, and has to be understood in relation to that history—an individual life history which unfolds within and takes its meaning from a larger social and cultural history. This becomes clear not only when we relate the perpetration of violence to the perpetrator's own experience of being a victim of violence—that is, to childhood trauma and abuse—but also when we ask epidemiological questions concerning the association between violence and such historical, cultural, and economic phenomena as race, gender, and social class.

Bringing this psychoanalytic approach to the study of violence reveals and illuminates many things that would otherwise be invisible, such as the connection between the inner world of the individual murderer (such as the emotions of envy or humiliation that motivate him in the moment of his committing an act of violence) and the outer world in which he lives and grew up (such as his inferior position in the status structure of his society; the historical heritage of a demeaned social status that is carried, and transmitted to him, by the group into which he was born; or the moral obligation he inherited to uphold the honour of his family or tribe by means of violence, even if it is at the cost of his own life).

In my attempts to understand the symbolic logic that motivates people to commit apparently senseless violence, as well as the unconscious logic that leads them to commit apparently rational but actually self-defeating violence, I have been inspired by a frequently quoted passage from the *New Introductory Lectures on Psychoanalysis*, in which Freud wrote that

pathology, by making things larger and coarser, can draw our attention to normal conditions which would otherwise have escaped us. Where it points to a breach or a rent, there may normally be an articulation present. If we throw a crystal to the floor, it breaks; but not into haphazard pieces. It comes apart along its lines of cleavage into fragments whose boundaries, though they were invisible, were predetermined by the crystal's structure. Mental patients are split and broken structures of this same kind. [1933a, pp. 58–59]

Freud's point was that neurotic or psychotic symptoms could throw light on aspects of the structure and functioning of the psyche that are universal, and apply both to the normal and the abnormal. I decided to see if the same might not be true of violent behaviour by treating it, for these purposes, as simply another symptom of individual and collective psychopathology or maladaptive functioning that is lethal both to individuals and, potentially, our whole species, unless we can improve our ability to understand and prevent it more effectively than we have up to now.

Adapting that point of view to the study of violence, I decided to study the most extreme examples of violence—the most horrendous atrocities, committed by the most incorrigibly and intractable violent people—on the assumption that they, too, were broken crystals, so that the motives that underlay their behaviour might be more apparent than they would be with more moderate levels of violence—the violence of everyday life. In our society, one of the few places in which it is possible to find exemplars of the most extreme violence is the prison and the prison mental hospital. If you were to ask me why I chose to work with violent criminals in such terrible environments, I would paraphrase what the American bank robber Willie Sutton said when he was asked why he robbed banks: "Because that's where the money is." I went into prisons, because that's where the violent people were.

To me, the exploration of those microcosms of murder derived its ultimate significance as an opportunity to use those settings as clinical "laboratories" in which to learn about the causes and prevention of the human propensity to commit acts of horrendous violence, wherever it manifests itself and on whatever scale—from homicide and suicide to war and genocide.

In the prisons and prison mental hospitals, violent individuals became my teachers and I their student in the effort to learn what could possibly lead human beings to treat other human beings as if they were not human, in ways that we call "inhuman", and whether there were any therapeutic interventions that could enable them to free themselves from the vicious circles of violence and retaliation that their lives had become, in which the more violent they were, the more harshly they were punished, to which they responded by becoming even more violent in return, and so on, *ad infinitum*. In the microcosm of the prison, this was a trap into which all of us—that is, the rest of society (as represented by our criminal justice system)—had fallen along with the prisoners, so that my task became to liberate the prisons as much as the prisoners from this mutually self-defeating vicious circle.

The clinical examples I want to summarize for you today are taken from among the most violent individuals, because they exemplify most starkly the fundamental features of all violent behaviour. In this sense, they function like myths and tragedies. The Greek tragedies and those of Shakespeare, the horrors described in Thucydides and the Bible, have seemed to me to map the universe of human violence that I have seen. And it is through thinking in terms of that literature that I personally have managed to find a way to mediate between ordinary sanity and humanity on the one hand, and unimaginable horror and monstrosity on the other. Compared to the tragedies I have seen and heard of on a daily basis, the abstractions of many of the "social sciences" seem like pale imitations of reality, like the shadows on the wall of Plato's cave. In the worlds I have worked in, Oedipus is not a theory, or a "complex". I have seen Oedipus, a man who killed his father and then blinded himself, not on the stage and not in a textbook, but in real life. I have seen Medea, a woman who killed her own children in response to her husband's infatuation with another woman. I have seen Othello, a man who murdered his wife and then took his own life. I have seen Samson (the archetypal "son of Sam"), and I have seen him many times: men who have brought the roof down on their own heads as the only means of expressing their boundless rage, when the whole world appeared to them as their enemy and they wanted to kill everyone, even, or perhaps especially, if it meant ending their own lives as well.

These experiences have led me to think that the classical myths and tragedies may have originated not so much as products of fantasy, as the symbolic, "conscious" representation of fantasies that are unconscious in the minds of healthy people, but, rather, as attempts to describe and represent, to cope with and make sense of, indeed to survive, emotionally and mentally, the actual crimes and atrocities that people have inflicted on one another for as far back into history as our collective memories extend.

"In the beginning was the deed," says Goethe, in Faust. He may well be right. In the violent men I have studied, the (violent) deed precedes the thought and the word. Much of the therapy we do with violent men consists of trying to help them find the words with which they could think and talk about their thoughts and feelings instead of acting them out in the form of impulsive, apparently "senseless" violence, or of premeditated, pseudo-rational violence. The blinding of Samson, Tiresias, and the Cyclops, the blinding of Gloucester in *King Lear*, are not so much mythic "fictions" as they are tragic depictions of real acts that real people commit in real life.

I say that as preface to my attempt to try to understand what could possibly have caused one particular act of violence that seemed to me to have pushed violence to the limit beyond which physical reality does not permit humans to go, just as it exemplifies the immemorial human propensity to push violence to the limit of what is physically possible. I want to begin with the story of a man I will call Ross L, because, of all the hundreds of murderers with whom I had spoken over the years, his crime had seemed to me the most senseless and incomprehensible, motiveless and meaningless. I had thought that I was beginning to be able to understand the individual and social forces that impelled men to commit truly terrible acts of violence, even when their motives had at first seemed cloudy or unclear. But the murder this man had committed seemed so totally senseless, so bereft of any motive that I could discover or imagine that might explain the connection between it and his horrible crime, that I felt totally perplexed. Then it occurred to me that the meaning of his crime was, all too literally, staring me in the face—that he had succeeded in communicating his message and his meaning not in words at all, but completely through actions. "In the beginning was the deed." This murder conformed completely to that principle; it could have been the primal paradigm upon which all murders are patterned, and it was going to have to be my job to translate his deed into words, if I were going to be able to understand why this particularly terrible murder, or any other murder, had occurred.

Ross L was a twenty-year-old man who was sentenced to prison because he had murdered a woman of his age, and, in the process, also cut out her eyes and tongue (ostensibly so she could not identify him to the police if she lived). His crime stood out for me not only for its brutality and its horror, for the extremes that it seemed to represent in the loss of that capacity for the most basic and normal human feelings that go to make up what we ordinarily mean when we speak of "humanity" itself, but also for its utter and total senselessness. If by some miracle she had lived, she still could have identified him, even without eyes or tongue, for she knew him. But in fact he had killed her, beyond any possibility of doubt, and dead men (and women) tell no tales; so why had he felt the need to add horror to horror by stabbing out her eyes and cutting her tongue apart as well? Doing this not only did not protect him from being discovered, it created even more evidence of his guilt for the murder. And, of course, murder itself is senseless and unnecessary; he did not "have" to kill her in the first place. The only effect of his doing so (if we think in terms of his "rational self-interest") is that now he will have to spend the rest of his life in prison.

So why did he do what he did? His actions not only constituted the extreme violation of another person's humanity, they also seemed to me to represent a kind of individual version, in their irrationality and their violation of every canon of common sense and what we normally call self-interest, of the many collective atrocities which have occurred throughout the history of warfare and genocide; to pose a kind of parallel, on a microcosmic scale, to what those kinds of collective violence represent on a macrocosmic one. Those are among the reasons why the very extremity of both the violence and the irrationality contained in his crime seemed to me to imply the possibility that it might reveal, more clearly than a more limited or moderate act of violence could, the psychological forces that underlie all violence, so that if we could learn to understand the psycho-logic that underlay this man's crime, we might come upon factors common to all murders.

When I began to ask myself what kind of person could have been capable of such atrocity, and what his real motivation could have been (for, as I have said, his ostensible purpose makes no sense at all), it occurred to me that his act had succeeded far beyond his purported intention: although the police caught him, the effect his crime had on the moral feelings of the people who then had to deal with him was that the sheer "inhumanity" of his crime was so extreme that he had become to others barely, if at all, recognizable or identifiable as human, as a human being. It had become very difficult to see him as a person, in other words—his crime kept getting in the way, concealing him, so to speak. And it occurred to me that that elemental fact might be the first clue in my effort to understand what could have caused him to do what he did.

Reflecting further on this man, talking with him at more length, and seeing his utter absence of remorse or guilt feelings and his feeling not only of total innocence but of wounded innocence (despite the fact that he did not deny that he had committed the acts of which he was found guilty); his feeling that other people were treating him unfairly and picking on him and always had; his attribution to others of all responsibility for his problems; his feeling that all the justification he needed for his crime was that "I didn't like the way she was looking at me" and "I didn't want her talking about me"; his extreme sensitivity to insult; his boasting and grandiosity; his assumption that he was entitled to have special privileges; his reiterated threats that if he did not get what he wanted he would kill himself or us and that whatever he did would be our fault; his unwillingness to accept responsibility for anything that would make him "look bad", I began to realize that his crime makes all too much sense, when one grasps the special logic that lies behind it.

How can we go about learning to see what that logic is? I will start with Freud's insight that thoughts and fantasies are symbolic representations of actions, so that they can precede actions and serve as substitutes for them as well. But it is also true that actions are symbolic (pre-verbal) representations of thoughts. Thus, actions can precede and serve as substitutes for (conscious) thoughts. That is, if the behaviour is never interpreted or translated into words and ideas, actions can simply take the place of "thinking" in terms of words.

The philosopher and literary critic Kenneth Burke wrote that in order to understand literature, we must learn to interpret *Language as Symbolic Action* (1966). I am suggesting that in order to under-

stand violence, we must reverse that procedure and learn to interpret action as symbolic language with a "symbolic logic" of its own.
Individuals or groups engaging in any given behaviour may or may
not be able to state consciously what the meaning of their action is,
or, in other words, what thought the action can be described as
having (in the medium of language). That is, they may not be able
to translate a symbolic action, such as a ritual, into that other
symbolic medium called language. Nevertheless, all behaviour is
meaningful; all behaviour is the embodiment or enactment, the
acting out, of a purpose or a wish; or, in a larger sense, of a wishful
fantasy, a story, a personal or collective myth; a plot, scenario, or
narrative, and sometimes a dream, nightmare or delusion, that can
also be expressed, by means of language, as a thought.

People with disorders of character, whose psychopathology
manifests itself in the form of abnormal, destructive, or life-threatening behaviour, act out in their behaviour the fantasies that normal
and neurotic people experience only in their unconscious minds
(such as in nightmares, or in the dreams of incest to which Plato
refers). They can also be described as acting out the fantasies that
psychotic people experience consciously in their delusions (which
is one reason why most of the violence in this world is committed
by people who occupy the "borderline" psychotic spectrum of character disorders, along with their near neighbours, those in the
"narcissistic" spectrum). In my attempt to understand murder and
the other forms of violent behaviour, then, I came to interpret that
behaviour, to translate its purpose or point or meaning into words
and thoughts. Just as Freud came to see the somatic symptoms of
his hysterical patients as a symbolic form of speech, so that the
body itself, rather than language, became the medium of communication, so we can see violence as a way of speaking with the body,
and apply the same processes and principles to the understanding
of violence that we bring to other non-verbal or non-logical modes
of communication, such as compulsive behaviour, repeated acci-
dents, magical rituals, and so on.

In other words, to understand murder and the other forms of
violence we must learn to understand what thought or fantasy the
violent behaviour is the symbolic representation of, or the ritual
enactment of, what it is "saying", as that can be re-stated in words,
and what unacceptable or threatening thought it represents,

through the symbolism of action, to deny or ward off. My hope was that if we could learn to understand this one murder, then the same principles of interpretation could be applied to any given act of violence.

One clue as to what the thought was that Ross L was expressing, or "acting out", in this senseless and apparently unmotivated murder and mutilation, is that the more time I spent with him, the clearer it became that his character—his habits and behaviour patterns, the moral value system in terms of which he justified his behaviour and goals—served as a defence against the threat of being treated with scorn and disrespect, of being perceived as a weakling, not a "real man", someone who could be "pushed around", laughed at, taken advantage of, and gossiped about. All of this suggested that he suffered from feelings of weakness, impotence, inferiority, and inadequacy as a man, and that as a result he might feel vulnerable and hypersensitive to any experience that would reflect that image of himself back to him. And as I talked with him further, I learnt that he had indeed had such experiences, and he had indeed found them intolerable.

For example, throughout his childhood, he said, he was regularly beaten up and teased by other boys, who taunted him as "a wimp, a punk, and a pussy". "Punk" is the derogatory, homophobic prison slang term for the passive sex-object, the sex-slave or "kid", of a more powerful man, and "pussy" is, of course, the equally derogatory slang term for the female genitals. So, he was being called an inadequate man, or non-man, in every possible way: as a wimp, he was a sissy, a Mr Milquetoast; as a punk, a homosexual; and as a pussy, not even male at all, but female.

When he was thirteen, however, he began drinking and taking street drugs (including cocaine), which he felt helped him to behave violently himself. That in turn bolstered his self-respect as a man. He boasted that he could rebuild the engine of any car within three hours. Mechanical expertise with cars was important to him, as it is to many teenage males, as a means of proving his adequacy as a man. But he committed his crime when he was without a car because he had been unable to pay the mechanic whom he had had to ask to rebuild its engine. The girl he murdered was a former high school classmate of his, to whom he had thus been forced to admit that he did not have either the money or the mechanical skills to have a car of his own, and upon whom he had to depend for a ride on a cold night. (A very trivial humiliation, of course, by any "objective" criterion, but, as I will discuss later, the intensity of humiliation is often inversely related to the magnitude of the precipitant.)

He also boasted of having become "the Don Juan" of his hometown, a "real stud" who had no trouble "getting girls". He claimed that he had not been hurt whenever he had been rejected by a girl, though he insisted that that had very seldom occurred. But, in fact, despite the "phallic narcissism" of his braggadocio, he had not succeeded in establishing his masculine sexual adequacy by forming a mutually satisfying sexual relationship with anyone. The task the police had in finding the murderer was made easier by the fact that he could not resist attempting to impress one of his acquaintances about how "tough" he was by boasting to him about the brutal crime he had just committed.

All of this suggests to me that the logic that underlay his murder and mutilation of another person was the emotional logic of the family of painful feelings called shame and humiliation, including feelings of weakness, inferiority, incompetence, sexual and financial inadequacy, painful feelings which, when they become overwhelming because a person has no basis for self-respect, can be intolerable, and so devastating as to bring about the collapse of self-esteem and the sense of self-worth—what some Asian cultures call "loss of face". And since the face is the physical symbol of the self, a person who "loses face" also loses the sense of having, or being, an intact, alive self. His behaviour, as we explore it further, can be seen as a desperate attempt—what could be more desperate?—to ward off these catastrophic experiences, and I will suggest that in its focus on eyes and tongues, his grotesque crime follows the logic of shame.

We all know that shame motivates the wish for concealment, the wish not to be seen; the word itself comes from Old Germanic roots meaning to clothe or cover oneself (cf. *Oxford English Dictionary*; Klein, 1966; Partridge, 1958; Schneider, 1977, pp. 29–30). As Otto Fenichel put it, "'I feel ashamed' means 'I do not want to be seen'" (1945, p. 139). Darwin pointed out that "Under a keen sense of shame there is a strong desire for concealment. . . . An ashamed person can hardly endure to meet the gaze of those present . . ." (1872, pp. 320–321). But Erik Erikson takes this common insight a step further, in a way that may help us to understand our murderer more deeply. He says,

> Shame supposes that one is completely exposed and conscious of being looked at . . . One is visible and not ready to be visible; which is why we dream of shame as a situation in which we are stared at in a condition of incomplete dress . . . 'with one's pants down.' . . . He who is ashamed would like to force the world not to look at him, not to notice his exposure. He would like to destroy the eyes of the world. [1963, pp. 252–253]

Erikson quotes the folk song that the poet Carl Sandburg used to sing, about a murderer who is standing under the gallows waiting to be hanged, to illustrate this aspect of shame, and the anger it stimulates towards the people in whose eyes one feels shamed (for one does feel shamed in other people's eyes):

> "My name it is Sam Hall, it is Sam Hall,
> And I hate you one and all, one and all:
> God damn your eyes!"

All of which is less surprising when we reflect that, as Aristotle realized long ago, ". . . *to en ophthalmois einai aido*", the eyes are the abode of shame. And, he added,

> For this reason we feel most shame before those who will always be with us and those who notice what we do, since in both cases eyes are upon us . . . we feel more shame about a thing if it is done openly, before all men's eyes. Hence the proverb, 'shame dwells in the eyes'. [1954, II. vi. 18–20]

But not only in the eyes, for, as he also realized, we also feel more shame "before those who are likely to tell everybody about you", and since "not telling others is as good as not believing you wrong", we can understand why preventing them from telling others about you, such as by preventing them from talking at all, is one of the oldest and most powerful ways of reducing one's risk of being shamed.

Leon Wurmser reached exactly the same conclusions more recently, when he wrote that "the eye is the organ of shame par excellence" (1987, p. 67). But not only the eye, for it is not only "the punishing look, the scornful expression", but also "the humiliating word, the derisive tone of voice and snickering, the rejecting gesture . . . sticking out the tongue . . . that signify shaming" (1981, p. 79). As long as shame is the operative emotion, these looks, this ridicule and gossip, are perceived as emanating from other people, who thus become the targets of the fear and rage that scorn and ridicule cause. It is only later, when people develop the capacity for feelings of guilt, that, as Wurmser says, "These physiognomic signs and signals may subsequently be duplicated metaphorically when the censor is introjected in the form of the 'eye' and the 'voice' of the conscience". The fear and anger and paranoia that shame provokes, and specifically towards eyes, is also captured in folk beliefs (and occasional individual delusions) about the "Evil Eye" (Maloney, 1976), though this anger can also, as in the case of this murderer, be directed towards the gossiping tongue that can repeat to others what the eye has seen.

Ross L's mutilation of his victim, which is senseless from any rational standpoint, thus becomes the concrete, non-verbal expression of the following thought (which has the structure, like all unconscious thought, of magical thinking): "If I destroy eyes I will destroy shame", for one can only be shamed in the (evil) eyes of others. In other words, "If I destroy eyes I cannot be shamed", and "if I destroy tongues then I cannot be talked about, ridiculed or laughed at; my shamefulness cannot be revealed to others".

Murder, in other words, is to behaviour what paranoia is to thought and hate is to feelings. That is, violence is the symbolic representation of a paranoid thought, but by means of actions rather than words, in people who are not necessarily decisional or psychotic, as those terms are conventionally defined. Violence towards others, then, can be seen as the behavioural equivalent of paranoia, or the behavioural version of it, its hypostasis, the translation into terms of physical reality of the waking dream (or nightmare) which paranoia expresses in the form of words and thoughts.

But paranoia itself is the form of psychopathology that results when a person's ability to differentiate between feelings and facts is overwhelmed by feelings of shame, so that the feeling of being shamed is mistaken for a fact, and the individual develops the delusion that he is actually being shamed, or, in other words, exposed and spied on and observed, talked about and laughed at behind his back, held up to ridicule and scorn, criticism, and scurrilous gossip. So, we can also see murder, from the standpoint of the feelings that motivate or cause it, as the ultimate defence, the last resort, against being overwhelmed by shame and "losing one's mind" by actually becoming paranoid.

People who are paranoid express their thoughts in words; this murderer expressed the same thoughts (that he was vulnerable to being spied on and gossiped about as "a wimp, a punk and a pussy", and that his victim would do those things to him if he did not take action to prevent her), not through the medium of words, but through the medium of actions—the actions of destroying the eyes and tongue that could spy on him and gossip about him.

My point here is not that violent people focus their hostility exclusively on eyes or tongues, for, of course, they do not. For example, Samuel Edgerton (1985, p. 132) mentions that in 1344 a man who insulted the City of Florence by kicking the Great Seal of the City with his muddy boot was sentenced by the Captain of Florence to have his foot cut off. In that case, the organ that commit-ted the insult was the foot, so, according to the laws of what Freud called "magical thinking", the shame could be removed only by having the foot removed. Lest we imagine that we have evolved beyond such barbarism, it is worth remembering that within very recent decades, in both Denmark and many of the United States, the punishment for sex crimes (rape, incest, paedophilia), the essence of which offences is that they are among the most humiliating and shame-inducing acts a man can inflict on another person, consisted of castration; again, the offender is punished, or, in other words, is humiliated himself, in the (sexual) organ with which he commits the (sexual) insult/assault. Thus, the shame of the rape victim is magically removed by being transferred on to the rapist instead; the victim's shame, in this construction, can only be removed by having the rapist's penis removed, since his penis was the vehicle by which the victim was shamed. My point is, rather, that I am attempting, by analysing a particularly extreme example of apparently unmoti-vated and irrational, senseless violence, to find symptoms that can serve as clues as to what is going on, and can help us to begin to make sense of the senseless so that we can improve our ability to prevent it. The fact that Ross L focused his attention and hos-tility on his victim's eyes and tongue is a valuable clue as to his corresponding preoccupation with, and morbid hypersensitivity to, the fear of being overwhelmed by shame and ridicule. If he is at all typical of other murderers, then we would have to conclude that the most dangerous men on earth are those who are afraid that they are "wimps". Wars have been started for less.

The living dead

One of the commonest and, to me, most surprising self-descriptions I heard repeatedly from the most extremely and incorrigibly violent men I worked with over the years was that they themselves had died (meaning that their personality had died), often at some identifiable time in the past, so that they feel dead, even though their bodies live on. What they mean is that they cannot feel anything—neither emotions nor physical sensations. I have seen many who admit to killing others without so much as a flicker of remorse or any other emotion. Moreover, they themselves have been battered in fights, and have mutilated themselves as horribly as they have mutilated their victims, which means very horribly indeed (blinded or emasculated themselves, torn out their toenails, swallowed razor blades, inserted screws into their urethras), without feeling any physical pain at the time. Common sense suggests that these men feel "dead" inside. For how else could they possibly murder others and mutilate themselves as they do, unless they lacked the normal capacity for the full range of feelings? The living dead need to kill others, because for them the most unendurable anguish is the pain of seeing that others are still alive.

The words they use to describe themselves refer to the living dead: they say they feel like robots, zombies, or vampires, that their bodies and souls, hearts and minds, are empty inside, or that their bodies are filled with lifeless stuffing like straw, not flesh and blood, that instead of having veins and nerves they have ropes or cords. Another murderer I worked with says he is a "vampire". If I call him the "living dead" I am only paraphrasing his description of himself: a vampire, in folklore, is somebody who by definition is dead even though he walks and talks. When this man says he is a vampire, he means it not metaphorically but literally, as the most exact and realistic way to describe his experience of himself. This is a man who strangled and stabbed his grandmother to death and then drank her blood. Once one knows that about him, one can see that his experience of himself as a dead thing is directly related to his committing a crime of violence, and even to the specific kind of violence he committed. We begin to see what Kafka described in his brilliant short story, "The penal colony", that violent acts are a form of expressing meaning; that they are an expressive language whose writing tablet is the human body, and whose vocabulary is only limited by the variety of violent acts that it is possible to inscribe on the body.

Once having seen that killing others does not bring themselves back to life, many murderers find that the only way to feel alive, since they cannot feel anything emotionally, is to feel something, even physical pain, so they attempt to induce such feelings by cutting or otherwise injuring their bodies. Self-mutilation is not merely an everyday, but a several-times-a-day event in the world of the prison. Over the years, innumerable inmates have told me that physical pain is preferable to feeling nothing. Nevertheless, even the most bizarre and extreme self-mutilations typically do not cause physical pain, or enable these men to have any feelings, even of pain, at the time they injure themselves. At most, that happens only later, when their bodies start to heal. Yet, as one man put it, the only time he felt any relief, any sense (fleeting though it was) of being alive, was immediately after he had cut or otherwise injured him-self. For another young inmate, only the sight of his own blood, and the awareness that he would feel something eventually, reassured him that he was alive, not a robot; until then he felt he had no nerves and blood vessels, only wires or cords. (This particular man's mother doused herself with petrol and set herself on fire in front of his eyes. He then ran away from home, supporting himself as a male prostitute.) His dilemma, faced with his history and with his life, was: which is worse, to feel or not to feel?

The death of the self—which is what we are talking about here—brings with it a sense of the intolerability of existence, one's own and everyone else's. Murder is an attempt not just to rescue one's self (for many, it is already too late for that, the self has already died), but to bring one's dead self back to life. When that does not happen, then one's own physical death can seem to promise the only relief possible.

These are among the reasons that many more murderers kill themselves than were ever killed by the state, even when capital punishment was the usual penalty for murder. The suicide rate among men who have just committed a murder is from a few hundred to a few thousand times greater than it is among ordinary men of the same age, sex, and race, in this country and elsewhere. This is also one reason, among others, why capital punishment does not deter violent crimes: if anything, it stimulates them, since, for the most violent men in our society, the very ones who are said to be the strongest argument in support of capital punishment, their own physical death is seen as the only means of ultimately escaping from the intolerable torment of their psychic death.

How can we understand the sense of inner deadness of the kind of man I am describing? These men's souls did not just die. They have dead souls because their souls were murdered. How did that happen? The degree of cruelty, humiliation, and violence to which these men were subjected in childhood is so extreme and so unusual that to me it gave a whole new meaning to the term "child abuse".

As children, the men I have seen were shot, axed, scalded, beaten, strangled, tortured, drugged, starved, suffocated, set on fire, thrown out of windows, raped, or prostituted by mothers who were their "pimps", their bones have been broken, they have been locked in closets or attics for extended periods, and, in one case I know of, deliberately locked by his parents in an empty icebox until he suffered brain damage from anoxia before he was let out.

How can violence to the body kill the soul (the self, the psyche), even if it does not kill the body? I believe the answer to that question is that violence—whatever else it may mean—is the ultimate means of communicating the absence of love on the part of the person inflicting the violence. Beating a child communicates the absence of love so directly that no words are necessary, and with a power that no words can undo. Even a pet dog knows it is unloved when it is beaten. A child can hardly be less perceptive. And love is as necessary for the survival of the self as oxygen is for the survival of the body. Without feelings of love, the self feels numb, empty, and dead.

There are only two possible sources of love for the self: love from others, and self-love. Children who fail to receive sufficient love from others fail to build those reserves of self-love, and the capacity for self-love, which enable them to survive the inevitable rejections and humiliations which even the most fortunate of people cannot avoid.

The word I will use to refer to the absence or deficiency of self-love is shame; its opposite is pride, by which I mean the presence of self-love, self-esteem, self-respect, and the sense of self-worth. When either self-love or love from others is diminished, one feels shame. But it may be somewhat paradoxical to refer to shame as a "feeling", for shame is actually the absence of feelings—the feelings of self-love and of love from others. And while shame is painful, calling it pain is paradoxical, for we usually think of pain as a feeling, and yet this pain results from the deadening of feeling, the absence of feeling. An analogous image comes to mind if we think about our experience of cold. If we say we are "cold", we experience cold as a feeling, as something that exists. But we know from physics that cold is really the absence of something, the absence of heat, or warmth. Shame is also experienced as a feeling, and an intensely painful one, but, like cold, it is, in essence, the absence of something, the absence of warmth—in this case, emotional warmth, or love for the self. And when it reaches overwhelming intensity, shame is experienced, like cold, as a feeling of numbness and deadness, an inability to feel anything. We know that cold starts out feeling painful, but when it reaches an intolerable extrème, it results in complete numbness and physical death. At first, only a limb may die, but when the cold is sufficiently severe, the whole body dies. Dante was profoundly correct, psychologically, when he described the lowest circle of hell not as a place of fire, but as one of absolute cold.

To suffer the loss of love from others, by being rejected or abandoned, assaulted or insulted, slighted or demeaned, humiliated or ridiculed, dishonoured or disrespected, is to be shamed by them. However it happens, to be overwhelmed by shame and humiliation is to experience the destruction of self-esteem, and without a certain minimal amount of self-esteem, the self collapses and the soul dies. That overwhelming shame is the cause of the death of the self is implicit in the double meaning of the word that means overwhelming shame: mortification, which also means "to make dead" (from *mors, mortis,* death, and *facere,* to make).

This should also help us to understand why people do not have to have been physically attacked as children in order to become violent as adults. Violent child abuse is not a necessary precursor to adult violence for the simple reason that violence is not the only way in which an adult can shame and humiliate a child; it is simply one of the most powerful ways. But words alone can shame and reject, insult and humiliate, tear down self-esteem, and murder the soul. All the evidence we have suggests that whether or not violent people were physically injured in childhood, they were deeply and fatally emotionally injured, by means of the other causes of humiliation and degradation. For example, Frazier and his colleagues found in their study of the childhoods of thirty-one multiple and mass-murderers that

> the high incidence of significant and repeated personal humiliation ... cannot be overlooked. The usual pattern is a series of repeated and memorable humiliations accompanied by severe feelings of shame. ... The recurrence of a pattern of verbal shaming and humiliation by parents before friends and other family members was recounted frequently and corroborated by family members. [Frazier et al., 1974]

Other sources of shame have been found to stimulate homicidal rage. For example, Stuart Palmer (1960) found that murderers were significantly more likely than their non-homicidal brothers to have physical deformities, whether congenital or acquired. They were more likely (beyond what would have occurred by chance) "to have been born with some extreme, severe, visible physical defect ... of the type that ... might well cause the individual social embarrassment ... [such as] an abnormally large head; a club foot [cf. Oedipus!] ... etc.". This finding has been replicated several times since it was originally reported, but, interestingly, more recent research has also found that these defects do not generate later violence when the child is raised by parents who are sufficiently supportive and loving. In other words, parental warmth can heal the narcissistic wounds, at least enough to neutralize their homicidal power.

So, I am saying that the motive or cause of violence is the wish to prevent or undo the condition of being overwhelmed by shame, humiliation, and disrespect, since that condition brings about the death of the self. While the resulting behaviour appears offensive to others, to the violent person it is defensive: killing others is self-defence in the most literal sense of the word—defence of that terribly vulnerable psychological construct called the self, whose death is feared far more than the death of the body. Those are among the reasons why these men feel no guilt, at least at the time of committing their murders, for, after all, even the law says there is no guilt in defending yourself.

Murder, and all violence, is the acting out of a narrative, a story, a plot, or, in other words, a myth, whether it is the myth of Oedipus, Medea, Cain and Abel, Othello, or any of the other variants on this archetypal form. Oedipus kills Laius because Laius disrespected and insulted him by wanting to take precedence and crowd him off at the crossroads. (The only thing that is new about "road rage" is the phrase used to describe it; the phenomenon itself is right at the heart of one of the archetypal murders of all time!) Medea killed their children as revenge on Jason for shaming her by choosing another woman. Othello killed Desdemona because she had shamed him by choosing another man (he thought). Cain killed Abel because "God had respect unto Abel and unto his offering; but unto Cain and his offering, God had not respect". In other words, God disrespected Cain—or, in the inner-city argot of many American criminals, He "dis'ed" Cain, and Cain responded to this act of shaming in exactly the same way as the murderers I see today.

There is a universal theme that reoccurs in one variation or another in all these myths: that submitting to overwhelming shame in any of its many varieties (inferiority and envy, insult and disrespect, rejection and jealousy, taunting and ridicule) brings about the death of the self, which can be warded off only by killing someone else.

Once we see shame, or an exquisitely heightened and unprotected vulnerability to shame, as the "red flag" signalling the approach of violence, it becomes a guide to both prevention and treatment. To emphasize the range of applicability of this approach across ethnic groups, gender, and social class, I will mention Matthew, the teenage son of a prominent clergyman, who was admitted to one of Harvard's psychiatric teaching hospitals following a long history of school failure, rejection by his peers, property destruction, repeated suicide attempts, and generally staying in the role of the family failure, a disappointment to his parents and clearly inferior to his better-adjusted siblings. His psychological testing report described him as having a "schizoid personality disorder", and then went on to state "he feels as if he had not lived up to parental expectations. His shame over failing is overwhelming to him". That last sentence is the red flag, warning of danger. Unaware of the relationship between shame and violence, the psychologist concluded that "this patient's potential for violence is not significant". However, less than a year later, Matthew attempted suicide; shortly after that he murdered his father, after his father slighted and rejected him, and his mother; and finally, several years later, he killed himself.

Towards a psychoanalytic theory of violence

In approaching the study of violence psychoanalytically, I have found that I can talk with violent people and ask what are, in effect, psychoanalytic questions concerning their motivations or reasons for doing the things they had done. When I do this, many of them tell me. Some, like Ross L, do not tell me in words. With them, I have tried to decode the symbolic language of their violent acts, like a cryptologist, or an anthropologist who tries to decipher the meaning of a bizarre and gruesome ritual. Yet, others do tell me, in words so simple and direct that I hardly need to do more than paraphrase and summarize what they have said in order to formulate a "theory".

For example, prisoners I have seen have told me repeatedly, when I asked them why they had assaulted someone, that it was "because he disrespected me", or "he disrespected my visit" (meaning "visitor"). In fact, the word "disrespect" is used so often by these men that they have abbreviated it into the slang term, "he dis'ed me". Now, any time a word is used so often that it gets abbreviated, we can begin to suspect that it might be centrally important, not just in the vocabulary, but also in the moral value system and the motivation of whoever is using it.

Let me cite an example. Chester T, a very angry and violent inmate in his thirties, in prison for armed robbery, was referred to see me in the Prison Mental Health Service, because he had engaged in a mutually self-defeating power struggle with the prison officers, in which the more violent he would become, the more severely he would be punished, and the more severely he was punished, the more violent he would become. By this time he was in solitary confinement, and there was no further punishment the officers could inflict on him, so they asked me to see him to see if I could find out what was going on and whether this vicious circle could be stopped. He was usually so inarticulate and incoherent that it was difficult to get a very informative answer to the simplest question. But this time, in an attempt to break through the vicious circle with this man, and acting on the assumption that all behaviour is meaningful, I asked him not just "What do you want?", but "What do you want so badly that you would sacrifice everything else in order to get it?", since it seemed to me that that was exactly what he was doing by that point. In response to my question, this man, who was usually agitated and disorganized, astonished me by standing up to his full height and immediately replying, simply and with calmness and assurance, with perfect coherence and even a kind of eloquence, "Pride. Dignity. Self-Esteem." And then he went on to say, in words closer to his more usual vocabulary (but still more coherently than usual), "And I'll kill every mother-fucker in that cell-block if I have to in order to get it! My life ain't worth nothin' if I take somebody disrespectin' me and callin' me punk asshole faggot and goin' 'Ha! Ha!' at me. Life ain't worth livin' if there ain't nothin' worth dyin' for. If you ain't got pride you got nothin'. That's all you got! I've already got my pride." And, referring to a man who had been taunting, ridiculing, and insulting him, "He's tryin' to take that away from me. I'm not a total idiot. I'm not a coward. There ain't nothin' I can do except snuff him. I'll throw gasoline on him and light him." He went on to say that the other inmate had challenged him to a fight, and he was afraid not to accept the challenge because he thought "I'll look like a coward and a punk if I don't fight him." The main thing one hears from violent men is one variation or another on exactly this theme—violence as the only alternative to being shamed, in other people's eyes and even in one's own.

I used to think that armed robbers committed their crimes in order to get money. And that is often the way they rationalize their behaviour, and they would like other people to think that is the reason. But if you sit down and talk with people who repeatedly commit such crimes, what you actually hear is, "I never got so much respect before in my life as I did when I first pointed a gun at somebody," or "You wouldn't believe how much respect you get when you have a gun pointed at some dude's face." For men who have lived for a lifetime on a diet of contempt and disdain, the temptation to gain instant respect in this way can be worth far more than the cost of losing their liberty, or even their lives.

Should we really be so surprised at all this? Doesn't the Bible, in describing the first recorded murder in history, tell us that Cain killed Abel because he was treated with disrespect? "The Lord had respect unto Abel and to his offering: But unto Cain . . . he had not respect" (Genesis 4: 4–5). In other words, God "dis'ed" Cain! Or rather, Cain was "dis'ed" because of Abel. The inextricable connection between disrespect and shame is emphasized by the anthropologist Julian Pitt-Rivers, who concluded that in all known cultures "the withdrawal of respect dishonors . . . and this inspires the sentiment of shame" (1968, pp. 503–504).

I have yet to see a serious act of violence that was not provoked by the experience of feeling shamed and humiliated, disrespected and ridiculed, and that did not represent the attempt to prevent or undo this "loss of face", no matter how severe the punishment, even if it includes death. For we misunderstand these men, at our peril, if we do not realize they mean it literally when they say they would rather kill or mutilate others, be killed or mutilated themselves, than live without pride, dignity, and self-respect. They literally prefer death to dishonour.

My thesis is that the different forms of violence, whether towards individuals or entire populations, are motivated, or caused, by the wish to ward off or undo the feeling of shame and replace it as far as possible with its opposite, pride. However, we all feel shamed at one time or another, and yet most people never commit an act of serious violence in their lives. So, shame is clearly not a sufficient cause of violence, even if it may be a necessary one. Hence, we need to recognize that shame does not lead to violence except when several other conditions also exist, of which I think three of the most important are these: first, that the degree of shame is so overwhelming as to bring about the death of the self. As Heinz Kohut put it, "the deepest level to which psychoanalysis can penetrate when it traces destructiveness [is to] the presence of a serious narcissistic injury, an injury that threatened the cohesion of the self" (1977, p. 116).

Second, that the individual does not perceive himself as having sufficient non-violent means available with which to maintain or restore his self-esteem, such as education, social status, wealth, or socially honoured achievements, for even the most chronically and recurrently violent people are not violent most of the time; even for them, violence is a last resort which is only resorted to when they see no adequate alternatives. Third, that the individual does not have the capacity to experience, at least under the current conditions, the emotions that inhibit or neutralize violent impulses, such as guilt and remorse over the impulse to cause pain or injury to someone else, love and empathy for the other person, and rational fear for the consequences one could bring on oneself by engaging in violence (such as retaliation or punishment). People who engage in serious violence tend to be strikingly lacking in the capacity for all of those feelings. Thus, violence towards others is most likely in someone who is experiencing a maximum of shame and a minimum of guilt.

Freud commented that no one feels as guilty as the saints, to which I would add that no one feels as innocent as the criminals; their lack of guilt feelings, even over the most atrocious of crimes, is one of their most prominent characteristics, but, of course, that would have to be true, for if they had the capacity to feel guilty over hurting other people, they would be less likely to have the emotional capacity to hurt them in the first place.

On the other hand, it is important to remember that people all too frequently resort to suicide also, when they feel that is the only means available to them, or likely to be successful, for wiping out their shame. And people with psychotic depressions and delusions of guilt may kill their loved ones for "altruistic" reasons (to spare them the pain that the perpetrator feels he or she has exposed them to) and follow that with a suicide (to expiate the guilt).

It is well known to anyone who reads the newspapers that people often seem to become seriously violent, even homicidal, over what are patently "trivial" precipitants. But it is precisely these trivial events that can be the most intensely humiliating, in a deeply paradoxical way that I think is only understandable through understanding the psychology and symbolism of shame, for it is the very triviality of those precipitants that makes them that much more overwhelmingly shameful to the person who is shamed by them. That is, nothing is more shameful than to feel ashamed. And the more trivial the slight or insult over which they feel shamed the more intense and shameful the feeling of shame is. (The logic here is: "Only a very 'slight'—i.e., small or unimportant—person will feel seriously slighted—i.e., shamed—over a 'slight'—i.e., trivial—slight".) So the intensity of the shame that a person feels may be inversely related to the "objective" magnitude of the insult. Both of the cases I recounted earlier illustrate this principle, which is why I originally found the case of Ross L so puzzling. It is also why the District Attorney who investigated the case of a female Harvard student who murdered her room-mate after feeling humiliated by her, and then committed suicide, said, "What makes this case seem so mysterious is that the thing which [precipitated all this violence]—the slight—was so slight."

That is also the reason that people who feel ashamed will go to such extremes to conceal from others the fact that they feel ashamed. This often misleads outside observers to conclude—mistakenly—that violent people have high self-esteem. Actually, they are concealing their overwhelming lack of self-esteem behind a defensive mask of "cool", and if we mistake that mask for their real self-concept then we are unintentionally entering into collusion with their own most maladaptive defence.

Bringing a psychoanalytic approach to the study of violence not only illuminates the psychology of violence; the study of violence also contributes to the larger psychoanalytic project, which is the understanding of human psychology and behaviour in general, through learning how to interpret the "symbolic logic" that underlies it all. We can also see how much is lost for psychoanalysis if we do not bring the study of violence into its purview. I am reminded here of Freud's metaphor for the clinical phenomenon of resistance against the fundamental rule of psychoanalysis, as he attempted to show how a patient's censoring of even one subject from examination would defeat the whole purpose of analysis. As he put it, if the police said they would patrol all parts of the city except one neighbourhood, where do you think the criminals would concentrate? The same principle applies here. If psychoanalysis does not go into the neighbourhoods in which violence occurs, by examining the problems and the populations in the slums and ghettoes and prisons, then psychoanalysis will miss much of what is important and relevant not only about the psychology of violence, but about all of psychology. And in doing that, psychoanalysis runs the risk of defeating its own project, just as the patient does who excludes one topic from psychoanalytic exploration.

Finally, I think it is important to notice how radical the implications are of substituting a psychoanalytic approach to violence for the traditional way of conceptualizing violence as a moral and legal problem. For the past 3000 years, since the time of the original moral and legal law-givers, such as Hammurabi and Moses and Solon, humanity has been engaged in a great experiment: to test the hypothesis that condemning violence morally and legally, and punishing it accordingly, will prevent violence from occurring. Now, 3000 years is long enough to test any hypothesis, and the results of this experiment are in: this has been the bloodiest century in all of human history, and during this century we acquired for the first time the technological means to become the first species in all evolutionary history to bring about its own extinction, which we are at risk of doing unless we can learn to understand the causes of violence well enough to improve our ability to prevent it. The main problem with defining violence as a moral and legal problem is that that point of view is incapable of informing us as to what causes violence and how we could prevent it. The only questions morality and law can answer take the form: "How evil was this particular act of violence, and how much punishment does the perpetrator of it deserve?" But this does not help us in the least to understand either what causes violence or how we could prevent it.

The psychohistorical significance of psychoanalysis is that it gave us a language and a cognitive structure—the structure of science—with which to replace moral and legal language. It leads us to ask a different question: "What are the causes of violence and how can we prevent it?" This is a question that can be answered by means of clinical enquiry and empirical evidence.

Increasingly, many individuals and groups, from the American Medical Association to the World Health Organization, are recommending that we approach violence as a problem in public health and preventative medicine. The analytic approach I have outlined here brings to this endeavour specific and relevant information concerning both the causes and prevention of violence, making it possible to isolate feelings of shame as the "pathogen" that causes violence, and showing what the vector is by which shame is spread in different concentrations into different sub-groups in our population (specifically, the social and economic structure, that is, the division of our society into upper and lower classes, castes, genders, and age groups). Again, the implications this has for the kinds of strategies that we would need to follow in order to diminish or prevent violence are radical, and, in this sense, the study of violence brings us back to the heart of the psychoanalytic project—that the analysis of the human psyche can guide not only the understanding, but the transformation, of the human world.

References

Aristotle (1954). *Rhetoric*, W. D. Ross (Ed. and Trans.). Oxford: Oxford University Press.

Burke, K. (1966). *Language as Symbolic Action*. Berkeley, CA: University of California Press.

Darwin, C. (1872). *The Expression of the Emotions in Man and Animals*. Chicago, IL: University of Chicago Press, 1965.

Edgerton, S. (1985). *Pictures and Punishment: Art and Criminal Prosecution during the Florentine Renaissance*. Ithaca, NY: Cornell University Press.

Erikson, E. H. (1963). *Childhood and Society* (2nd edn). New York: W. W. Norton.

Fenichel, O. (1945). *The Psychoanalytic Theory of Neurosis*. New York: W. W. Norton.

Frazier, S. H. et al. (1974). A clinical study of serial and multiple murder. In: S. H. Frazier (Ed.), *Aggression. Proceedings of the Association for Research in Nervous and Mental Disease*. Baltimore, MD: Williams & Wilkins.

Freud, S. (1933a). *New Introductory Lectures on Psycho-Analysis. S.E., 22*. London: Hogarth Press.

Klein, E. (1966). *A Comprehensive Etymological Dictionary of the English Language*. New York: Elsevier.

Kohut, H. (1977). *Kohut, Heinz. The Restoration of the Self*. New York: International Universities Press.

Maloney, C. (Ed.) (1976). *The Evil Eye*. New York: Columbia University Press.

Palmer, S. (1960). *A Study of Murder*. New York: Crowell.

Partridge, E. (1958). *Origins: A Short Etymological Dictionary of the English Language*. New York: Greenwich House, 1983.

Pitt-Rivers, J. (1968). Honor. In: D. Sills (Ed.), *International Encyclopedia of the Social Sciences* (pp. 503–511. New York: Macmillan.

Schneider, C. (1977). *Shame, Exposure and Privacy*. Boston, MA: Beacon Press.

Wurmser, L. (1981). *The Mask of Shame*. Baltimore, MD: Johns Hopkins University Press.

Wurmser, L. (1987). Shame: the veiled companion of narcissism. In: D. L. Nathanson (Ed.), *The Many Faces of Shame* (pp. 64–92). New York: Guilford Press.

Discussion of James Gilligan's paper

*A*ugust Ruhs, Vienna: "If no act without language has a mean-ing, there are maybe acts which have no meaning. I think of the differentiation between acting in and acting out and what the French call a kind of action without signification, no symbolized action. For example, when Freud discussed the case of the nineteen-year-old homosexual girl and he tried to interpret the jump into the ditch, the suicidal act, he said it was a significant act translating the wish to be pregnant by jumping down, which means in German *niederkommen*, like to give birth. Then there was a re-reading of this by Lacan, who said no, it's not, it's out of the symbolic—it's when she as a subject is disappearing, she's identi-fying with a falling object and now it's going into the Real and in the Real there is no symbolic. I wanted to discuss whether the sentence is true that there is no act without meaning."

James Gilligan: "It's a good theoretical question. I've implicitly been trying to distinguish between behaviour that I think does have a symbolic meaning the way that rituals have a symbolic meaning—for example, religious rituals such as the holy communion. Giving the wine and bread is meant to symbolize the body and blood of

Christ, or in a courtroom, standing up when the judge enters the courtroom is a symbol of one's respect for the law and, by implication, for the court and the judge. So, there are many kinds of rituals in our society that permeate all aspects and all institutions in it and they really do have a symbolic meaning. All of what we call courtesy and politeness, standing up when someone enters the room, all of these are symbols of respect or similar messages. I've asked myself the question: are there some behaviours that are just behaviours that have no meaning that can be put into words? We do things all day long, we tie our shoes, does that have a symbolic meaning? It does and it doesn't; it's a symbol purely of being an adult with a certain competence. I have grandchildren who are learning to tie their shoes and they become very proud when they show they can tie their own shoes—a symbol of competence, adulthood, of being a worthwhile human being. The more I think about it, the more I'm beginning to think that almost all behaviour can be translated into some kind of symbolic meaning. If we drink a cup of coffee, it symbolizes something that we choose coffee rather than tea. They have different social connotations in our minds. Let me get to what I think is the essence of psychopathology. I think Freud says this repeatedly: the essence of psychopathology is, or one of the criteria is, dissociation. Freud talked about, in most of his descriptions of neurosis, obsessive compulsive neurosis, a consequence of isolation of thoughts from affects in which you over-emphasize thoughts producing intellectualization and you de-emphasize affects, make them unconscious. His theory is more the opposite: you repress thoughts and become flooded with affect. Another way to think about the human psyche is that the psyche is divided into three parts but they are not geographical areas, they are three areas of function, cognition, affection, or emotion and action. Ordinarily these are integrated and synthesized in the "normal" psyche. We act according to thoughts and feelings that we can explain and that we are consciously aware of. Psychopathology results when these get dissociated from each other. If you think about diagnostic categories, we speak of affective disorders like depression and mania and we speak of thought disorders, schizophrenia, paranoia, and the like. I would say that character disorders or personality disorders could be seen as action disorders, that is, "people behaviour" is the pathological symptom. I put the violent person in the realm of character disorder and action disorder. The problem with the violent is that they have dissociated their actions from their thoughts and feelings. That is putting it very abstractly, so let me be concrete: when I worked with prisoners the first thing that struck me about them was that any time I walked into a prison and started talking to a criminal, I got the impression that I was talking to somebody who responds with actions, without the actions passing through the filters of thought and feeling, which they do for most of us. In other words, when I work with violent criminals I get the impression that it's almost as if they have a short-circuit in their brains so that everything immediately goes straight to action rather than being slowed down by thoughts or being accompanied by feelings. They've dissociated action from thoughts and feelings, and what I'm trying to do is to undo that dissociation by showing the association between the thoughts and the feelings that they have not developed, or else they have lost the capacity for. That's not putting it in Lacanian language, but it's ordinary English, which is the way I understand it."

Dave Someikh: "Professor Gilligan, thank you very much for a fascinating and rich presentation. I've been a forensic psychiatrist for nearly thirty years and also trained as an analyst like Carine, and indeed worked in the same place as her for years. My career has involved meeting many, many people who have killed and having to write reports making sense of what seems senseless. The starting point for me in your talk was something I have total sympathy with, which you were just really iterating, because my interest clinically, has been in what in this country is called personality disorder and the treatment of people with exactly the lack you describe: a short-circuit to action. For me, violent acts are one category of acting out where someone has an affect which they are unable to digest and it has to be dealt with by immediately expelling it in the form of action, and the work that Carine describes so beautifully is an example of how one provides an environment that allows people to learn to put things into words as a substitute for action. Where I think there is something missing in the way you present the phenomenology of murderous acts is that they don't always represent their psychopathology in symbolic terms, in terms of what they do to the victim. In other words, the victim, in a funny way just like the Kafka example you gave, becomes a sort of message about the psychopathology and that's the symbolic element which is absent in terms of the perpetrator's mind, there being no symbol in their mind. Instead it's acted out on the victim. My problem with this is twofold. First, and it's a minor thing, I think there are limits to symbolic interpretation that are well recognized, and I thought Anne Alvarez also gave a nice example when she was talking about the child destroying the doll. Before I got into forensic psychiatry I worked psychodynamically with people who cut themselves. There is a great deal one can understand in terms of what the act of cutting your skin represents in terms of penetration, in terms of something about the relationship with the mother, and so on. If cutting becomes a ritual, the meaning can get lost and the ritual develops another function, which is anti-symbolic. It's like getting drunk in the sense that you are losing touch with reality rather than understanding something. In the language of the schizophrenic, or indeed in the language of the politician, when you have empty words, you hear a string of words which apparently have meaning, but in reality they have no content. I think this phenomenon is one that can be seen in symbolic acts, too. There can be a diversion. There is, on the one hand, a symbolic representation that a killing may make, but, on the other hand, there is the whole matter for the psychodynamic therapist of the nature of the mechanism that leads some people to kill and some people to not kill. That seems to relate to the nature of the act and what makes it possible to treat the victim as a non-person."

Carine Minne: "James, would you like to respond, or shall we collect some more comments?"

James Gilligan: "I would like to respond as briefly as I can. First of all, the question of whether acts are symbolic or a result of an inability to symbolize through language or other means. It's almost a semantic difference, you could say, what it means to really symbolize. To reduce it to a practical level, my feeling is that when we were working with violent criminals in prisons one of the main sources of therapeutic effects, to the degree that our work has therapeutic effects, is in enabling prisoners to find words with which they can express their feelings and seek to achieve their goals. Once they find the words, there is less need to act out violently. I found that words were the only alternative to action, including violent action. With respect to why some people, and there is only a tiny minority of people who actually cross the line into physical violence, why they do that and other people don't, one of the central focuses is what determines the transition from fantasy to action. Let me reformulate what I said earlier. I would suggest that shame is a necessary, but not sufficient, cause of violence. I'd say it is necessary because I think it is always present when there is violence. On the other hand, all of us feel shame at one time or another; it's a universal human emotion and we have all been humiliated or we have felt ashamed of something we have done that we thought was foolish. I would say that there have to be several other pre-conditions before shame will lead to physical violent action. One I would suggest is when the intensity of the humiliation is so extreme that it threatens to bring about what I call the death of the self. That is when people feel overwhelmed by it. There can be a variety of reasons for this; you can also speak of not having enough ego strength, or their being so already damaged by previous humiliations that they are hypersensitive to shame and hypervulnerable. A second pre-condition, I think, is that the person who resorts to violence is one who lacks the resources, emotional and cognitive, that the rest of us have that would prevent us from committing an act of violence. no matter how humiliated we might feel. For example, all of us have felt insulted or rejected at one time or another, but we have other resources available with which to restore our self esteem. We have some degree of education or achievement or respect, self-respect or respect from our social environment, and so on. The people in the prisons were almost totally lacking in these things. The people in prisons are very disproportionately uneducated; many are illiterate adults who can't read or write and are deeply ashamed of this. They are among the poorest members of our society. The prisons are filled with the poor, by and large. There are a few, very few, rich people, and they're the ones who get in the headlines, so people overestimate how common they are. Ninety-nine per cent of the people in prisons are poor. They are often homeless, unemployed members of minority groups that are subject to systematic humiliation and are treated as inferior in America—African Americans, Hispanic Americans, and so on. In other words, the violent people don't have the non-violent resources available with which to maintain their self esteem. Violence is the only thing they have got. A third thing I mentioned that I haven't gone into is being raised as a male in our patriarchal society: men are raised to be violent and also to not flinch from becoming victims of violence. After all, who is drafted into the military, where your job is to kill and run the risk you would be killed—it's men. Our language says something about that: both in Greek and Latin the words for masculinity also mean courage. In Greek *andrea* means courage, in Latin *vere* is man and soldier, to be a man is to be a soldier, but it's the route of another Latin word, *vertus*, which is the route of our word virtue, but in Rome, that militaristic society, the master virtue was courage, so *vertus* really means courage. You have to have courage to be a soldier and to be violent. This is a roundabout way of saying that in our cultural tradition masculinity is associated with violence and to be a real man you have to able and willing to be violent. I also often had the sense that if prisoners could fantasize they would be less likely to commit violence. Fantasy can be an alternative to action, and we all know that with our non-violent patients. How many masturbatory fantasies are alternatives to perverse sexuality, which people don't act out in reality, but for which the fantasy serves as an alternative. What is so missing and so striking to me about the violent is their incapacity to put things into words. Yes, they act out feelings by action, but a lot of us can discharge our feelings by words. Words can also serve the purpose of diminishing the intensity of certain feelings.

Siobhan O'Connor: "Thank you, I'd like to say how much I enjoyed your talk. I use your system when I'm lecturing on violence, so I'm hugely indebted to you for that. I wonder if you could say a little bit more about the relationship between shame and guilt and how that plays a part in the acts that you are describing. I understand that at the point of the act, which is an act of self-defence in some senses, there is an absence of guilt, but, of course, we can all have acts of defence which are attacking but also feel some sense of guilt about having done that, and what I was wanting you to tease out a little bit more was whether, in the kind of ongoing process of endlessly being humiliated, the capacity for guilt is diminished in these individuals and, therefore, the capacity to use guilt as a brake on action is also diminished."

James Gilligan: "That is exactly what I think. What is typical of people who commit severe violence is their lack of capacity for normal feelings of guilt and remorse that any of us would feel when we contemplate such an act. You are also right that sometimes, and these are rare exceptions—I'd say over forty years of working with violent people I've seen maybe a couple—who felt severely guilty after having committed a murder, and in both cases they were highly suicidal. One succeeded in committing suicide and the other made an extremely serious attempt but, by sheer luck, he survived. They were more like Othello, in that they committed the homicide when motivated by feelings of shame, but then, when they realized what they had done, they felt guilty and committed suicide. What's most striking about 99% of criminals is the incapacity for guilty feelings. I used to be amazed to see how it was precisely the people who committed the most atrocious violence who were the least able to feel guilty, and then it struck me that maybe that makes sense. How else could they be capable of committing such horrible crimes if they had the capacity for guilt feelings? Regarding shame and guilt, I wrote my doctoral thesis on that and I can't quite summarize it here, but I drew a lot on the work of Franz Alexander and his student Gerhard Peers, who conceptualized shame and guilt as antagonistic emotional systems, rather like comparing the parasympathetic and the sympathetic nervous systems—they have opposite effects. I would also say that shame is a more primitive, an earlier, more primitive motive of defence, with guilt occurring later in development. One thing this means is that the first emotion that children feel in each stage of psychological development is shame over a lack of confidence at meeting the tasks of that stage of development. Whether you think of it in psychosexual or psychosocial terms, shame motivates self-aggrandizement in the service of self-preservation, even at the expense of other people, and it will stimulate anger out and love in. Guilt, I would say, does just the opposite; it stimulates anger in and love out, and when people develop the capacity for guilt, they are much less likely to become capable of violent behaviour. I would say that shame motivates defence against passive dependent libidinal needs to be loved and taken care of by others, which, for example, for a grown man would mean saying I am like a little baby, I need to be loved and taken care of by other people. The macho, hyper-masculine image is one of a person who is tough, strong, independent, who has no needs, who can take care of himself, and so forth. Shame motivates that macho defence against a dependency that, in fact, we all have. It is a universal human characteristic that we all need each other, we're all dependent, but shame denies this. Guilt can motivate suicide more than homicide, although people can commit suicide as a way of avoiding shame just as they can commit suicide as a way to atone for their feelings of guilt. On rare occasions, guilt can motivate violence and homicide, and an example of that is a mother going through a post partum depression who develops a psychotic depression, delusions of guilt, feels she has ruined her children's' lives and the only way to rescue the children from the awful fate she has created for them is to kill them and then to kill herself because of her guilt for all that. This is called altruistic homicide: it's meant as mercy killing, that's the meaning of it to the person committing it. I would say that would be a rare exception where guilt can motivate homicide. It's almost always motivated by shame, and guilt will tend to militate against violence against another. These are complicated issues; it's not as if there is one simple formula that fits all, but I think there are some universal principles that we can understand."

Liz Miller: "I'm a general adult psychiatrist in North Yorkshire. One of the things that struck me when you've been talking about the client you see is that in a sense they have almost accidentally ended up where they are, that what has been done to them has been done inadvertently by people who didn't necessarily plan for their actions to have the consequences they did on the psychological development of the children who then became murderers. I'm wondering if you've come across people who have deliberately been corrupted by adults as part of a kind of ritual behaviour. The reason I ask is that not only me, but several of my colleagues have occasionally come across patients who claim to have been ritually abused, and in my area I understand the police have been aware of at least three circles of ritual abusers. I have two patients currently who claim to have had that happen to them, and the stories they give are very consistent with the reading I've done about it, and I've often wondered about the people who carry out these acts because I know of one person who, if my patient is to be believed, is currently in one of our local high secure prisons, and quite how this begins to happen and how these people, if they are helpable, can be helped."

James Gilligan: "I certainly have seen many examples of it, although it is still somewhat of a rarity, but I have seen repeated examples of adult violent criminals and prisoners who were ritually abused by parents. One of the most violent people I ever worked with was such a person. His mother said to him when he was a child that the devil was inside him, the devil possessed him, and he was then subjected to voodoo-type rituals. He describes being in a completely darkened basement, no light at all, in which there was a voodoo priest whose job was to exorcise the devil out of him, and he describes being terrified. He also developed what Erikson calls a negative identity, in that he *did* come to feel that the devil was inside him and he acted that out in a whole series of murders that he committed as an adult. There are neo-Nazi skinhead groups that are like this, not exactly involved in ritual abuse in the same sense, but who are connected to a lot of symbolism and ritual behaviour. I knew of one young child who was used as a sexual toy by the adults. Both of his parents would have sexual orgies in their home and their friends would participate. This boy would be passed from adult to adult for sexual purposes and he later committed a murder. He got involved with a woman with a young child and set fire to her house with the idea that he would rescue her from the fire and that would prove what a hero, what a masculine, powerful, adult man he was, but unfortunately the fire killed her and he was not able to rescue her. This is what he was put in prison for, but his background story was corroborated by his brother after the man had committed suicide in prison. Another example is of a child who was tied to a bedpost by a drug addicted, sexually perverse mother, who was a nurse, and the mother and the mother's sister would sexually abuse the little girl. It's a ritual in so far as they tied her to the bed. There are a variety of different kinds of ritual abuse, some of which are associated with a kind of quasi-religious cult or its equivalent, some of which are quasi-political cults, and some of which are for the purpose of sheer paedophilia and incest and their perverse acts."

Dermott Davison: "I'm a family doctor, a GP. I enjoyed your talk and found it fascinating, but I'm struck with a thought and perhaps a question. I was very taken with 'in the beginning was the deed' and, of course, your mind goes to 'in the beginning was the word'. I was thinking about how you talked about the shaming and humiliating experiences of many of these adults from their early days. I found myself wondering, well, perhaps did it begin with the word in terms of the words that were spoken and taken in by the child, even the example you've just given where the child was told he was possessed by the devil. My thought, slightly parallel to it, is, is the acquisition of language and language skills in childhood at an appropriate age, is that somehow protective against violent acts in adulthood because you mentioned several times that a lot of the people you dealt with have struggled to find words for what they are experiencing?"

James Gilligan: "Yes, I'm glad you raised this, because it enables me to revisit the discussion on the relationship between words and deeds. I do think the acquisition of language gives the developing child an alternative to action. They can ask for something instead of grabbing for it, or they can express their anger, which is less violent. I think what is normal in human development is to integrate words and deeds so that, in a way, in the beginning is both the word and the deed. At birth, we don't have words, but we develop them; it's one of the first major acquisitions of early childhood. Normally, these go together, we have words and deeds. The violent either have lost or never fully gained the capacity to express themselves in words, and deeds is all they have with which to express their feelings or try to achieve their goals. For the rest of us, you could say in the beginning is the word and the deed and the emotion— they are all co-ordinated with each other. Pathology consists of splitting them from each other, dissociating them from each other, and that is what I was struck by with the prison inmates who were so lacking in the capacity for words and feelings. All they had was actions, and once they got words it made a huge difference. For example, we did a study in the Massachusetts prisons to find out which of the programmes we had were most effective in prevent-ing recidivism or re-offending after they left the prison. We found one programme that was 100% effective over a twenty-five-year period: this was getting a college degree while in prison. There were several hundred inmates who'd got a degree. Boston University provided college level courses in the prison for free. We couldn't find anyone who'd returned to prison! Then we discov-ered the State of Indiana had the same result, and Folsom State Prison in California had the same result, and throughout the coun-try there have been studies of the relationship between education and crime. They are not 100% in every state but they are certainly statistically the most powerful crime reduction tool we have. Naturally, I say rather perversely, once our politicians discovered this they got rid of the programmes. When I presented this in Massachusetts in a series of public lectures I'd been invited to give at Harvard, a friend of mine gave a copy of my lectures to our new Governor, who had been elected to office on the campaign promise to reintroduce prisoners to the joys of breaking rocks. He was truly back to the Stone Age in terms of his criminological theory. He gave a press conference after he read my account of this study, and said we've got to stop this programme of giving a free college education to prisoners, otherwise people who are too poor to go to college are going to start committing crimes so they can get sent to prison to get a free college education. So, he abolished the programme, and then the entire US Congress, influenced by Newt Gingrich, a right-wing Republican congressman, repealed the system grants that had been set up to provide free college tuition and free college text books for prisoners. If you live in the community you can still get these education facilities, but in the prisons throughout the country, you can't."

Carine Minne: "They are all gone?"

James Gilligan: "All gone, so in the name of being tough on crime and law and order we have systematically eliminated the most effective single programme we have yet discovered for reducing crime and violence. A college degree is an intensification of the capacity to use words and language. I should also add reading and literacy is an additional safeguard against violence. The more you can use your mind, the less you are reduced to violence. When I was a college student and a medical student and then a psychiatric resident, we were taught so much that we were all obsessive–compulsive and we intellectualized far too much. Then I got into the prisons, and I realized they intellectualized far too little. What they need is to gain the capacity to intellectualize, which can provide a higher order defence and, in some ways, a defence against violence. Look at Freud's interpretation of the dynamics of obsessive–compulsive neurosis and intellectualization as a defence against violence. That's something prisoners can't get too much of."

Carine Minne: "We've got several more people who want to make some comments."

Jessica Yakeley: "I'm a psychiatrist at the Portman Clinic in London and a psychoanalyst. I wondered whether you could say something more about the importance of history, which I think you mentioned at the beginning of your paper, about how it is important to understand the meaning of the violence in the context of the patient's history. I've been recently quite concerned and worried about what I see as a trend in forensic psychiatry and forensic psychotherapy in forgetting history. It's very common to go on to a forensic ward where the nurses will be looking after a patient, and if you ask about the index of events it can be as if they have no knowledge of it, and I think that this protects them from the horror of it. I think this coincides, or perhaps it's not a coincidence, with a trend in psychoanalytic theory and technique of prioritizing the here and now and the transference at the expense sometimes of history and the technique of reconstruction. I think this is, at times, a toxic, dangerous combination, as we're really forgetting the power of the repetition compulsion, another classical psychoanalytic concept that's become a bit unfashionable, but if you forget history then your risk assessment is flawed, things will be repeated. I wonder whether you might say something about that."

James Gilligan: "I totally agree; I'll not comment further as I want to give as much time as possible for others but I totally agree with you. It's a good point."

Siobhan O'Connor, psychiatrist and psychoanalyst: "I am fascinated by the issue of shame and the fact that you used Sam Hall as an example. Coming from Ireland, I've become increasingly aware of how powerful mockery and sadistic humour is and how children are kept under control by them. Relatively recently, a very important politician here, Ian Paisley, would have been very popular, charismatic, and I think a lot of it was due to his vicious, sadistic humour that is often missed. I have a depressed analytic patient who can say something lively one minute and then wham, he kills it, "that was pathetic", and he can also be quite humorous as well, and I think it links in both with the Irish violence and with the Irish depression. The question I have for you is in terms of identification. Gerry Anderson is a well-known talk show host who is very good at humorous mockery. He says that the English laugh at nothing and it's because it doesn't have the Irish mockery in it. I wonder if there is something in the identification with the victim."

James Gilligan: "Let me relate that to the first violent person I talked about today. I mentioned that Ross L destroyed the eyes and tongue of his victim. I did not mention how he also attacked her genitals. To me, I thought that was his way, among other things, of trying to destroy what he thinks of as his own femininity. Remember he was as a child shamed about being called a 'pussy', so he destroys the 'pussy' of his victim. I think it's a way of trying to exorcise his own sense that he himself as a 'pussy'. It's a projective mechanism."

Carine Minne: "We've time for one more comment."

Eileen McCourt, art therapist: "I wondered if you might say something about the opportunities for symbolization afforded by the art therapies when working with offenders."

James Gilligan: "I couldn't over-emphasize the importance of that. After working in the Massachusetts prisons, I spent ten years running a violence prevention experiment in the jails of San Francisco, and this was a multi-model intensive programme in which they were in programmes six days a week, twelve hours a day. An important component of it was several different arts programmes, regular art therapy, music therapy, and drama therapy. We pulled out every stop and it worked, it really did. We would have them write a one-act play describing what we called the 'end of innocence moment' in their lives and experience what turned them on the path towards violence. Usually, these were traumatic incidents, but they would write a play about it and then act in the play, cast their fellow inmates in other roles, and by doing that, and all of these arts, it gave them an alternative to violent action. I think the treatment of the violent has to be multi-disciplinary. It's a team project, it's not just one psychoanalytic therapist like myself, it's a whole team."

Carine Minne: "We have to stop this session now, but there is an hour-long discussion later in the day. One thing I'd be interested in hearing about is what James was referring to as the age of genocide and terrorism. The most violence, James was saying, is carried out by people suffering from borderline or narcissistic character or personality disorders and I would love to hear more about any terrorists that have been examined analytically.

Thank you all for your comments and questions and thank you, James."

CHAPTER FIVE

From action to communication: the transformation of aggression in childhood

Marie Zaphiriou Woods

Introduction

This short paper outlines the development of aggression in childhood in the context of relationships which, when all goes well, enable the transformation from action to communication. My approach is rooted in a psychoanalytic understanding of normal development, emphasizing the interaction between the infant and young child's evolving internal world, and that of the parents (caregivers). In line with Yakeley's multi-dimensional viewpoint (Yakeley, 2010, p. 24), the role of trauma and loss, the capacity for representation and mentalization, unconscious fantasy, and the defensive system are also considered.

The development of aggression

There is a vast psychoanalytic literature on aggression. I will give a brief overview, starting with Winnicott (1950), who equated the infant's aggression with activity, muscularity, a "life force". Winnicott describes how the mother's capacity to survive, without retaliation, her infant's ruthless instinctual expressions enables him to realize his full aggressive potential, to feel real, and, over time, to recognize that she is separate, outside his omnipotent control (1969). Combined with her empathy and readiness to perceive and receive his spontaneous reparative gestures, the mother's survival also enables the fusion of aggressive and erotic drives, and the transformation of the infant's anxiety about losing or destroying her into concern and a sense of responsibility (Winnicott, 1963). Aggression can then be integrated into the personality as a useful energy in work and play. When fusion does not occur, aggression is split off, leading to enactments of violence and destruction (see Abram, 1996).

In her writings, Anna Freud gave aggression the same status as sexuality, seeing it as an inborn urge, a basic motivating drive in human development. She noted (1949) that the sexual instincts need an admixture of aggression to achieve their aims, and saw aggression as "mind building", stimulating the development of mental capacities in order to enable it to achieve its goals, and contributing to assertiveness, mastery, and, sometimes, necessary self-preservation. Like Winnicott, she stressed the importance of consistent loving relationships to promote the fusion of sexuality with aggressive urges, which otherwise became destructive and uncontrollable. According to Anna Freud, environmental failure in the anal phase (1–3 years) was particularly risky because it left unbound the young child's sadism and destructiveness (see, too, Edgcumbe, 2000). Both Anna Freud (1949, 1965) and Winnicott (1956, 1986) saw pathological aggression and antisocial behaviour as arising out of early deprivation and trauma. More recently, attachment research has shown that prolonged absence or loss of attachment figures can cause the infant's natural angry protest at their absence to develop into more pathological destructive aggression (Yakeley, 2010).

From the beginning of life, the infant discharges tension through the body (squirming, sicking, pushing away). The way in which a mother receives these earliest bodily expressions—her voice, facial expression, and physical care (handling)—has a profound effect on the way the infant comes to represent his activity and aggression. To quote Mayes and Cohen (1993) "any aggressive act and fantasy is embedded in a social matrix" (p. 152). The mother's response will be largely determined by her own inner world—her conflicts and her representations of self and other and her relationship with her baby. Unresolved maternal trauma or loss, leading to frightened or frightening behaviours (Main & Hesse, 1990) or a hostile or helpless stance (Lyons-Ruth, Yellin, Melnick, & Atwood, 2005) have been associated with disorganized infant attachments (see, too, Sleed & Fonagy, 2010). For the normal development of aggression, the mother needs to do more than meet his physical needs; she needs to be receptive and empathic. "It lays the foundations for the capacity to tolerate vulnerability because helplessness is associated with a protective object" (Parsons & Dermen, 1999, p. 331). Confident that he will not be left in unbearable states of "going to pieces" or "falling for ever" (Winnicott, 1962, p. 58), the infant gradually learns to differentiate different shades of feeling until not every internal state has the same urgency. He learns to manage his own feelings and experiences, and to internalize his mother's protective function (see Parsons, 2007).

Toddlers make exuberant use of their bodies to express activity and aggression in increasingly skilled ways. Walking, climbing up on furniture, making a huge mess, they revel in their growing sense of agency and power, and resent adult restriction, whether it be to keep them or others safe, or to begin to socialize them. They may throw a huge tantrum, biting, hitting, screaming, throwing themselves about to express rage at having their omnipotence limited, but also anxiety about being small and helpless, and of losing their beloved mother, whom they desperately need. Lacking a clear distinction between fantasy and reality, they fear that angry feelings can actually kill people, and that they might lose their loving feelings. The mother's firmness, or "opposition" (Winnicott, 1969) helps the child to learn to delay gratification, tolerate frustration, and channel his anger.

Faced with the onslaught of toddler ambivalence (their passionate love and equally passionate hate, their fierce independence alternating with clinging dependence), the mother (or care-giver) may be hard put to stand her ground, to be firm but also loving, and ready to repair the relationship after inevitable breakdowns. *Her* conflicts around aggression, and mess, closeness, and separateness, will have been evoked; she is likely at times to feel anxious, overwhelmed, guilty, and ashamed, tempted to externalize her own repudiated impulses on to her toddler and to reject or even hurt him. The support of another adult can rescue the mother–toddler couple from becoming enmeshed in murderous battles. Fathers can help their toddlers to separate from their mothers and to modulate their aggression (Herzog, 1982). Firm loving consistency from *both* parents helps the toddler to balance his ambivalence, to avoid split-ting (Klein, 1935), and to develop concern (Winnicott, 1963). Both parents' containment of the toddler's unmanageable feelings and anxieties will, over time, be internalized by the toddler and con-tribute to his growing capacity to regulate his own negative feeling states.

The regulation of feelings and of closeness is facilitated by the development of language and play, which can become intensely enjoyable ways in which a toddler and parent can communicate, while at the same time fostering the recognition that they have separate minds. Being able to name angry feelings ("cross"), to state aggressive wishes ("kill the cat") and express them in play are huge strides on the way from action to symbolic communication. After the third year, there is a decrease in physical aggressivity and an increase in verbal aggressivity (shouting, name-calling) (Mayes & Cohen, 1993). Once negative feelings and experiences can begin to be talked about and played with, they are not necessarily acted on. This aids mastery, impulse control, and the differentiation of fan-tasy from reality.

In their shared communications, around toilet training, for example, the parents' feelings about control and mess will be communicated at a conscious and unconscious level. The older toddler, who is concerned to please his parents and keep their love and approval, will identify with these attitudes, which will then contribute to superego development. He may develop reaction formations against unacceptable impulses to be cruel or messy, complying with the parents' demands that he become kind, clean, even tidy. Transformed by such defences, aggression can contribute to useful character traits. Excessive compliance, however, can lead to false self-development with insufficient aggression available for normal moves towards separation.

Nursery school aged children may use their bodies for aggres-sive display, to seek admiration for being big, strong, and attractive to their loved ones. Frustration of these wishes may leave them feeling shamed and humiliated and can lead to outbursts of narcissistic rage. Moving on to the Oedipal phase, they may become jealously possessive of one parent, competitive with, and rejecting of, the other. They become curious about their origins and the parents' sexual relationship. Their fantasies may be imbued with rage and jealousy at being excluded, which, when enhanced by earlier (pre-Oedipal) feelings and fantasies and perhaps the witnessing of actual fights, may lead them to imagine intercourse as a violent battle. Fearing retaliation and physical damage, and the loss of their parents' love and approval, the young child gradually relinquishes his desires, accepting the reality of sexual and generational difference. If all goes well, his conscience (superego) becomes increasingly structuralized, gaining strength from paternal introjection. The child's growing sense of right and wrong may not always enable him to control his impulses, and may lead to tale-telling with blame externalized ("look what he/she did"). Fearing punishment for his aggressive wishes, he may project them, developing fears and phobias.

The young child begins to understand that other people's motives and intentions may be different from his (theory of mind). He begins to own responsibility for his wishes and fantasies, and to experience guilt and concern about the people he loves. He struggles to repair what he perceives as resulting from his own aggressivity (Mayes & Cohen, 1993). This process may be interfered with if he has experienced actual violence or abuse (Fonagy, Gergely, Jurist, & Target, 2002). If it feels too dangerous to contemplate the other's mind, the child is less likely to develop awareness of others' thoughts and feelings, with adverse consequences for the development of empathy and the inhibition of aggressive impulses. He may identify with the aggressor (A. Freud, 1936), becoming aggressive and meting out to others the sorts of experiences of helplessness and fear to which he has been subjected.

Primary school aged children still display physical and verbal aggression in playground fights. However, most develop a sense of fairness, and learn to abide by rules (written and unwritten). They can divert their aggression and competitiveness into learning, games, and sports. Mayes and Cohen (1993) have noted an interesting paradox: that as aggressive behaviour decreases, it tends to be more personally directed, instigated by threats to the child's self esteem, and more intended to do harm to the offending other. Children with a fragile sense of self will be inordinately sensitive to feeling ostracized, bullied, or ignored, and will defend themselves with violent means (Fonagy, Moran, & Target, 1993; Gilligan, 1996).

Post scriptum

The clinical material presented at the conference has been omitted for reasons of confidentiality. It described the referral and treatment of two aggressive primary school aged boys, whose parents, for different reasons, had not been able to facilitate the move from bodily to symbolic expression (see Parsons, 2007). From early on, both children were perceived as aggressive and difficult ("a nightmare"), and compared unfavourably with an idealized sibling. They were each seen in three times a week psychoanalytic psychotherapy (one for 1½ years and the other for just over two years). This work, combined with fortnightly meetings with each mother (by a separate parent worker), enabled the boys to achieve some of the transformations described above. They became able to progress at school and to develop good relationships at home.

References

Abram, J. (1996). *The Language of Winnicott*. London: Karnac.

Edgcumbe, R. (2000). *Anna Freud. A View of Development, Disturbance and Therapeutic Techniques*. London: Routledge.

Fonagy, P., Gergely, G. E., Jurist, E. L., & Target, M. (2002). *Affect Regulation, Mentalization and the Development of the Self*. New York: Other Press.

Fonagy, P., Moran, G., & Target, M. (1993). Aggression and the psychological self. *International Journal of Psychoanalysis, 74*(3): 471–485.

Freud, A. (1936). *Ego and Mechanisms of Defence*. London: Hogarth Press.

Freud, A. (1949). Aggression in relation to emotional development: normal and pathological. In: *Indications for Child Analysis and Other Papers*. London: Hogarth Press.

Freud, A. (1965). *Normality and Pathology in Childhood: Assessments of Development. Writings of Anna Freud, Vol. 14*. London: Hogarth Press.

Gilligan, J. (1996). *Violence: Our Deadliest Epidemic and its Causes*. New York: Grosset/Putnam.

Herzog, J. (1982). On father hunger: the father's role in the modulation of aggressive drive and fantasy. In: S. W. Cath, A. R. Gorwitt, & J. M. Ross (Eds.), *Father and Child* (pp. 167–174). Boston, MA: Little, Brown.

Klein, M. (1935). A contribution to the psychogenesis of manic depressive states. In: *Love, Guilt, Reparation and Other Works 1921–1945* (pp. 262–289). London: Hogarth Press.

Lyons-Ruth, K., Yellin, C., Melnick, S., & Atwood, G. (2005). Expanding the concept of unresolved mental states: hostile/helpless states of mind on the Adult Attachment Interview are associated with disrupted mother–infant communication and infant disorganization. *Development and Psychology, 17*: 1–23.

Main, M., & Hesse, E. (1990). Parents' unresolved traumatic experiences are related to infant disorganised attachment status; is frightened and/or frightening parental behaviour the linking mechanism? In: M. T. Greenberg, D. Cicchetti, & E. Cummings (Eds.), *Attachment in the Preschool Years* (pp. 161–182). Chicago, IL: University of Chicago Press.

Mayes, L. C., & Cohen, D. J. (1993). The social matrix of aggression— enactments and representations of loving and hating in the first years of life. *The Psychoanalytic Study of the Child, 48*: 145–169.

Parsons, M. (2007). From biting teeth to biting wit; the normative development of aggression. In: D. Morgan & S. Ruszczynski (Eds.), *Lectures on Violence, Perversion and Delinquency* (pp. 117–136). London: Karnac.

Parsons, M., & Dermen, S. (1999). The violent child and adolescent. In: M. Lanyado & A. Horne (Eds.), *The Handbook of Child and Adolescent Psychotherapy* (pp. 329–346). London: Routledge.

Sleed, M., & Fonagy, P. (2010). Understanding disruptions in the parent–infant relationship. Do actions speak louder than words? In: T. Baradon (Ed.), *Relational Trauma in Infancy* (pp. 136–162). London: Routledge.

Winnicott, D. W. (Ed.) (1950). Aggression in relation to emotional development. In: *Collected Papers: Through Paediatrics to Psychoanalysis* (pp. 204–218). London: Hogarth Press.

Winnicott, D. W. (Ed.) (1956). The anti-social tendency. In: *Collected Papers: Through Paediatrics to Psychoanalysis* (pp. 306–315). London: Hogarth Press.

Winnicott, D. W. (1962). Ego integration in child development. In: *Maturational Processes and the Facilitating Environment* (pp. 56–63). London: Hogarth Press.

Winnicott, D. W. (Ed.) (1963). The development of a capacity for concern. In: *Maturational Processes and the Facilitating Environment* (pp. 73–82). London: Hogarth Press.

Winnicott, D. W. (1969). The use of an object. *International Journal of Psychoanalysis, 50*: 711–716.

Winnicott, D. W. (1986). *Deprivation and Delinquency*. London: Tavistock.

Yakeley, J. (2010). *Working with Violence. A Contemporary Psychoanalytic Approach*. London: Palgrave Macmillan.

Note

Regrettably, due to technical reasons on the day, a recording and transcription of the discussion of Marie Zaphirou Woods' paper is unavailable.

CHAPTER SIX

Aggression and violence in adolescence

Marianne Parsons

Introduction

Marie has given a very clear account of the normative development of aggression in childhood, with some vivid clinical material about a boy whose development went off track, leading him to enact in very aggressive ways until his anxieties could be worked through in psychotherapy. My task is to extend the theme into adolescence, and then I want to focus on a concept pertinent to untransformed aggression: the core complex. My interest in aggression was stimulated in the Portman Clinic Violence Research Group under the leadership of Mervin Glasser, and I will use material from one of my Portman Clinic patients, an adolescent boy, to illustrate how thinking about the core complex can help with understanding and working with a violent patient. I will begin with the impact of the adolescent process.

The developmental process of adolescence

Erikson (1956) defined adolescence as the years when the mind develops the capacity to integrate the profound physical changes that start in puberty in relationship to the self and to others. It is a "normative crisis situation" (Tonnesmann, 1980) and a time of necessary "developmental disturbance" (A. Freud, 1958), when the typical "fluctuations between extreme opposites would be deemed highly abnormal at any other time of life" (A. Freud, 1958, p. 165). It is like an age-appropriate transient madness in which everything is in a state of bewildering and unpredictable tension and change, with rapid shifts between wild excitement and deep depression. Such upheavals show that necessary internal adjustments are in progress.

The ego is put under enormous strain due to the changes in the sexual and aggressive drives at puberty (both quantitative and qualitative) and the need to face the many developmental tasks of adolescence, chiefly taking ownership of a maturing body, loosening the tie to the parents, and forming a differentiated identity (Blos, 1967; Laufer, 1978). In a healthy adolescent, the development of the ego and superego will accommodate all this, but in some cases the heightened instinctual impulses "succeed in creating utter confusion and chaos in what has been an orderly, socially directed ego during the latency period" (A. Freud, 1958, p. 258) and the adolescent's defences may break down. As their bodies mature, adolescents face the excitement, responsibilities, fantasies, and fears that accompany the approach of adulthood, including the reality that they will soon be as big, powerful, and sexually active as the parents. Previously, they could rely on adults to intervene if their aggression got out of hand, but their increased physical strength means taking further responsibility for the damage their body could do.

The adolescent swings from needy dependence to rebellious independence and rejection of the parents, and both fears and longs for intimacy. Recently, a friend spoke wryly of "losing" her "lovely and loving child" and being faced now with an eleven-year-old who was sulky, moody, and resentful and wanted little to do with her, except at those times when the mum wanted a bit of peace! She understood this was the beginning of a healthy adolescent process and was able to take it in her stride. Nevertheless, she, like her child, was facing the painful experience of loss of the previous intimacy of the parent–child relationship as well as the typically increased ambivalence. A succinct quote about adolescence from Winnicott fits well here: "You sowed a baby and reaped a bomb"!

(Winnicott, 1971, p. 145). Hostility and aggressivity, which in a healthy adolescent is used to facilitate the necessary separation from parents (Winnicott, 1950), may instead be directed against the self, leading to depression, self-denigration, abuse of alcohol or drugs, promiscuity, anorexia and bulimia, self-harm, and even suicide (Friedman, Glasser, Laufer, Laufer & Wohl, 1972).

In adolescence, aggression is heightened and impulsivity increases because of the temporary weakening of inhibitory forces and the increase in regressive ones. There is a frantic turn to the outside world, to sensory stimulation and to action (Blos, 1966). Winnicott thought that the adolescent needs to "prod society repeatedly so that society's antagonism is made manifest and can be met with antagonism" (Winnicott, 1961, p. 85). Typical healthy passions concern matters of world importance (world peace, racism, animal rights), in their view treated complacently by adults. Such ideals provide a focus for transforming and directing aggression in adaptive and socially useful ways, while also allowing the adolescents to feel superior to the parents as they individuate from them. Referring particularly to the wild aggression that can arise in adolescent groups or gangs, Buxbaum wrote, "Just as the river, swollen with melting snow and torrential rains, breaks through its dams and floods the land, so the inordinately increased aggression floods the adolescent's whole system, explodes, and inundates society" (Buxbaum, 1970, p. 263). Delinquent and destructive enactments of aggression constitute the adolescent's rebellion not only against external authority, but also against a tyrannical superego, where guilt is ignored or unavailable as a signal and has to be defied and triumphed over.

Narcissistic balance is disturbed alarmingly, causing the youngster to be self-absorbed, preoccupied, and struggling to feel real (Winnicott, 1961). Adolescents typically experiment with different fantasy self-images until making the final adjustment to a more realistic view of their capabilities. Some risk-taking behaviour is expectable as the teenager tests his limits and tries to find his own identity and values as distinct from those of his parents. However, risk-taking may represent an unresolved sense of omnipotence, the avoidance of independent mastery and self-care, and a rebellion against parental and superego guidance. Some narcissistically vulnerable adolescents develop an omnipotent grandiose self-image, such as the "tough guy" or the "dictator" to defend against feelings of inadequacy, helplessness, and humiliation. As well as providing an idealized self to live up to, this is also a tyrannical model of both internal and external control. To avoid fears of regression and dependence, they may engage in risky and dangerous behaviour, such as delinquency, substance abuse, and violence. Others may avoid all conflictual situations, especially competition, out of fear of their own or their parents' uncontrollable aggression. They gain self-esteem from living up to an ideal self-image as "good" and by perceiving others as aggressive, but when faced with an extreme situation, their defensive compliance may break down, causing a violent outburst.

If the adolescent's earlier development has been good enough, he will have established healthy modes of relating in which aggression is bound by loving feelings (A. Freud, 1949, 1972) and can be used for protection of self and others and for self-assertion. Aggression is sublimated through various hobbies, interests and skills, and channelled into activities (such as competitive sports and verbal debate). Language becomes the major medium for the expression of aggression. For those with weak spots in their development and without the internal resources to deal adequately with the developmental tasks of adolescence, puberty may precipitate the onset of significant problems with aggressivity.

I now want to look at the roots of violence, especially in relation to how core complex anxieties contribute to the release of untransformed aggression.

The roots of violence

The main difference between aggression and violence is that violence involves a *physical* attack on the body of another person when this is not developmentally age-appropriate (Parsons, 2006). The toddler who physically attacks someone is being aggressive, not violent, because it is expectable for toddlers to express their anger and frustration in bodily ways, and the teenager who attacks another with verbal abuse is also being aggressive, not violent, but if that adolescent were to resort to physical attack, that would then constitute an act of violence.

Marie described how the young child internalizes the mother's capacity to provide for his needs and protect him from both external and internal dangers, such as sensations, feelings, and fears that he cannot yet process himself. If the mother is able to act adequately as a protective shield (Freud, 1920g; Khan, 1963), keeping her baby safe until he gradually develops the resources to do this for himself, he will develop a sense of basic safety and trust, and will form a secure attachment to her. He will internalize her ways of looking after him and will gradually be able to tolerate small amounts of anxiety and frustration as he learns that she *will* do something to help. In time, vulnerability and helplessness can become linked to hope for something better, and the world feels a potentially safe and good place. Internalization of the mother's protective function involves the gradual development of a permeable psychological membrane, which allows for fluid movement of sensations, feelings, and experiences into and out of the psyche. Acting like a filter, it hinders the outward expression of raw unprocessed impulses and also protects the ego from being swamped by the incursion of overwhelming stimulation, thus allowing for some flexible give and take in relation to helplessness, frustration, and criticism, and for the appropriate use of aggressiveness for self-assertion and protection (Parsons, 2009).

Violence can be understood as an attempted solution to the overwhelming *unprocessed trauma of helplessness in the absence of a protective other*. Environmental failures that amount to cumulative trauma prevent the internalization of a protective function in the ego that would regulate fear and anxiety. Instead of being able to establish a flexible psychological membrane, the child erects a rigid protective internal barrier, like an impenetrable fortress. He may feel omnipotent and invincible, but is, in fact, extremely vulnerable. He cannot register anxiety as a danger signal to help him to make use of appropriate defences to deal with his helplessness, anger, and frustration, and any threat that penetrates his rigid barrier will feel traumatic and trigger the most primitive defences of flight or fight. With the accompanying development of an insecure or disorganized attachment, he will be narcissistically vulnerable with no reliable sense of feeling loveable. Even slight disappointments will feel like catastrophic attacks and threaten his self-esteem and psychic integrity, and may lead to violent outbursts of narcissistic rage (Khan, 1963; Kohut, 1972). He may also develop a false or precocious independence, something often seen in violent individuals, who tend to act out their frustration and anxiety, unable to use their minds for self-reflection or containment of feelings.

Feeling completely helpless and without protection brings forth terror of annihilation, which is expressed through the unconscious anxieties that form the nucleus of the core complex (Glasser, 1979, 1998). These are of *engulfment* (that is, fear of annihilation because of feeling smothered or taken over by another and therefore losing one's self) and of *abandonment* (fears of annihilation through feeling deserted and left alone to starve and die). Although developmentally appropriate in toddlerhood, core complex anxieties become especially acute in adolescence, when thoughts of genital intimacy are stimulated by the physical and psychological effects of puberty, and when the adolescent is struggling to become independent of his parents, especially mother. If the adolescent has severe unresolved conflicts in relation to his parents, particularly with regard to aggression and separation, is confused about his sexual identity and feels a failure among peers, core complex anxieties become overwhelming and threaten him with fears of madness. When feeling abandoned and alone, he will have the regressive longing to merge with an idealized image of an omnipotent, all-satisfying mother and will try to seek closeness, but then faces anxiety about annihilation of his separate, differentiated self and so has to withdraw to protect himself. Swinging back and forth between these two extremes, he is caught in a vicious circle and desperately needs to find a position of safety. Sadomasochism is an effective, though crippling solution (Glasser, 1979, 1998). By actively engaging in a sadomasochistic style of relating, he keeps a grip on the other but at arm's length, within his control but at a safe distance. If this sadomasochistic defence fails to hold the core complex anxieties at bay, self-preservative violence will be "mobilised for psychic self-preservation, and may be aimed at his own body or another's" (Campbell & Hale, 1991).

A major factor in unresolved core complex problems is the extent of the mother's narcissism. By neglecting her child's needs and putting her own first, such a mother both abandons as well as engulfs her child, leaving him at the mercy of an ongoing threat of annihilation. This inconsistency leaves the child neither emotionally close to the mother nor able to separate from her, and increases his anxiety and aggression. He may enact this for the rest of his life, always longing for intimacy but also fearing it. If, when faced with her child's angry demands, the mother always gives in to him or reacts aggressively by yelling at him or hitting him, she is unwittingly setting up a sadomasochistic pattern for his future relationships. For the child, getting what he wants is gratifying, but it is a hollow gift because he is being given something only to be kept quiet, instead of containment and help to manage his frustration. If the mother hits the child, he feels punished, but he also gets some contact with the mother, though of a negatively exciting kind. This sadomasochistic mode of relating, with its mixture of control, punishment, humiliation, and excited contact with the other, can become a fixed part of the child's personality. Instead of having a view of relating that is based on mutuality and give and take, the child learns that there are two opposing sides, the attacker and the attacked, the controller and the controlled, and his sense of identity will inevitably include both these opposing sides.

As violent-prone people are extremely sensitive to feeling engulfed, neglected, and shamed, extra care is needed in relating and communicating with them. Saying too much will be experienced as intrusive, being silent will feel dismissive and abandoning, and anything we say may be experienced as threatening, humiliating, or punitive. This was one of the technical problems I faced in working with my patient Tom.

Tom

Seventeen-year-old Tom had no compunctions about his violence; he gloried in it and his whole sense of identity was shaped by coldly calculated violence. He was referred to the Portman Clinic for once weekly psychotherapy after an attempted rape. A girl whom he had wanted to ask out had recently rejected him and chosen to date another boy instead, so he had planned to lie in wait for someone who looked like her and commit rape at knifepoint. He got as far as holding the knife to a young woman's throat, but was unable to carry out the rape and demanded money from her instead. Unsatisfied, he returned to the same place the next day determined to carry out his plan fully this time, but the police had been alerted to the previous incident and laid in wait to arrest him.

Tom came from a very corrupt family: they were all involved with theft and violence and the use of force. As a child, Tom was treated both dismissively and violently by both parents and would run to his grandparents' house to escape being beaten. He was firmly set in action mode and could see no point in thinking about his past or his feelings in therapy, saying that such things were irrelevant and did not matter. He denied any hatred towards his parents, and shrugged his shoulders as if his history had had no effect on him. Later, it became clear that he nursed a strong sense of grievance that his younger brother had received the attention and care Tom had been denied. Tom was bullied at primary school, but now loved getting into fights. He planned to join the violent wing of the BNP and had fiercely racist opinions. He terrorized Asian boys, whom he described resentfully as "keeping themselves to themselves, taking our jobs, always getting their way, and having their own shops." He felt morally justified in attacking them because he thought they were looked after and given everything they wanted. It seemed clear that his early experiences of being treated violently, feeling unacknowledged and unprotected by his parents, especially mother, and his sense of abandonment that his brother got what he had missed, were carried as an unprocessed trauma that could only be enacted.

He had no wish to give up his violence towards boys, but hoped that therapy would somehow get rid of his fantasies of violently raping a woman, as he was worried that he might re-enact them. He was not concerned from a moral point of view, but was fearful only of getting punished. It gradually became clear that his sexual fantasies were linked to feelings of murderous rage towards his mother, whom he experienced as humiliating and utterly rejecting. The rape fantasies stopped when he had his first sexual relationship soon after therapy started. Significantly, in terms of transference acting out, this relationship was with an older woman who was in a position of authority over him—in fact, one of his schoolteachers.

The experience of being in the room with Tom was extremely difficult and I felt a constant, heavy emptiness that was very hard to bear. The sessions felt lifeless and as though they would never end, but something boiled dangerously underneath the surface. It was like being at the edge of a volcano, where the cold grey ash might make one forget the raging power that could erupt at any moment. The wish to be number one and in control were his driving forces, and not winning aroused extreme vengeful rage. His excitement about the World Cup was in terms of the football hooligans, and he relished the thought of extreme violence arising from the Argentina *vs.* England match. He was contemptuously scathing about almost everyone: about all women (who should stay at home and not compete with men for outside work), about all authority figures (such as teachers or the government, who wanted to impose their rules on him), about anyone who might be in competition with him and with other white British men (such as Asians, the French, and the Irish), about weakness in any form. His ego ideal was that of a forceful dictator who squashes the weak underfoot. He seemed to have no notion whatsoever of care, tenderness, or empathy, and could not believe that anyone might really be interested in, or concerned about, him.

Tom was unable to retain anything from one session to the next, so each week it felt as if we were starting from scratch. Although I often felt lost and clumsy in my work with him and frequently felt like giving up, I tried to hold on to some hope of making a connection with him so as not to act on my countertransference wish to be rid of him.

Tom's fear of trusting me made it very hard for him to engage in the therapeutic process. He was polite, but mostly silent. Unlike most adolescents, who are silent in therapy and tend to avoid eye contact, Tom stared at me in a challenging and expectant way that was extremely uncomfortable. I felt held in a controlling vice-like grip, both shut out by him in the silence and also intruded on because of his penetrating gaze. One can see the link here with his fantasy of invading a woman forcefully by rape. Tom found the silences very awkward too, and wanted me to ask him questions, but when I did, he experienced me as forcefully intrusive. This was a very powerful dynamic. As I thought about it, I began to understand how he was trying to defend himself against terrifying core complex anxieties of abandonment and engulfment through a sadomasochistic engagement with me. And through identification with the aggressor (his violent father and his neglectful but also intrusive mother), he made me feel both engulfed and alone. Using these countertransference feelings as a guide and aware of the defensive sadomasochism, I told

Tom that I had a dilemma to think about with him: that my words as well as my silence made him feel awful, and he seemed to feel very uncomfortable and unsafe in the room with me.

I tried to explore his discomfort with me, checking if I was understanding correctly how it felt for him, and it gradually emerged that he found all verbal communication difficult. He felt he had nothing interesting to say and that nobody noticed him. I said that this could make him feel terribly lonely; it might be very hard for him to feel he was a "somebody" worthy of notice, and perhaps it was as if he felt invisible. He agreed, and said that the only thing that always made people pay attention to him was when he talked about his (racist) political opinions. It did not matter whether the person agreed or disagreed; all that mattered to him was to get an intense reaction. I linked this urgent need to get through to people with his helpless isolation of never having felt noticed in a good way by his parents, especially his mother. I wondered if the only way he felt he could have an impact on some-one was by force—by his forceful political views or physical violence. This seemed to reach him, and he responded reluctantly but thoughtfully by saying for the first time that he felt helpless and vulnerable sometimes.

Some months later, he described women as grabbing like mum—men's ideas were the only things worth listening to. He agreed when I suggested that he probably felt contemptuous of anything I might say. A week later he brought a memory from when he was five, during a long period of time when his father was away at sea. Mum was very irritated by his little brother's crying, but she yelled at Tom and hit *him*, not his brother. He told me he hated his mum. This was the first time that he had been able to voice his anger about her. By now, it was more possible to think about feel-ings with him, and he was able to listen when I spoke about how confused, helpless, hurt, and frightened he had been when he was little. I said that he had felt attacked rather than protected by his mum, and had then found a way of protecting himself by building a picture of himself as powerful and strong and incapable of being affected by anything or anyone. Tom nodded, so I ventured to add that it might feel very risky to allow himself to get in touch with any feelings of hurt and helplessness and he needed not to let anything matter.

A few weeks later, when he was talking about going abroad to university, he suddenly fell silent. When I wondered why he had stopped, he mumbled, "It doesn't matter", then agreed that he felt I was not interested and said, " I don't think people *are* interested." I suggested that he felt I was only pretending to be interested and he said, "Well, you just do this for the money." I took up how lonely he might feel coming here each week, convinced that I am not interested and only seeing him for the money, and then he has to keep things hidden inside because he cannot trust my motives. I also said that it was very hard for him to believe I might *really* be interested in him. A few weeks later he was able to express his ambivalence. Although irritated with me because he thought I had been pompous and nagging in the previous session, he also said, "I don't know why I come here, but I do . . . I do think you have good intentions."

In her paper "Sadistic and violent acts in the young", Professor Sue Bailey links adolescent violence with deep-seated fears of failure and sexual inadequacy in a narcissistically vulnerable psyche, and stresses the importance of omnipotent grandiose fantasy and the first sexual experience (Bailey, 1997). This was the case for Tom. His story shows how an adolescent may end up acting violently. Due to his childhood experiences of traumatic helplessness, he was caught in the vicious circle of core complex anxieties. With violent and negating parents, Tom experienced the smallest slight as utterly traumatic. Defensively, he relied on sadomasochism and had built a pseudo-identity for himself as the "tough guy", which fortified his rigid internal barrier as a substitute for the missing protective function. Desperate to avoid feelings of shame and inadequacy, he resorted to fantasies of world domination through the BNP and of controlling and subjugating women sadistically with his rape fantasies. But underneath the posturing of the would-be dictator, there was a frightened and humiliated child whose only way of protecting himself from an overwhelming sensitivity to feeling a rejected nobody was to act violently. He turned the passive experience of being neglected, humiliated, and battered into an active experience of being dismissive and contemptuously violent towards others: through identification with the aggressor, Tom as victim turned into Tom the perpetrator.

He presented himself as an immaculately dressed adult in a smart suit, with none of the typically adolescent anxieties about growing up. The capacity to acknowledge regressive wishes implies healthy narcissism and an internalized image of a protective other who can be relied on. Without these, Tom could only deal with his sense of being rejected by his mother and give vent to his murderous rage towards her by sexually attacking other women. He also denied his regressive wishes and externalized them on to the ethnic minorities whom he then enviously attacked for being greedy children, like his brother, who got everything they wanted.

Psychotherapy lasted for eighteen months until Tom left for university. It was only possible to scratch the surface of his underlying difficulties in this short time, but he did make some progress. His rape fantasies stopped, as did his deliberate seeking out of fights with others boys, though if provoked he still enjoyed getting the upper hand forcefully. He had had his first sexual relationship, albeit with an inappropriate person, and this brought relief from his sense of inadequacy and gave him confidence for his future as a man. He began to recognize that he mattered and so did his feelings and past experiences, and sometimes he was able to reflect on them. Although he was still determined to become a member of the BNP, by the end of therapy he had decided not to join its violent wing but to become an MP, thinking it would be more efficacious to try to bring people round to his way of thinking by oratory. Not the most successful outcome of psychotherapy perhaps, but at least a step in the right direction of the transformation of his aggression—from action to words (Parsons, 2006).

Post scriptum

In the Portman Clinic Violence Research Project, we noticed that all the violent men in the research study attempted to protect themselves by habitual sadomasochistic modes of relating. When this defence broke down, their core complex anxieties surfaced and self-preservative violence then erupted to destroy the person who had become the source of the ultimate danger—annihilation of the psychic self. These violent men all had *extremely vulnerable phallic-narcissism*, which was linked to their *experience of a narcissistic mother as well as to the lack of a reliable, strong father* who might offset the over-close mother–child tie and also provide a model for secure masculine identification. Anything that called into question the masculinity of these patients, for example, a jibe about being a mummy's boy, weak, small, homosexual, etc., was likely to trigger their violence. In therapy, they often recalled extremely humiliating slights on their masculinity from their mothers in childhood and adolescence. The *self-preservative violence* that erupted when their masculinity was called into question in the present, even if instigated by a man, seemed to be *aimed unconsciously at the castrating and annihilating mother*. Although both men and women can act violently towards others and towards themselves, Estella Welldon at the Portman Clinic found that men mostly tend to attack other people and women tend to attack their own bodies or the products of them, their babies and children (Welldon, 1988). There may be a biological factor here in terms of anatomical differences, but of major significance is the woman's identification of her body with that of her mother. Like the violent man, the woman's violence towards her own body or that of her child may unconsciously represent an attack on the annihilating mother.

References

Bailey, S. (1997). Sadistic and violent acts in the young. *Child Psychology & Psychiatry Review*, 2(3): 92–102.

Blos, P. (1966). The concept of acting out in relation to the adolescent process. In: *The Adolescent Passage: Developmental Issues* (pp. 254–277). New York: International Universities Press, 1979.

Blos, P. (1967). The second individuation process of adolescence. *Psychoanalytic Study of the Child*, 22: 162–186.

Buxbaum, E. (1970). *Troubled Children in a Troubled World*. New York: International Universities Press.

Campbell, D., & Hale, R. (1991). Suicidal acts. In: J. Holmes (Ed.), *Textbook of Psychotherapy in Psychiatric Practice* (pp. 287–306). London: Churchill Livingstone.

Erikson, E. (1956). The concept of ego identity. *Journal of the American Psychoanalytic Association*, 4: 56–121.

Freud, A. (1949). Aggression in relation to emotional development: normal and pathological. *Psychoanalytic Study of the Child*, 3(4): 37–42.

Freud, A. (1958). Adolescence. *Psychoanalytic Study of the Child*, 13: 255–278.

Freud, A. (1972). Comments on aggression. In: *Psychoanalytic Psychology of Normal Development* (pp. 151–175). London: Hogarth, 1982.

Freud, S. (1920g). Beyond the pleasure principle. *S.E.*, 18: 7–64. London: Hogarth.

Friedman, M., Glasser, M., Laufer, E., Laufer, M., & Wohl, M. (1972). Attempted suicide and self-mutilation in adolescence: some observations from a psychoanalytic research project. *International Journal of Psychoanalysis*, 53: 179–183.

Glasser, M. (1979). Some aspects of the role of aggression in the perversions. In: I. Rosen (Ed.), *Sexual Deviations* (2nd edn) (pp. 278–305). Oxford: Oxford University Press.

Glasser, M. (1998). On violence: a preliminary communication. *International Journal of Psychoanalysis*, 79(5): 887–902.

Khan, M. (1963). The concept of cumulative trauma. *Psychoanalytic Study of the Child*, 18: 286–306.

Kohut, H. (1972). Thoughts on narcissism and narcissistic rage. *Psychoanalytic Study of the Child*, 27: 360–400.

Laufer, M. (1978). The nature of adolescent pathology and the psychoanalytic process. *Psychoanalytic Study of the Child*, 33: 307–322.

Parsons, M. (2006). From biting teeth to biting wit: the normative development of aggression. In: C. Harding (Ed.), *Aggression and Destructiveness* (pp. 41–58). London: Brunner-Routledge, 2006. Also in: D. Morgan and S. Ruszczynski (Eds.), *Lectures on Violence, Perversion and Delinquency: The Portman Papers* (pp. 117–136). London: Karnac, 2007.

Parsons, M. (2009).The roots of violence: theory and implications for technique with children and adolescents. In: M. Lanyardo & A. Horne (Eds.), *The Handbook of Child and Adolescent Psychotherapy* (revised edn) (pp. 361–380). London: Routledge.

Tonnesmann, M. (1980). Adolescent re-enactment, trauma and reconstruction. *Journal of Child Psychotherapy*, 6: 23–44.

Welldon, E. (1988). *Mother, Madonna, Whore*. London: Free Association Books [reprinted London: Karnac, 1992].

Winnicott, D. W. (1950). Aggression in relation to emotional development. In: *Collected Papers: Through Paediatrics to Psychoanalysis* (pp. 204–218). London: Hogarth, 1975.

Winnicott, D. W. (1961). Adolescence: struggling through the doldrums. In: *The Family and Individual Development* (pp. 79–87). London: Tavistock, 1965.
Winnicott, D. W. (1971). Contemporary concepts of adolescent development and their implications for higher education. In: *Playing and Reality* (pp. 138–150). London: Tavistock.

Discussion of Marianne Parsons' paper

*B*rian *Martindale* (Chair): "We have about twenty minutes for discussion."

Question: "Can I ask about how Tom came to you in the first place? I'm interested in his motivation. We heard about his motivation once he was seeing you, but I'm wondering about his motivation before his first appointment."

Marianne Parsons: "It's a very good question. He was referred by his probation officer, like many of the Portman adolescent patients. In my early years at the Portman we used to treat patients who were sent under a probation order and we stopped this because as soon as the probation order stopped, the patient stopped coming. It was like 'you can take a horse to water but you can't make it drink'. The patient would turn up and you would do your best and you might say a few things that were helpful. You might provide a different experience in the room with you, but most of it would go over their heads. By the time I was seeing Tom things had changed. He had a genuine wish to stay out of prison and I think he thought 'I'll go to that stupid effing place and see if they can make my fantasies disappear. He wasn't worried about raping for moral reasons or out of concern for his victim, he was worried about going to prison, so there was some motivation in him of a very primitive kind, but at least it got him to us. However, he did leave when he reached an age when he could go off to university."

Brian Martindale: "So a self preservative motivation".

Marianne Parsons: "Yes."

Question: "I was really surprised when you said he was going off to university. I wasn't expecting that at all and I'm wondering whether there was some kind of resilience in him. From the picture you presented, I'm surprised he managed to learn anything, as he seemed in such an oppositional place to anybody in authority, women in particular, and I imagine a lot of his teachers would have been women."

Marianne Parsons: "Yes there was a resilience in him."

Question: "What led him to do that? What did he study? Politics?"

Marianne Parsons: "Yes, his aim was to study politics. He was quite bright. He'd managed to get through a lot of schooling without bowing to any authority figures because he was bright. It's a strange background. Most of the kids we had at the Portman came from deprived backgrounds and his was a deprived background in many ways, but he wasn't deprived in terms of his intelligence and he was able to make use of that. I think he was fascinated by listening to BNP people speaking on the radio, so he went to meetings, was part of their junior wing, and was very active. I think he was fired up by that kind of authority and took on board some of their ideas. He used to like to debate with them and think about their ideas. He got some of his education from a bad source, but at least there was some to and fro, some debating going on, albeit from a corrupt superego type of organization or authority figure."

Brian Martindale: "He also got some education from his teacher."

Marianne Parsons: "He got a lot of interesting 'education' from his teacher, yes he did!"

Question: "It is interesting that he uses that negative way forward, being interested in aggression and conflict, in the service of some kind of development. The description you gave earlier was of the kind of kid you'd expect to end up joining the army."

Marianne Parsons: "Absolutely, most of the Portman patients did join the army or the sea cadets or something similar. I think that was partly because it was a good way for them to rationalize their use of aggression, but it was also a home where you could be looked after. Tom didn't want to do that probably because his main aim was to use violence against ethnic groups."

Question: "I'm working with a young man at the moment who also raped. Mother committed suicide when he was seven years old and this is always in the background, and because he refuses to speak about the mother's death in any detail, I've never been able to make the link with him. I'm wondering about a sequence of conversations that could lead into that where he makes the connection, if there is one. Can you give me any guidance on that?"

Marianne Parsons: "Did people hear the question sufficiently? Good. I think it is going to take a long time and I imagine you'll have to be quite patient, but the fact that you've got it in your mind and that you can consider that there might be a link between these two things means that there may come a point when you feel that the ground is ready for you to say something about that, as there came a point when Marie began to recognize she could do something differently, and I recognized in my patient that I could now say something about what was going between us. I think one would have to be very gentle about how one approached it if he has not been able to talk about his mother and what his fantasies are about why she killed herself. He might think he was responsible in some way. It would be very typical of a child of seven to think this."

Question: "What about an ADHD child who may or may not have been told that the mother killed herself because of him?"

Marianne Parsons: "Many mothers who are emotionally unstable will say 'you'll be the death me' or 'you kill me when you do that', and thereby give the child all the information they need to think they are responsible. It's invariably a very slow process before one gets to that, and with some young patients, such as an ADHD child, one might need to help them quite early on to face the reality of what happened as well as look at how they fear their murderous wishes actually killed someone. Can your patient recognize any feelings of vulnerability and helplessness or is he rigidly defended against them?"

Questioner: "He's been in treatment now for a year and a half and is now acknowledging that he does have feelings, he does feel vulnerable, he does feel scared, he does feel alone."

Marianne Parsons: "So you are laying the groundwork with time."

Questioner: "Our difficulty is I'm a psychologist, not a psychothera-pist. We may never get the time."

Brian Martindale: "Both cases presented by Marie and Marianne showed no evidence that they could use you to think about them-selves outside of the session for quite some time. That seems to be the crucial shift that needs to happen, because in some ways what's the good of someone understanding something in the session unless they can take it outside and use it in the world. It seems that any sort of idea of you being available to them, in a thinking way, might feel terribly intrusive, invasive even. In some ways, I think the core complex has to wipe you out all the time, and that seems to be crucial in what we are talking about. What would be the point in making links unless it was of some use to him in his daily life?"

Questioner: "I suppose my aim is to not only leave him a better inte-grated individual as an adult but that he will not re-offend. Unfortunately, we don't have the luxury of being able to predict if this young man will have a normal sexual experience."

Marianne Parsons: "There's a difference between your case and mine. Mine was an attempted rape and your patient actually raped somebody. There must have been something healthy in Tom that stopped him from crossing the body barrier and actually commit-ting rape."

New questioner: "I was wondering if there was a bit more to say about fathering and fathers and whether the transference to you was necessary always as a mother. I was thinking of Marie's anecdote about knuckles. As you know, boys, when they hit knuckles, it's both aggressive and intimate at the same time. Could you explore that a bit?"

Marianne Parsons: " I have said something about the transference in relation to me as a father but not very much, it's true. I think he did see me sometimes as being battering. He was beaten by both mother and father and I think father was the more battering one, although he came to idealize his father and think that only men had good things to say. I think the fact that I was an older woman was always going to make it more likely that he would relate to me more as a mother, and it was very interesting that quite soon after therapy started he acted out in the transference. One could say he had a transference wish by having an affair with his older teacher. His father was very abandoning as well as intrusive, and his mother was also very abandoning as well as intrusive, so I suspect I was both to him."

Brian Martindale: "Was he seductive?"

Marianne Parsons: "He was seductive in a forceful 'raping' way through, for example, the way he stared at me. Does your patient do this?"

Questioner: "Not at all."

Marianne Parsons: "He absolutely fixed me with his gaze. He would gaze and gaze and gaze at me—non-stop."

Questioner: "I wonder what your thoughts are about being hit by a mother or being hit by a father, for a boy?"

Marianne Parsons: "Yes—that's an interesting one—I'd like to think about it."

Questioner: "There is a sense that the mother must indulge the omnipotence of the child. When the mother hits the child, that's not an indulgence of that at all, and for a boy it must be a block to masculinity somewhere. Then you get into rape fantasies: is there any way of overcoming this block?"

Marianne Parsons: "Yes, I think that's right . . . Tom's masculinity was posturing, it didn't feel real at all. I think a boy being hit by a father can somehow, perhaps perversely, confirm something: but not an appropriate masculinity. It's humiliating and the essence of the core complex is about humiliation, which is one of James Gilligan's points that he often talks about. There is a difference for a boy to be beaten by the mother rather than the father; it is more castrating and does more damage to a boy's phallic narcissism. When I was part of the violence research workshop at the Portman, the adult male patients we studied had extremely vulnerable phallic narcissism. In other words, they were extremely sensitive about themselves as masculine men. Anything that might touch on them being mummy's boy, not strong, weak, wimpish, gay, whatever, something that might prod them in such a very sensitive area, was what released the violence. I think that point you've made is a very pertinent one."

Brian Martindale: "Chris Brogan now. Anyone else? Shall we gather the three last questions together? Don't forget we've got the plenary session this afternoon."

Chris Brogan: "I think this follows the last two comments. I wondered if you could expand a little on technique. You said 'look, I've got a dilemma' and you put it almost on the table in front of you so the two of you could look at it. I wonder if you triangulated something so you actually got into a more paternal position, which enabled him to say something, to show interest. I may have got this wrong, but there was something that shifted afterwards and I thought it was a lovely way of getting over an impasse and of getting out of that sadomasochistic fix. My thoughts were of *Jungle Book*, where Ka hypnotizes all the animals and they are drawn to him with his reptilian stare and Mowgli, of course, being human, doesn't fall into the trap. I wonder if you'd like to say a bit more about this".

Questioner: "I don't know if we'll have time to talk about this, but I was wondering whether you might elaborate a little bit about the process that might be happening in females in adolescence who are violent, which I think will be a little different."

Questioner: "At the outset of your contact with these patients, do you share their knowledge of their parent and if so, does that actually create a platform for more openness and discussion from the client?"

Marianne Parsons: "When you say share, what do you have in mind?"

Questioner: "Share your knowledge of the background they've had with their parents."

Brian Martindale: "Share with the parents?"

Questioner: "No, share with the client, because that would create a sort of jumping off point, or do you wait for everything to come from the client?"

Brian Martindale: "So we have three questions."

Marianne Parsons: "I'll take them in reverse order. I normally wait for the patient to say whatever they can and sometimes what I might do with a Portman patient, because they know we'll have been sent material about them, is say 'look, I do know there are some things in your history that have been really difficult, perhaps we can talk about those.' I might try to give them a feeder to give me a bit more, so there's not really a straight answer to your question. It would depend on the patient, how intrusive it's going to be for me to do that, or how helpful it might be.

"With regard to female violence, that's a big one, and perhaps we could save that. I feel that's going to come up in the plenary along with the question of triangulation. You answered your own question beautifully—that's exactly what it's about. I realized I was stuck in a sadomasochistic conflict I couldn't break. If I broke through his sadomasochistic defence, it could make him feel humiliated and abandoned or engulfed by me. He could then become violent, and it wouldn't be good for him and it wouldn't be good for me. So I have to find a way of standing outside it and what you say is exactly what I did, to create a third, perhaps bringing in the father, or a transitional space in the Winnicottian sense. Ann Horne, one of my colleagues at the Portman, used to do this with young patients who were using their bodies in a sexually perverse way. She would say 'isn't it interesting what your body does'. Bringing in the body as a third invites the patient's curiosity, tries to engage a reflecting ego and so creates the triangulation. And the triangulation does have a paternal function that can break the sado-masochistic tie with the mother in the transference."

Brian Martindale: "That's a way of thinking you hope he will internalize."

Marianne Parsons: "Exactly."

Brian Martindale: "Thank you to both our speakers."

CHAPTER SEVEN

The perverse fascination of destructiveness*

Paola Capozzi and Franco De Masi

> The war of absolute enmity knows no bracketing. The consistent fulfillment of absolute enmity provides its own meaning and justification.
>
> (Schmitt, 1962, p. 52)

Professor Paul Williams (Chair) introduces Dr Franco De Masi

"It is with great pleasure that I introduce Dr Franco De Masi from Milan. Franco, as many of you know, participated in the first International Psychoanalytic Conference in Belfast, and it is a pleasure to have him back with us. He has long experience in treating patients with psychosis and severe disturbance, and has published widely on these subjects. He is a training and supervising analyst of the Milan Psychoanalytic Society. His paper today was written in collaboration with his wife, psychoanalyst Paola Capozzi, who, unfortunately, is unable to be with us today due to illness. We shall have a good amount of time to explore Franco's

---

* Translated by Philip Slotkin MA Cantab. MITI.

paper, so please make a note of questions, as I am sure Franco will be pleased to respond. Dr De Masi . . ."

* * *

Although psychoanalytic thought has long concerned itself with aggression, it has never achieved a unified conception of this subject, but has instead formulated a variety of contrasting theories. Two basic positions can be distinguished. According to the first, aggression (with its corollaries of hate and destructiveness) forms part of the human instinctual endowment, while the second holds that it is a consequence of frustration and trauma. The champions of the first position include Sigmund Freud and Melanie Klein. Freud saw aggression as an innate component of libido—that is, of the force that presses for the achievement of pleasure and the conquest of objects. As we know, Freud initially regarded aggression not as a specific drive, but rather as the active component necessary for the achievement of the drive's aim; in other words, it was a component of the sexual drives of the ego. In this sense, perversion, too, was deemed to be a fixation on anal sadism. In 1920, however, Freud introduced the notion of the death drive, whose aim was the dissolution of the individual, or Nirvana; the death drive, which was originally directed inwards, gave rise, when turned outwards, to destructiveness. The working of the death drive was based on the activity of the libidinal drive, thus forming destructive impulses directed against external objects. Its virulence was mitigated by its fusion with the sexual drive, but in its defused form it entirely dominated the personality.

Melanie Klein (1932), on the other hand, held that the conflict between love and hate (the latter being an expression of the destructive instinct) was the engine of development and the foundation of mental functioning. The stronger the destructive endowment with which an individual was born, the more difficult would be that individual's path to integration and the achievement of healthy ambivalence.

The group of psychoanalysts who regard aggression as a primal disposition that is reinforced in response to a traumatic experience (i.e., deprivation of basic needs or exposure to violence) includes Anna Freud, Fairbairn, Winnicott, and Kohut. Anna Freud (1949), for instance, stresses that traumatic experiences result in the de-fusion of aggressive and libidinal drives, so that the former are not neutralized, but find expression in an urge towards destructive aggression. Such cases, in her view, involve a deficiency in emotional development, and it is this to which therapy must be directed.

Kohut (1978) links aggression to a narcissistic self-image: this grandiose, omnipotent self-image will not brook offence and frustration, which unleash narcissistic rage whose degree of violence is proportionate to the image's grandiosity. Kohut emphasizes not only the reactive nature of aggression, but also the self's predisposition to develop along narcissistic and grandiose lines.

A third group comprises the authors who see aggression as a reaction to a negative environment, or to unsatisfactory object relations; it includes Khan, the attachment theorists, and Fonagy. Fonagy (2001a,b; Fonagy, Gergely, Jurist, & Target, 2002) postulates that, when the capacity for mentalization fails to develop, the subject is unable to distinguish reality from fantasy and physical from psychic reality; hence the instrumental and manipulative use of the object and the body. This mode predominates in violent patients, who tend to express and confront their thoughts and emotions by means of physical action directed against themselves and others. That is to say, when someone is unable to feel himself[1] from within, he is compelled to experience the self from without. Trauma plays a significant part in the psychogenesis of violence. One need only think of severely abused children who exhibit a persistence of psychic equivalence, a tendency to resort to the pretending mode (with consequent dissociation) and an inability to reflect on their own and others' mental states. A patient who is destined to become violent lacks a fundamental image of self, but instead internalizes representations of the parental affective state; in this way there arises an alien self that destroys the sense of the self's cohesion. The patient himself subsequently uses the alien self as a part of a defensive manoeuvre—that is, he identifies with the abuser's mental state in order to regain a sense of control. The crucial processes linking the failure of mentalization to violence follow from the fact that, without a stable sense of identity, the subject does not feel responsible for his actions and is, therefore, unable to anticipate the psychological consequences of an act. Such patients exhibit a certain fluidity of the representational system, so that emotions and thoughts are not experienced as real and meaningful. Violence also has the aim of combating an intolerable mental state, which is equivalent to a defence against the humiliation experienced in the psychic equivalence mode.

In this contribution, we shall attempt to distinguish aggression, which can assume the form of hate and violence, from destructiveness. In so doing, we shall follow Glasser (1998) in distinguishing between self-preservative and sadomasochistic violence. Whereas aggression can be regarded in certain contexts as a defence useful for survival, destructiveness is directed against the very roots of life. In the sphere of mental phenomena, destructiveness underlies severe psychopathologies such as perversion, anorexic and borderline syndromes, drug addiction, and psychoses. In the social and political field, destructiveness was responsible for the greatest tragedies of the last century, such as Nazism and the derivatives of ideological communism (e.g., the regimes of Stalin and Pol Pot).

Hate

Hate, a feeling that is inevitably present in human beings, is charged with the wish to harm one's adversary. Hating means wanting to cause the object that harms us to suffer and wanting to destroy that object. The difference between reactive and destructive aggression lies not in the intensity of the hate, which may be extreme in both cases, but in the quality and character of the attacked object. Hate is defensive when turned against a bad object, but destructive if the aim is to destroy a good object. The definition of a good object is, of course, problematic: is a good object one that is useful and gives pleasure, or is it one that gives rise to unpleasure and sometimes pain? According to Freud (1915), hate comes before love: the ego hates, abhors and pursues with intent to destroy all objects which are a source of unpleasurable feeling for it, without taking into account whether they mean a frustration of sexual satisfaction or of the satisfaction of self-preservative needs. Indeed, it may be asserted that the true prototypes of the relation of hate are derived not from sexual life, but from the ego's struggle to preserve and maintain itself (Freud, 1915c, p. 138).

A little later, he writes, "Hate, as a relation to objects, is older than love. It derives from the narcissistic ego's primordial repudiation of the external world with its outpouring of stimuli" (*ibid.*, p. 139). From this point of view, hate will be aroused by any stimulus that disturbs the primitive ego's maintenance of pleasure. In order to preserve narcissistic well-being, aggression is deployed against the frustrating object with a view to its elimination. The narcissistic ego thus makes no distinction between the inevitable frustration that is necessary for growth and an intentional, malevolent attack; in the narcissistic position, any object that interferes with personal well-being is bad, because the primitive ego is incapable of understanding the nature of frustration, but wishes only to eliminate it. People who act violently are often found to be linked to their victims in a sadomasochistic circuit. Hate, which stems from a narcissistic wound or an injustice sustained, is always an unpleasant feeling that is hard to tolerate. Recrimination and ill-will excite violence to an uncontainable pitch. By killing, the murderer severs the negative bond between him and his object. Violence is resorted to for internal reasons, to expel an intolerable state of mind, and relief is obtained by ridding oneself not so much of one's enemy as of an intolerable mental state. Hate is sometimes bound up with anxiety aroused when a person feels humiliated, ignored, or threatened (whether in objective or subjective reality). The dynamic of shame, hate, and revenge demanded by wounded narcissism cannot be described here for reasons of space; it was alluded to earlier by the reference to Kohut. The most intransigent and violent reactions occur when trauma strikes a person living in a state of paranoid omnipotence. However, even when hate arises out of omnipotence, it is still human reactions and emotions that are involved, albeit primitive and abnormal ones.

Emotional indifference

In Carol Reed's fine film, *The Third Man*, Orson Welles plays the character of Harry Lime, an unscrupulous racketeer wanted by the police in immediate post-war Vienna, then under Russian and American occupation. His old friend Holly Martins (Joseph Cotten), unaware of Harry's activities, arrives in Vienna to look him up just a few days after he has seemingly been killed in a road accident. Holly is unconvinced by the official version of events and, after many vicissitudes, finds out from certain clues that Harry is alive, but does not know that his friend pretended to be dead so that he could operate undisturbed, without fear of detection by the police who had been hunting for him. Concerned that his cover has been blown by Holly, Harry decides to meet him in secret; he wants to learn how much his friend knows. He intends to eliminate him before he can talk to the police. They meet at the Prater amusement park, where, in order not to be overheard, the two men take a ride on the giant Ferris wheel. When the pod reaches its highest point, Harry, who has been contemplating getting rid of his friend by thrusting him out and causing him to plunge to the ground, says to him, "Take a look down below: if one of those dots you see down there were to disappear, would you feel sorry? If I were to offer you 2000 pounds for every dot that disappeared, would you tell me to keep my money? Or would you count how many dots were left?" This memorable scene describes one of the possible versions of the process of dehumanization. The mental condition concerned could be defined in terms of Harry Lime's statement that men are little dots that can be eliminated. With the seduction of power and contempt for the shared values of solidarity, Lime attempts to corrupt Martins; in other words, he tries to use the same arguments that seduced his own mind as propaganda. His words express a cynical, perverse attitude in which empathy with the fate of others is totally lacking. Perversion coincides neither with aggression nor with hate, but is the absence of love—that is, indifference. Its nucleus is pleasurable destructiveness, which thrives in indifference and the absence of passion.

Dehumanization

Nowadays, achievement of the mental state of emotional indifference, which underlies the process of dehumanization, is facilitated by the use of technology, which enables a person to kill without the perception of killing. They are so remote from their so-called enemies, and they have to aim from such a distance, that they are no longer really *aiming*; they no longer have any perception of their victims, they have no knowledge of them, and cannot even imagine them. Not before, not while it is happening, and not afterwards. Can such things be called *soldiers*? And how could such soldiers hate people they have never met and (considering that they will have been eliminated) never will meet? And these soldiers, who no longer engage in hand-to-hand combat, who no longer share a battlefield with the enemy, but are at best manipulating instruments in some ill-defined place from which not a single enemy soldier is within sight—why would these soldiers need hate? Is it not, would it not be, an utterly superfluous feeling? One that is absolutely outdated? This long quotation is taken from an essay whose title translates as "The out-datedness of hating" by Günther Anders (1985),[2] an author who always spoke out against war and the destructiveness of man, and who drew particular attention to the danger of dehumanization that is characteristic of our age. Destructiveness differs from aggression in that it expresses indifference and lack of hostility towards a specific object; it is an anti-relational operation that takes place in silence, is planned, and develops in a special mental state in which feelings and emotions are abolished. It is possible to be destructive without hating, for hate is unpleasurable and entails conflict, whereas destructive sadism is pleasurable. It is not always easy to distinguish between these two concepts in the psychoanalytic literature, even in the work of Freud himself, and they are sometimes found to overlap.

Trauma

In thinking about some of our patients' histories, we have become increasingly aware of the importance for mental growth of the overall emotional responses of adults. These early experiences interfere with children's maturational potential and may have the consequence of psychopathology. Even if a child has not been subject to actual violence, he will have suffered a *trauma*, which could be termed *emotional*, caused by the overall set of responses of his caregiver. Such a trauma not only leaves "holes" in the personality, but also affects its structure, giving rise to anxieties, arrests, and disturbances of emotional development that can lead to loss of contact with the emotions.

This very early pathogenic configuration could be described as the *traumatic distortion of emotional experience*—that is, a set of responses from adults that interfere with children's maturational potential and result in a psychopathological development. The nuclei that eventually lead to the loss of emotional contact and underlie the processes of dehumanization may well be structured at this time.

A receptive object

According to Bion (1962), human beings are not born with an apparatus for perceiving their emotions, but have the potential to develop it; in order for this apparatus to develop, there must be a mother who offers suitable responses and confirms the child's preconceptions. The mother must be capable from the beginning of understanding the fear, anxiety, and wishes which the infant, as yet lacking language and thought, projects into her in order to be understood (Bion describes this action by the infant as *projective identification for the purpose of communication*). If the mother is unable to be receptive, the newborn will not acquire the capacity to understand his own sensations and needs, because he fails to obtain a response that confers meaning on his projections. A child who is constantly ignored or devalued may ultimately develop within himself a hatred for the world and a deep-seated death wish.

It was Ferenczi, in "The unwelcome child and his death-instinct" (1929), who had the insight that linked the death wish to infantile emotional trauma: in this contribution, he postulates that the lack of vitality and the wish to disappear into the void that characterize certain lives have their origin in the child's conscious or unconscious perception of maternal rejection. In view of the important role of the earliest infantile experiences in strengthening or weakening the vital aspects of the personality, it will readily be understood that a child exposed at an early stage to psychologically unfavourable events may ultimately tend to destroy the life drive within him. Similarly, where the conditions of dependence impose intolerable suffering on an individual, a wish for self-annihilation may be the response to prolonged exposure to trauma.

Sharing of emotions

Certain findings of neuroscientific research confirm long-established insights by psychoanalysts, who are in continuous touch with the human mind. The neurosciences are, at present, particularly concerned with the problem of how human minds perceive each other and how feelings are transmitted from individual to individual. After all, a human being's capacity to communicate his emotions allows his interlocutor to share in and feel something of the relevant experience for himself without thereby forfeiting his separateness. That is the only way an individual can respond empathically to a fellow human being and help him.

Rizzolatti and Gallese (1998) discovered the existence of "mirror neurons", a group of nerve cells that are activated when we see someone perform an action involving movement. In other words, certain cell groups begin to resonate and activate the same muscles in the observer as those used by the person who is at that time performing a purposive action. This kind of activation is not equivalent to the initiation of an *imitative process*, but instead tends to establish sensorimotor procedures that are unconsciously learnt in the early phases of life; their unconscious repetition facilitates access to a motor alphabet that permits a better understanding of the intention of the person performing the relevant action.

The same mechanism, based on a preparedness to internalize and reproduce what is perceived of the other, may underlie the ways in which the individual learns to apprehend not only the meaning of actions, but also other people's sensations or emotions. To arrive at an understanding of the mental states of others, however, imitative procedures are not enough. An emotional world is also required, in the absence of which an individual will not acquire the capacity to understand other people.

The place in the mind that enables us to understand others emotionally comes into being because we have been understood in turn and have fully internalized the experience of emotional contact with the other. In order to be born and to develop as individuals, we must have been received emotionally in the mind of an adult (primordially, that of the mother). Without the specific experience of being understood, we cannot introject this same function, which is used in emotional communication with others. In such a case, the *emotional mind* fails to develop. A child deprived of emotional reception may fully develop the functions of cognition and logic, but will not possess the capacity for an internalized relational life. It is insufficient to assert that one must have been received in someone's mind in order to acquire a sense of identity; the ways in which this process takes place must also be considered. The quality of the parental response may either help a child to acquire a realistic self-perception that will enable him to relate to the world or stimulate him to negate truth and to develop an altered, grandiose, narcissistic personality. The mother may see her child as exceptional and make him believe he is special, destined to become master of the world. Such an attitude reinforces grandiosity and legitimizes the assumption of being privileged and consequent arrogance. The adult subject will then remain in the paranoid–schizoid mental position and regard anyone who threatens his supposed superiority as an enemy.

Omnipotence and destructiveness

In addressing the problems presented by the analytic treatment of difficult patients who are seemingly refractory to psychoanalysis, we face considerable uncertainty when seeking to establish a link between severe pathologies and infantile traumas. While acknowledging the role of infantile trauma in the generation of adult suffering, we find that with the majority of severely ill patients it is not easy to establish evidence of repeated violent trauma in infancy. The common element favouring such pathology is in fact the mental absence of the parents—their indifference to the child's emotional development. This emotional remoteness allows a child, already in early infancy, to stand aloof from reality and to take refuge in (megalomanic, fantasy-related or sexualized) psychic withdrawal involving incipient pathological identification with grandiose characters who are felt to be providers of pleasure, so that the world of relationships is progressively abandoned. In our view, two equally important factors, which eventually potentiate each other, together facilitate the distortion of growth: the lack of empathy from the environment, and the child's formation of psychopathological structures that cause him to deviate from normal development. In other words, it is not only infantile traumas that are responsible for adult suffering and psychopathology.

The prolific Swiss psychoanalyst Alice Miller (1980) wondered why the children of violent, abusive parents tended in turn to ill-treat others. An unloved or unwanted child is potentially destined to become a violent adult who will take revenge on others for the traumas he has sustained or who will beat his own children, and is thus likely to generate further oppressors or criminals-to-be. In Miller's view, a child's aggression is positive, necessary for survival, and derived from the life instinct; it is events subsequent to birth that result in negative psychic development. Since a traumatic environment calls for the suppression of feelings and idealization of the aggressors, a child in this situation will grow up without developing an awareness of what was done to him. His split-off feelings of anger, impotence, and despair will continue to find expression in destructive acts against others (criminality) or himself (drug addiction, alcoholism, prostitution, mental disorders, or suicide). In her passionate defence of the ill-treated child, the Swiss analyst also examines the case of Adolf Hitler, who, as a child, was constantly beaten by his father. Miller claims that the German dictator's traumatic infancy partly explains the destructive nature of his political leadership.

In our opinion, Alice Miller does not sufficiently emphasize that, although in conflict with his father, Hitler enjoyed the boundless admiration of his mother and, later, of his sister, and that this maternal exaltation may have fuelled his conviction of being a superman. In other words, we take the view that the relationship between trauma and the process of dehumanization is not always so straightforward. It is not only trauma that favours human destructiveness; seduction by grandiose figures who make for confusion between good and evil may be even more telling. In such cases, a part of the personality justifies the destructive behaviour in the name of a moral imperative. The individual is then subordinated to a value system that stems from a perversion of conscience. That is the psychological condition of Harry Lime, the protagonist of *The Third Man*, discussed earlier.

Psychopathological constructions

In clinical work, it is in our view useful to distinguish defences from *psychopathological constructions*, as this distinction will provide us with a clearer conception when treating severe cases involving pathological structures that can no longer be defined as defences. In the use of defences such as, for example, repression or projections, the unconscious perception of the defensive transformation undertaken is preserved, whereas in the case of a psychopathological construction a radical alteration of awareness and of personality structure is observed. Inherent in defences is an equilibrium that does not completely destroy psychic reality, while psychopathological constructions tend to distort it radically, with a consequent process of dehumanization in the internal world.

Edna O'Shaughnessy (1981, p. 362) writes, "Unlike defences . . . which are a normal part of development, a defensive organization is a fixation, a pathological formation when development arouses irresoluble and almost overwhelming anxiety". Expressed in Kleinian terms, defences are a normal part of negotiating the paranoid–schizoid and depressive positions; a defensive organization, on the other hand, is a pathological fixed formation in one or other position, or on the borderline between them. Furthermore, according to the same author, the defensive organization becomes increasingly invasive, and is transformed in such a way that it takes on an omnipotent, triumphant and cruel character.

Destructive narcissism

The author who has best explained the mode of action of the psychopathological structure is Herbert Rosenfeld (1971). Describing destructive narcissism, he postulates that in certain severe psychopathologies a bad internal entity—a bad self—is idealized. This pathological nucleus removes the subject from contact with emotions and from relating to others. The sick part, which is idealized, progressively comes to hold sway over the rest of the personality, using propaganda that promises an easy solution to every problem. This structure resembles a delusional object whose healthy parts tend to allow themselves to be captured because in this way pain completely disappears and the subject is free to indulge in any

transgressive activity. These patients' destructive narcissism is organized in the same way as a criminal gang dominated by a leader
who controls all its members in order to increase their destructiveness. A pathological superego allied to the sick part of the personality is often present. For this reason, blind obedience is demanded
and any insubordination is punished by attacks and intimidatory
accusations. A psychopathological construction cannot be regarded
as a mere expression of the mechanisms of primitive aggression, but
represents a pathological distortion of psychic development—that
is, an idealization of a bad part of the self. Its supremacy results from
the perverse transformation of the superego, which causes destructiveness to appear innocent and exciting.

It was only after two years of analysis and following the estab-
lishment of a trusting relationship with the analyst that Vincenzo, a
young characteropathic patient who was a drug addict with suicidal tendencies, allowed exploration of the destructive withdrawal
in which he had long been imprisoned. In this withdrawal he was
Nero, a tyrannical character with whom he identified because he
represented unbridled destructiveness. When opposed, Vincenzo-
as-Nero would become furious and, seeing himself as the victim of
unwarranted persecution, would feel entitled to take revenge. Just
as Nero destroyed and set fire to the city, so Vincenzo took a
perverse pleasure in sowing confusion among his love objects and
acting violently towards them.

The power acquired by the pathological organization over the
rest of the personality depends on the role of the superego. This
perverse superego is unlike its primitive counterpart described by
Melanie Klein: whereas a superego in which primitive aspects
predominate is observed in some clinical situations, in the case of a
psychopathological structure an intimidatory, perverse superego is
at work. In such instances, the psychopathological transformation
occurs because the narcissistic organization forms a perverse superego structure that assumes a dominant character.

The psychotic part of the personality

It is well known that, in order to keep excitation alive, the perverse
action must constantly increase the dose of "badness". A work of

literature in which this is demonstrated is de Sade's "The one hundred and twenty days of Sodom" (1784). Just when the libertines have their victims completely at their mercy and can do anything they like with them, including killing them, they realize that they are habituated to excitation; they then recognize that, however much they raise the pitch of violence, they will never be satisfied. The real crime, rather than a sequence of wretched misdeeds, would be to put out the sun in order to destroy the universe. A similar process is involved when the psychotic or perverse part of the personality comes increasingly to hold sway over the healthy part, as in the following case history.

Fifteen-year-old Alfredo was sent for therapy by his parents when they learnt from one of his schoolmates that he intended to commit suicide. A highly intelligent youngster who did not look anything like a normal adolescent, he dressed in black like an old man (he wore a double-breasted jacket and black shoes) and behaved accordingly. As was discovered during the course of the therapy, his parents had always remained emotionally remote from him. His upbringing with them had been cold, dutiful, and, in many respects, crushing. His only significant relationship had been with his grandfather, who had cared for him but had treated him like an adult, thus stimulating the logical and mathematical aspects of his intelligence.

Alfredo had always been an isolated child who did not like to play with others of his own age. Even now he had no friends. He excelled academically and had a privileged relationship only with his teachers, who were often astonished by his intellectual performance. When he grew up he wanted to be a doctor, not because he wished to help the suffering, but because he aspired to the role of anatomist/pathologist so that he could dissect corpses.

During his first few sessions, Alfredo mentioned several times that he spent many hours of his day designing a bunker in which he wished to live. In this refuge he would be able to create all the reality he wanted; this reality could be magnificent (he was a scientist or a famous mathematician), but also bloody and grim. He fantasized that in his bunker he was a great surgeon who could disfigure or cut into his patients or tear them to pieces. The withdrawal into fantasy had recently become so invasive that he was afraid of being utterly colonized by it. He confessed that, in class, he allowed himself to be carried away by these fantasies to such an extent that he would lose touch with his fellow-pupils and teachers.

Alfredo's mind had now been well and truly taken over by the pleasure of violence and the thrill of blood. He announced that he had begun to eat raw meat, and in his sessions he showed the analyst the cuts he had inflicted on his body; he also described certain fantasies which came to him in his bunker-cum-mortuary and which had the power to excite him. In one of them he was working as an anatomist/pathologist in a disused, dilapidated hospital with blood everywhere. A voice called him by a German name; the woman on whom he was operating was not at all dead, even though she was nailed to the operating table. He had given her a very fine nose, but, just when his work was finished, he was seized by an irresistible impulse. While being complimented by the nurse, he decided to demolish the patient's entire face because it seemed to him to be flabby. His scalpel savagely disfigured the woman's face, leaving it bathed in blood. In the second part of the fantasy, a girl led him into a dark corridor. She was accompanied by a French poodle. Alfredo ordered her to kill it. The girl did not want to sacrifice her pet, stroked it and wept. He insisted. The girl began to wring the puppy's neck; although in tears, she broke its neck. The sound of the bones breaking could be heard. At the moment when the girl killed the dog, Alfredo felt pleasure.

Since his earliest infancy Alfredo had succeeded in fleeing from emotional reality and taking refuge in pathological withdrawal (a megalomanic state of being flushed with power). In this psychic retreat, pathological identifications took place with grandiose, destructive characters, such as the hangman, the dictator, the great surgeon, and the anatomist/pathologist. In deploying all his omnipotence, Alfredo distorted reality. While seeing a corpse as a thing of beauty, he could at the same time destroy it; he could do anything he liked.

The serial killer

It was astonishing to observe the sequence of events that could have led this young man to become a serial killer. In one session Alfredo produced an extremely insightful description of the relationship between destructiveness and destructive pleasure:

"Maybe I like this stuff because it makes me powerful . . . I imagine myself as a powerful person like a hangman . . . a doctor . . . a dictator; I spend the whole day in my imaginary bunker . . . I'm always a dictator with my army or a mad surgeon . . . what makes me happiest is to be a hangman, as I hold people's lives in my hands; having someone's life in my hands, I like that . . . it amuses me until I decide to kill them. When I imagine myself as a dictator, I am living in a huge bunker; there aren't many other people—apart from myself, there are just the guards and my family . . . then I imagine all the stylish furnishings . . . I spend hours just imagining."

Alfredo was obviously getting more and more fascinated by the possibility of becoming a diabolical being, and this frightened even him. Dehumanization, the fascination of the negative, the pleasure of blood and death, and the ecstasy of destruction—all these elements were taking him over and beginning to form part of a new and dangerous personality. The puppy that was killed was not only the good infantile part which succumbed to the diabolical part that took pleasure in destruction, but also his infantile aggressive vitality which had been extinguished. In his relational life, for example with his schoolmates, Alfredo could not tolerate any conflict. In any contest or situation of rivalry or jealousy, he would give way, but would then spend hours in fantasies about torturing his enemy, tearing him to pieces or dissecting him. This behaviour greatly facilitates understanding of the difference between aggression and destructiveness: Alfredo was not at all *aggressive*; he was unable to assert himself with his schoolmates, to make demands on them or to defend himself if he was attacked by them. On the contrary, he was constantly engaged in imagining acts of *destructive cruelty* that fuelled and exalted his omnipotent self. The risk in his case was that he himself might fall victim to his mad part, from which the fascination with murder and the pleasure of destructiveness stemmed, so that he was liable to attack and harm himself.

Criminality and perversion

There is a voluminous psychoanalytic literature on criminality and perversion, on the connections between them and on their distinguishing features. Freud postulates that the sexual pleasure obtained by a pervert can mitigate aggression. According to another interpretation, however, the fact that pleasure is achieved through violence makes that violence more redoubtable and dangerous. We shall now describe a perversion which gradually turned into actual criminal behaviour, and which may be regarded as evidence in favour of the second hypothesis. The description is taken from the notes of the social worker in charge of Jürgen Bartsch, whose case is described in Alice Miller's *For Your Own Good* (1980). After a number of failed attempts, Jürgen Bartsch finally succeeded in killing four youths aged between sixteen and twenty. Even if each crime varied in detail, the basic procedure was always the same: having lured the youth into an old air-raid shelter, Jürgen would beat him, terrorize him into a totally submissive state, tie him up, manipulate his genitals, and finally strangle him or beat him to death. Although Jürgen himself, and the doctors who surgically castrated him, believed the contrary, sexuality seems to have had little to do with the motivation of his criminal acts. Jürgen confessed that, from the age of thirteen or fourteen, his mind had been increasingly disturbed, so that he was ultimately powerless to influence the events that were to overwhelm him. For a long time he prayed, hoping that this at least might be of some help. He reported that he was particularly aroused by the dazed eyes of his victims: paralysed with terror, these young men became so small and submissive that they were unable to protest or defend themselves in any way. The victims' helplessness inflamed the aggressor's sadism even more. According to the detailed description given to the court, the acme of excitation was attained not during masturbation, but only when the victim's body was cut. This meticulous operation gave rise to a kind of permanent mental orgasm. There is not enough information to reconstruct the progressive and inexorable seizure of power by the sadistic, murderous part over the rest of Jürgen's personality. Since feelings of friendship and brotherhood for his young companions persisted in other parts of his person, he must surely have struggled to rein in and neutralize the perverse part of himself. Ultimately, however, just as his victims appeared submissive and incapable of defence, so the good part of his personality became totally helpless and colluded with the murderous part. This case history presented by Alice Miller, despite the summary nature of the autobiographical account, confirms that—in some cases at least—the achievement of lustful mental pleasure underlies the criminal impulse. Jürgen's testimony again suggests a continuity between perversion and criminal sexuality. We do not know why the acting out of cruelty and the infliction of suffering give rise to orgasmic mental excitation. We can only record the fact that the link with sexual ecstasy makes cruelty increasingly devastating and dangerous. This type of pleasure seems totally detached from the sexual act and the associated grat-ification (libido), and is therefore inconsistent with the Freudian paradigm. Destructiveness triumphs through the criminal act because such an act can trigger this type of pleasure.

Our example falls more within the category of a criminal perver-sion than in that of sexual criminality proper. In the latter, the victim is a hated object, the killing of whom gives rise to pleasure. When the victim is a woman, she is experienced as a rejecting narcissistic object. The sexual crime is committed in revenge for an excessively persistent humiliation: having sexually abused his victim, the criminal kills her. He retains memories, body parts, or items of personal clothing as trophies. None of this is seen in sexual perversion. On reflection, we find that the sadomasochistic perver-sion usually coincides not with the "pleasure of doing evil", but with the excitation that accompanies the perverse act and fantasy. The master in the sadomasochistic game derives sexual pleasure from the fact that the servant does everything he wants, and not from any hatred of him. The structured perversion is relatively benign not because of the docility of the perverse subject, but because of the absence of destructive hate or envy of the victim. The pervert loves cruelty, but does not hate his victim. However, in perversion, too, a dangerous escalation, intimately connected with the nature of the perverse excitation and pleasure, must be kept under control. Even if the extreme positions are never fully attained in perversion, but kept within the play of the imagination, the perverse subject nevertheless often pushes himself to the limit with a view to achieving an ever more voluptuous orgasm. Since sexual excitation arises out of the omnipotent idea of having the partner totally in one's power, the determinant of pleasure tends to shift increasingly towards the wish to have the subjugated victim totally at the pervert's disposal.

The pleasure of sexuality

"I maintain that sexuality is an immensely wide field that has never been fully explored." These are the words not of an academic, but of Gianfranco Stevanin, a serial killer who committed his crimes in a small village near Verona. Stevanin killed a number of prostitutes, whom he lured to his farm, where he dismembered their bodies and buried them. When he described the committing of his murders to the court assessor, the memory could apparently arise only when he was in a trance-like state. Recalling his crimes as if they had been carried out in a state of altered consciousness seemed to be not only a convenient defence against the criminal charges. Stevanin had, in fact, probably been gradually colonized by a particular type of criminal sexuality and had then committed terrible acts without any awareness of what he was doing. This murderer is mentioned here in order to show that perverse fantasy can not only drive a person to commit criminal acts, but also give rise to a quasi-hypnoid state of dissociated consciousness. Having been committed, Stevanin's criminal acts were dissociated from the memory of them, and, as it were, buried with the bodies of the hapless murdered women. Indeed, he may well have obtained a particular kind of pleasure from dissecting his victims' corpses. This of course is reminiscent of young Alfredo's fantasies and of Jürgen Bartsch.

"You can do anything you like!"

What is the origin of the pleasure of doing evil—of perverse criminal pleasure? Homicidal destructiveness is attributable not to hate (neither Stevanin nor Jürgen Bartsch hated their victims), but to its allowing the maximum possible degree of licence and transgressive omnipotence: "You can do anything you like; you can even kill!" Hence, the possible escalation of perversion into a criminal act is due to factors inherent in the nature and dynamics of perverse pleasure and not to hatred of the object. A perverse individual commits crime in the world of fantasy and fiction, whereas a criminal pervert does so in actual reality. For this reason, the connection between cruelty and mental ecstasy is especially dangerous. What is involved is a pleasurable destructiveness, which thrives in indifference and the absence of passion: "Rape has nothing to do with impotence. Absolute domination of another body becomes a drug. You rape, torture and murder for the sense of being the master of other people's fate," said Angelo Izzo, who killed two women after imprisoning them and torturing them and who repeated the same crime after an interval of thirty years, murdering a mother and daughter whom he had befriended while on day release from a semi-custodial sentence. According to the British psychoanalyst Arthur Hyatt-Williams (1998), who undertook the therapy of criminals, murder is often committed in reality when it has already been perpetrated many times before in waking fantasies or nightmares, and sometimes in unconscious fantasies that have never attained consciousness. This is also partly true of de Sade, who, while incarcerated in prison and in an asylum for the criminally insane owing to his sexual excesses and perse-cution of the authorities, was able to express his unceasing per-verse fantasies in concrete form by describing them in his novels. In this way, he could contain the horror in the disturbing fascina-tion of his literary oeuvre, without acting it out as he had begun to do and would surely have continued to do had he remained at liberty.

Conclusions

Discussing the problem of masochism and sadism in the context of the death drive, Freud (1924c) points out that masochism is incom-prehensible if it is accepted that the pleasure principle—the custo-dian not only of mental life but of life in general—dominates the mental processes. Masochism would be a great danger, whereas sadism would not. Freud also accepts the existence of a primary masochism, seen as deriving from the holding back of the death drive by the libido, and postulates that destructiveness directed against oneself or others is simply a consequence of the de-fusion of the libidinal and destructive drives. When the latter are no longer bound and moderated by the former, less and less restraint is placed on their expression. However, a weakness of Freud's theory lies precisely in the difficulty of postulating a meeting or fusion of two antagonistic drives that are destined to cancel each other out.

As stated earlier, destructiveness coincides not with aggression or hate, but with the absence of love—that is, with indifference. This type of pleasurable destructiveness, which thrives in indifference and the absence of passion, exerts an irresistible fascination over some patients. Rosenfeld (1987) rightly points out that, when fusion occurs, it is a successful attempt by the destructive part to colonize the rest of the personality. In this case the violence of the destructive impulse is not tempered, but greatly potentiated.

A more useful model for understanding this fascination invokes the split between the healthy and perverse parts of the personality. However, the two parts are not in static equilibrium, because the perverse part of the personality will eventually colonize the healthy part. This process is clearly visible in the case history of Alfredo, who is taken over by the destructive propaganda to such an extent that it drives him to use his own body as an object on which to direct his murderous impulses. The infantile part, represented by the girl with the puppy, submits masochistically and fails to oppose the pleasure of cruelty and the spilling of blood. In our view, the psychoanalytic arguments outlined above help not only to identify a comprehensible link between the problem of evil and that of pleasure, but also to explain the degree and quality of the "evil" at work. We have postulated the existence of various sequences or levels seeking to distinguish themselves from each other: there is a psychically "comprehensible" evil and an evil that is utterly remote from any possibility of comprehension.

Freud (1911b) emphasized the priority of the pleasure principle, which operates even after the consolidation of the capacities for attention, memory, and consciousness characteristic of the reality principle. The sexual drive, fantasy, and dreams, as expressions of the pleasure principle, in effect constitute a parallel thought activity, harking back to the primal condition in which withdrawal from the world is achieved at the expense of contact with reality. We contend that, unlike hate, destructiveness leads to a form of mental orgasm that allows the subject to act outside the realm of awareness and responsibility. Aggression can thus be clearly distinguished from destructiveness. Whereas aggression stems from hate and is exhausted once the aim of lowering tension has been accomplished, destructiveness, sustained as it is by pleasure, tends to be self-perpetuating. Destructiveness is not the opposite of love, but, in particular, an attack on emotions and on relations between human objects. As Eric Brenman (1985, p. 273) notes, it gives rise to a specific form of narrow-mindedness without which evil cannot be continuously kept up:

In normal development, love modifies cruelty; in order to perpetuate cruelty, steps have to be taken to prevent human love from operating. My contention is that in order to maintain the practice of cruelty, a singular narrow-mindedness of purpose is put into operation. This has the function of squeezing out humanity and preventing human understanding from modifying the cruelty. The consequence of this process produces a cruelty that is "inhuman".

The conception we have explored in this paper shows that the problem of pleasure is more complex than Freud thought: pleasure does not depend on the defence of the self against the demands of external reality, or on drive discharge. In its production, the destructive mechanisms, directed against the subject's own self or others, seem to be much more efficacious than those involved in the survival of the individual through self-affirmation and satisfaction of the drives. Destructiveness gives rise to a mental excitation that makes evil pleasurable and irresistible. Hence, Sacher-Masoch's (1875) specific emphasis on the "over-sensitive" and "over-sensual" character of perverse pleasure. Ecstatic and sensual pleasure is bound up with evil, by which it is fuelled. The good does not give pleasure: it is not visible, but only thinkable. Evil, by contrast, is anchored in the body and is concretely sensual.

Notes

1. [Translator's note: For convenience, the masculine form is used for both sexes throughout this translation.]
2. [Translator's note: This essay does not appear to have been published in English. The quotation is here translated from the Italian edition.]

References

Anders, G. (1985). Die Antiquiertheit des Hassens. In: R. Kahle, H. Menzner & G. Vinnai (Eds.), *Hass. Die Macht eines unerwünschten Gefühls* (pp. 11–32). Reinbek bei Hamburg: Rowohlt.

Bion, W. R. (1962). *Learning from Experience*. London: Heinemann.

Brenman, E. (1985). Cruelty and narrowmindedness. *International Journal of Psychoanalysis, 66*: 273–282.

de Sade, D.-A.-F. (1784). The one hundred and twenty days of Sodom. In: A. Wainhouse & R. Seaver (Ed. & Trans.). *The One Hundred and Twenty Days of Sodom and Other Writings*. London: Arrow, 1991.

Ferenczi, S. (1929). The unwelcome child and his death-instinct. *International Journal of Psychoanalysis, 10*: 125–129.

Fonagy, P. (2001a). The psychoanalysis of violence. Paper presented on 15 March 2001 at the DSPP professional seminar "Preventing mass murder in schools: understanding violent children from 'peaceful' families".

Fonagy, P. (2001b). The roots of violence in the failure of mentalization. Paper presented at the Milan Psychoanalysis Centre on 18 May 2001.

Fonagy, P., Gergely, G., Jurist, E. L., & Target, M. (2002). *Affect Regulation, Mentalization and the Development of the Self*. New York: Other Press.

Freud, A. (1949). Aggression in relation to emotional development: normal and pathological. *Psychoanalytic Study of the Child, 3–4*: 37–42.

Freud, S. (1911b). Formulations on the two principles of mental functioning. *S.E., 12*: 213–226. London: Hogarth.

Freud, S. (1915c). Instincts and their vicissitudes. *S.E., 14*: 109–140. London: Hogarth.

Freud, S. (1920g). *Beyond the Pleasure Principle*. *S.E., 18*: 1–64. London: Hogarth.

Freud, S. (1924c). The economic problem of masochism. *S.E., 19*: 155–170. London: Hogarth.

Glasser, M. (1998). On violence: a preliminary communication. *International Journal of Psychoanalysis, 79*: 887–902.

Hyatt-Williams, A. (1998). *Cruelty, Violence and Murder: Understanding the Criminal Mind*. London: Karnac.

Klein, M. (1932). *The Psycho-Analysis of Children*. London: Hogarth.

Kohut, H. (1978). *The Search for the Self*. New York: International Universities Press.

Miller, A. (1980). *For Your Own Good: Hidden Cruelty in Child-Rearing and the Roots of Violence*, H. & H. Hannum (Trans.). London: Faber, 1983.

O'Shaughnessy, E. (1981). A clinical study of a defensive organization. *International Journal of Psychoanalysis, 62*: 359–369.

Rizzolatti, G., & Gallese, V. (1998). From action to meaning: a neuro-physiological perspective. In: J. L. Petit (Ed.), *La philosophie de l'action et les neurosciences* (pp. 217–229). Paris: Librairie Philosophique J. Vrin.

Rosenfeld, H. (1971). A clinical approach to the psychoanalytic theory of the life and death instincts: an investigation into the aggressive aspects of narcissism. *International Journal of Psychoanalysis, 52*: 169–178.

Rosenfeld, H. (1987). *Impasse and Interpretation*. London: Tavistock.

Schmitt, C. (1962). *Theory of the Partisan*. New York: Telos Press [reprinted 2007].

von Sacher-Masoch, L. (1875). *Venus in Furs*. New York: Sylvan Press, 1947.

Discussion of Paola Capozzi and Franco De Masi's paper

*P*aul Williams: "Thank you, that is food for thought.

Question from the floor: "I'm trying to reconcile Stoller's title, *Perversion: The Erotic Form of Hatred*, with your comments that perversion has nothing to do with hatred. There seems to be a conflict there."

Franco De Masi: "Stoller's conception is that perversion is a defence against a trauma. Stoller thinks of the pervert as being a child who was submitted to traumas of being beaten, perhaps of receiving violent aggressive sexuality from an adult. I think that for my conception, the origin of perversion is more complicated. I think the perverse child [is one] who has withdrawn from reality and from emotions and has filled his mind with fantasies that are not necessarily the product of trauma in infancy."

Questioner: "You don't think it's revenge against the object?"

Franco De Masi: "For me it is not, because there are many children who have not been submitted to trauma. For twenty years I have analysed a perverse, sadomasochistic, paedophile individual who was not a traumatized youngster but who lived in a good enough family, but without emotional bonds to the father or other people. It is not trauma in the way Stoller is thinking."

Paul Williams: "I think this is an important issue—the role of indifference or neglect that allows a developmental vacuum and then in order to feel alive excitation is generated. Many very disturbed individuals don't complain of specific traumatic events, but their lives have felt meaningless and often it is connected to indifference, which I think is the opposite of love, as opposed to hate."

Franco De Masi: "I think the more frequently a child is beaten and traumatized, the more likely he is to become psychopathic. This can be seen in certain borderline patients."

Question: "You said something about the badness that has to keep on increasing. With Alfredo, you say it came to a stage where there was something suicidal. I was wondering whether there might almost be a healthy part in him that turns against his torment. I'm curious about when there arises such a need for some kind of balance that he would turn on himself and if you could say more about that."

Paul Williams: "The suicidal impulse and how does that come about?"

Questioner: "How he goes that way instead of turning on someone else?"

Franco De Masi: "Alfredo's is a case of a supervision I was undertaking. I don't know if Alfredo had the intention to kill himself. I know he said this to his schoolmates perhaps to triumph over them. Anyway there was a danger that he could harm himself in a serious way. When this happened, my supervisee and I were afraid that harm could take place because he was very excited by blood. During the psychoanalytic therapy he identified more and more with a destructive Nazi character and was excited by self-harming. He was not violent or aggressive towards older people: he was mute and without emotion because he was in a psychical retreat. The suicidal patient is filled with hatred for himself and the whole world. Alfredo does not hate himself nor the others, but is excited by the destructivity against his own vital and infantile parts."

Paul Williams: "I imagine that if the level of excitation starts to fail, something then isn't working and he is at greater risk of feeling suicidal."

Question: "Where do you place intentionality and conscious choice as opposed to unconscious processes, where he arrives at this colonization of the personality by this destructive, idealized path?"

Franco De Masi: "I think that it is a complicated situation because the psychotic or perverse part of the personality acts as a superego, a perverse superego that dominates the rest of the personality. Why is this part of the personality submitted, subjugated, to the psychotic part? I think that the psychotic part promises pleasure. The sane part of the personality is acting without insight because a true colonization by the psychotic over the sane part creates a failure of responsibility. These patients are conscious, but without responsibility."

Paul Williams: "I would add one thought to Franco's; namely, the systemic, organized quality of pathological organizations. It colonizes and takes over in a way that the individual doesn't have awareness that they are colonized: the patient, to all intents and purposes, believes they are thinking and acting objectively."

Franco De Masi: "Perhaps it's possible to see unconscious intentionality in some dreams, insightful dreams where the sane part appears and is very anxious and alarmed by the actions of the psychotic part. These kind of dreams permit the analyst to speak with the patient about his psychotic part. If you speak to the patient without those dreams, the problem is that you are seen to be making propaganda against other propaganda. When the patient dreams, it is not my dream, it is his dream, and the patient illustrates his anxiety towards the psychotic part."

Question: "You mentioned incomprehensible evil. What do you mean by that?"

Franco De Masi: "Incomprehensible evil is destructiveness, pure destructiveness. It is incomprehensible because it is not fuelled by hate. I can act out a criminal act because I hate a person—my wife, my son, my friend. I hate the individual. The fact that I succeed in killing him is comprehensible. What is not comprehensible is killing without hate. We do not comprehend that. We normal or neurotic people can't comprehend criminality without hate."

Question: "I wondered in terms of how it related to empathy. Incomprehensible evil is presumably the product of a person who cannot imagine experiencing empathy."

Franco De Masi: "I quoted the beautiful film *The Third Man* in which it is shown how you can kill anyone because he is not seen as a human being. Its precondition is that it is done without any empathy towards the other people. Let me also quote a writer, Gunter Anders, who is not translated in English, but in Italy was translated. He illustrates the achievement of the mental state of emotional indifference that underlies the process of dehumanization that is further facilitated by the use of technology which enables a person to kill without the perception of killing. In the words of Gunter Anders, soldiers can be so remote from their so-called enemies, and they have to aim from such a far distance that they are no longer really aiming, so they no longer have any perception of their victims. They have no knowledge of their victims: they can't even imagine them, not before the killing, not while it's happening, and not afterwards. Can such people be called soldiers? How could such soldiers hate people they have never caught sight of, who no longer engage in hand to hand combat, who no longer share a battlefield with the enemy? At best, they are manipulating instruments in some ill-defined place from which not a single enemy soldier is within sight. Why would such a soldier need to hate? Wouldn't it be an utterly superfluous feeling? Hate becomes superfluous and absolutely out-dated. There is an essay entitled "The out-of-dateness of hating" by Gunter Anders, written in 1985, which draws attention to the danger of dehumanization that is a characteristic of our age."

Paul Williams: "You've described graphically the kind of chilling, computer-controlled attacks we see on television of villages in Afghanistan. Thank you, Franco, and thank you everyone for your comments and questions."

CHAPTER EIGHT

Aggression:
social and political aspects

Lord Alderdice

*D*r *Philip McGarry* (Chair): "Thank you for returning for the last session of the conference and I'm sure you'll all agree we have had three tremendous sessions this morning. I am delighted to introduce my colleague and long-standing friend, Lord John Alderdice. John and I go back many years. John is a man of many parts and there are two particular roles that John has performed over the years. One is as a very distinguished consultant psychiatrist in psychotherapy. My first memory of John was as a medical student. I was a medical student at Holywell and he was a registrar. Tom Freeman was the consultant, and that's where John's interest in psychotherapy burgeoned, from that particular point. John has been an Honorary Fellow of the Royal College, he has been awarded many distinctions around the world, is a Visiting Professor in Virginia, Lima in Peru, and also Chair of the International Dialogue Institute in Istanbul. John was the founder of the Centre for Psychotherapy in Belfast, which is one of the key organizers of this meeting. The Centre for Psychotherapy in Northern Ireland has a very distinguished role in assessment, treatment, and, in particular, training of staff across a range of disciplines and is a very important institute for Northern Ireland. As well as being very distinguished as a psychiatrist, John has had another life as a politician. John was leader of the Alliance Party for many years and John and I spent some years in the City Hall chamber together during some interesting times. John was also the inaugural speaker at the Northern Ireland Assembly in 1998, once devolution was restored, and he managed a fantastic job of getting that fragile institution up and running. John also has been the President of Liberal International between 2005 and 2009 and, of course, he has a very active role in the House of Lords. There is nobody better placed to marry the principles of psychoanalysis and politics and social aspects. John, unusually for him, has written his presentation. One of the amazing things from the time when I was Chairman of the Alliance Party was the annual conference, in which the leader's speech is viewed as extremely important. One year the TV journalists used the advance script of his speech to identify the highlights and so did not record the full forty-minute speech. The next year John turned up and I said to him, "Where's the script for the journalists?" "No script, they'll have to listen", was his reply. He gave a forty-five-minute speech unscripted and it was the most coherent, constructed speech I'd heard in my life. No other politician I know has ever attempted to do this and no sensible politician should attempt to do it unless they are of John's ability. Amazingly, today John does have a script, so I'll leave you in the capable hands of John, Lord Alderdice."

John, Lord Alderdice: "Thank you, Philip, it's always a pleasure to work with you and really a word of thanks and congratulations to everybody who was involved in organizing in this conference and coming along. It's tremendous to see such a warmth of interest in psychoanalytical work, because for a long time it was very much a minority sport, and it's tremendous not only to see our friends from outside here to encourage us, but also so many people from Ireland, north and south, contributing and working together and giving each other support in what is at times a very challenging, if ultimately very rewarding work. Thank you all very much."

* * *

Just over a month ago, I retired as a consultant psychiatrist to focus my full attention on applying what I have learnt over the last thirty years in psychoanalytically informed work with individuals to deal with disturbances of communal life and politics. In truth, this has always been my interest, and presenting this paper on certain social and political aspects of aggression at the end of my clinical psychiatric career is an appropriate closing bookend. The very first paper I presented as a young trainee psychiatrist was at a conference here in Belfast in June 1982, and it was entitled "Aggression—nature or nurture". In those days there was no training scheme in Ireland and, in addition to my daily psychoanalytic sessions with Dr Tom Freeman, I had to travel each month to Dublin for supervision with Dr Mike Fitzgerald, who had recently returned to his native soil, and to London for supervision with Dr Clifford Yorke at the Anna Freud Centre and Dr Sheilagh Davies at the Royal Free Hospital. But Dr Davies also gave me an hour of her marvellous supervision by telephone every Sunday evening during my training, so having to use communications technology to overcome the isolation of our island home, as we have had to do at this conference, is nothing new for us here in Belfast.

One benefit of travelling to London every month was that I could sometimes get along to distinguished lectures at the Tavistock, the Maudsley or one of the other centres of excellence, and I remember as a trainee in February 1985, twenty-five years ago, hearing Nina Coltart deliver her famous paper "Slouching towards Bethlehem . . . or thinking the unthinkable in psychoanalysis". She spoke in the paper of the importance of being able to have faith in the psychoanalytic process, which can help us through the necessary experience of not knowing, especially when dealing with things which cannot as yet be thought by us or our patients, much less put into words. The title of her paper came from the last line of "The Second Coming", a short poem by the Irishman, W. B. Yeats, and the lines express optimism that something of hope may be emerging,

> And what rough beast, its hour come round at last,
> Slouches towards Bethlehem to be born?

On this day, after the UK General Election, we are indeed still wondering what kind of beast our new government will be. Yeats's poem starts with a stanza that, given Yeats's Irishness, I have often felt expressed my own experience of Northern Ireland, and some of you might also feel is more widely relevant:

> Turning and turning in the widening gyre
> The falcon cannot hear the falconer;
> Things fall apart; the centre cannot hold;
> Mere anarchy is loosed upon the world,
> The blood-dimmed tide is loosed, and everywhere
> The ceremony of innocence is drowned;
> The best lack all conviction, while the worst
> Are full of passionate intensity. [Yeats, 1921]

Ten years into the new millennium, with its many opportunities and challenges, the aggression of people against other people is still top of our list of concerns. Of course, we are also troubled by the violent, unpredictable forces of nature, which have not only inconvenienced our conference, but, much more importantly, have led to the deaths of hundreds of thousands of people in storms, earthquakes, hurricanes, and tsunamis in the past few years alone. Despite the fact that we sometimes refer to these as "acts of God", few of us see them as intentional occurrences with a malign or angry purpose at their source; indeed, our concern is that the apparent increase in their number is a result of environmental damage to which we as humanity have made a direct, but certainly not intentional, contribution. No, it is not the violence of nature, but the violence of *human* nature that makes us most fearful, and in recent years especially, the violence of those who use terrorism to promote their political and social causes, spreading fear, not as an unfortunate side effect of their activities, but as a purposeful tactic. That this planned use of the tactic of terror is carried through with "passionate intensity" adds to our fear, but must also surely propel us into serious thought and reflection. How can it be that "twenty centuries", as W. B. Yeats puts it, after the life of the Jew who proclaimed the new possibilities of better relationships, the place of his birth is such a focus of violence and instability for the whole world? The tradition from which Jesus emerged (and, incidentally, from which psychoanalysis emerged) has brought us the three great Abrahamic faiths, but, despite their transcendent visions, it is their inability to find ways of living together which fuels the most dangerous current divisions in our world. Their relationships with each other are not only less than transcendent, but often less than human.

As analysts, we try to develop a context in which we can observe and explore what lies at the back of our patients' internal conflicts in order to help them become free of them. Using this model, I set myself to apply a similar approach to the conflict here in my own community, treating the community as a patient. This is not the place to describe how I developed this approach, save to say that as I got to know those who represented the different strands of life in Ireland, North and South, I was struck by the powerful and universal wish to be treated with respect. Listening through the process of our talks to their different stories and the reasons which they identified as most the significant causes of violence, it was experiences of disrespect and humiliation which seemed most salient. In individuals and communities, the sense of injustice which comes from humiliation produces a deep wish for vengeance and the righting of the wrong. Communal memories of times when they have been degraded and their existence threatened provoke deep fears and create a capacity for responses at least as violent as those which have been experienced. It is not necessary that each person has been individually disrespected; indeed, some of those who feel most strongly have not experienced it personally, but iden-tify strongly with the community which has experienced it. So, Muslims in one part of the world will respond with anger at the perception of Muslims in another part of the world being badly treated. I have tried to explore whether this dynamic of humiliation and its relationship to the outbreak of terrorism is particular to Northern Ireland, and to this end I have examined many other countries that have also experienced violent insurgencies. Perhaps a few examples will suffice.

My attention was drawn to Peru by my friend Moisés Lemlij, a psychoanalyst who returned to his native country and tried to assist his people explore the roots of the Maoist insurgency there. The main terrorist organization, Sendero Luminosa, or "Shining Path", began among students in Ayacucho, a university town in the moun-tains. Their claim that native people were not receiving fair atten-tion to their needs was indisputable. Centuries after the Spanish conquered the region, the minority of Spanish descendents still control all the main elements of wealth and governance. However, this picture of a minority ruling elite is not a merely Spanish colonial phenomenon, for they had defeated and replaced the Incas, who had occupied a similar position. It was not difficult to appreciate that the Quechua-speaking Indian people and others like them had not been accorded any respect. This lack of recognition and respect was borne in on me as I participated in a ceremony when the remains of seven of the tens of thousands of the "disappeared" were returned to their families. As I walked with the families through the streets of Ayacucho following the coffins, few people paid any attention. They just went about their business, ignoring this multiple funeral. These grieving people and their dead relatives seemed to be of no import. What is, in fact, striking about the Maoist strategy, whether conducted here or elsewhere, is that despite its angry and profoundly violent promotion of the cause of these oppressed people, their treatment of these same people is appalling. The lack of humanity in the treatment of those in whose cause they claim to fight is remarkable.

The same abuse of a downtrodden group is evident in Nepal, another mountainous country, but one in which violence and political instability is still very current. The background is not quite the same. Nepal has no colonial past. Even at the height of the British Raj in India, Nepal remained independent, and, until the recent revolution, was the world's last remaining Hindu kingdom. The country is a poor one, but it seemed to me that the problems that led to the violent Maoist insurgency were not so much economic deprivation *per se*, but the caste system and its results. Power in that country was held by those who come from the upper castes. The army, in particular the officers who supported the monarchy and the status quo, were largely drawn from this upper caste background and were extraordinarily dismissive of those of lower caste, who were not treated as deserving of any regard. The failure of a brief earlier attempt at democracy to enable the lower caste population and their representatives to play a proper role in the country led to a withdrawal into violence, from which, as yet, the exit is uncertain.

Although the situations in Northern Ireland, Peru, and Nepal are widely divergent when assessed on economic grounds, and the history, politics, and forms of government are also different, all three have experienced violent internal insurgencies characterized by the use of terrorism. I would argue that in all three cases, these insurgencies stem from the long-standing sense of humiliation and disrespect felt by a significant section of the population. Similar remarks could also be made about South Africa and Israel/Palestine, but these are more complex both in their origins and presentation and they deserve further exploration on their own. In particular, it is clear that when humiliation was visited on the local indigenous population by the incomers, it had elements of a repetition of the abuse that they (that is to say, the Afrikaaners and the Jews) had themselves experienced in their own places of origin, and so their behaviour towards the indigenous people they now lived among was characterized by what we would call "identification with the aggressor".

In short, when the question is asked, "Why do people engage in the dreadful violence we call terrorism?", it seems likely that experiences of humiliation play an important role. My main intention in this paper is to engage with a different, but equally common, question. "How can people engage in the dreadful violence and aggression we call terrorism?" This is not a technical enquiry as to the ways and means of a terrorist insurgency, but an expression of astonishment and distress that human beings can do such terrible things to each other.

In discussing my observations about the importance of humiliation in the origins of terrorist violence with Dr Estella Welldon some years ago, she drew my attention to the work of Professor James Gilligan (who I am delighted is with us and contributing to this conference). As you know, Professor Gilligan has done remarkable work with mentally disturbed individuals who had committed very serious violent crimes and with the institutions in which they were incarcerated in the USA. He had made observations about what he called "shaming" in the earlier experience of these prisoners, who had gone on to commit very violent crimes against other persons. This was similar to what I was noting as "humiliation" of a whole community, as well as of individuals, in the origins of IRA terrorism. When working with the prisoners, he became aware that, despite the awfulness of their crimes, they believed themselves to be justified. It became apparent that they saw themselves as righting some terrible wrong, some humiliation, a deep disrespect that had been done to them. This is similar to those who engage in terrorism. While the rest of the world may see them as evil, they believe that theirs is a moral and courageous activity motivated not by personal material gain, but by principle. The question remains, however: how is it possible for one human being to do such a thing to others?

In the closing scientific presentation on the theme of "Aggression", delivered at the 27th International Psycho-analytical Congress in 1971, Anna Freud (1982a) made two observations about aggression in young children. She noted that toddlers are not easy to control because they are extremely aggressive to each other, not only in order to have what they want (sweets, toys, attention), but sometimes for no very obvious reason they will bite, scratch, hit out, and kick. The toddler who is attacked may be unable to defend himself, and may just as easily be the aggressor or have been an aggressor shortly before or after. She took from this that the direct expression of aggression is an earlier stage in development than the use of aggression for the purposes of defence. The second observation she made concerned the attitude to the hurt being inflicted. She noted that the toddlers were, at least initially, oblivious of the damage they were doing, which had to be drawn to their attention. In other words, the basic purpose of aggression is not to inflict hurt, although, of course, subsequently it can be marshalled to this effect. Although it was not the term she used, another way of putting this could be that the appreciation of the effect of one's aggression on the other is part way along a developmental line to humanization. Becoming a human being is a developmental task or process—the "rough beast . . . slouching . . . to be born". To lose this capacity of being aware of the effect of one's aggression on the other would then be a slipping back, or reversal, in the process. Not only would one be treating the other as less than human, one would also be losing some of one's own capacity for being human: that is, de-humanization not only affects how one treats the other, it also affects oneself.

Miss Freud's observations came at the end of a very cautious discussion about the source, aim, object of, and defences against, aggression, in which she advised against simply applying the understanding we have gained from work on libidinal development. She took the view that much more observation was required, and subsequently, in "Study guide to Freud's writings" (1982b), she encouraged the view that observation and application of psycho-analysis should include the social and cultural as well as that which emerged and may be applied in the treatment of patients. Thus encouraged, I will continue to explore the question of aggression, combining our clinical understandings with other social, political, and cultural observations.

Returning to the work of James Gilligan, it seems clear that while his patients may well have regressed into psychosis, they did not fail to appreciate that their victims were suffering. They had not simply fallen back to a point in childhood development where they did not understand the damaging nature of their actions. Their violence was, after all, retributive. There may have been a conden-sation of their object representations of their victim with those of the aggressor from the past, but the intention was to still to exact primitive justice. One explanation of the regression into psychosis would then be that it occurs because the aggressive drive, which has been given enormous added power from the experience of humiliation, comes into conflict with more advanced components of the superego that appreciate the human-ness of the other, which situation can only be satisfied by a dissolution of the ego and a regression into primary process thinking. Neurotic defence or compromise formation in this situation is inadequate to prevent a descent into psychotic illness. Precisely why humiliation should be so profoundly toxic, and whether the strengthening of the power of aggression is related to some primitive superego component is not entirely certain to me, but the result with these patients was an unthinkable rage, which burst out with tragic consequences.

Is something similar at work at a group level with those involved in terrorism? That there is venomous resentment cannot be doubted, and that it has been strengthened by communal and individual experiences of various kinds is also a matter of observa-tion by anyone who takes seriously the thinking of those involved in terrorism. Often thoughtful and articulate young people, they may try to protect themselves from the enormity of the injuries that they inflict on others. Activists in some places may take alcohol before going out on an operation, and some have noted that they make a point of not watching the news of their atrocities. Others strengthen themselves with words from a piece of their movement's literature, a team talk, or other encouraging or displacement activity. There is, however, no evidence of individual psychosis; on the contrary, vulnerable people are carefully weeded out by handlers within the organizations, but there is often a "fundamentalism" in the beliefs held by the group. This is not just a matter of the content of their beliefs, but is represented by a more primitive mode of thinking, and one which is difficult to engage in rational debate or argument. This group thinking is also characterized by denial in word and action of the individual humanity of those who are about to suffer. Their perception of the people who will die in the Twin Towers or a bomb in Belfast or Tel Aviv is that they are Americans, or Protestants, or Jews, and that this is all that is to be said. That part of their identity stands for the whole of them. As Amartya Sen has pointed out, in such circumstances the complex web of identities which makes us up as individual people is reduced down to one single component which we share with the rest of our "group"—much the same as the part standing for the whole that we see in individual psychosis. That some of those who will be killed may not even share the position of the government or state that is hated and being attacked, or that they may even have campaigned for the cause espoused by those who will now kill them, is shut out from thinking. The victims are set aside as the "unfortunate collateral damage of war". But, in using such terminology, we immediately become aware that this defence is the same for those involved in official armed forces as in terrorist groups. The need to set aside the humanity of the enemy is a necessary and common defence for the soldier or the bomber pilot as much as for the terrorist.

As we do with people whom others call mad, our approach is not to deny what seems disturbed and disturbing about what they do and say, or to dismiss it, but to take it seriously and try to understand the underlying meaning. So, I have tried to understand the meaning of the words and actions of those groups who employ the tactic of terrorism, examining their arguments, and asking whether or not there is any element of veracity in them. We know that those defences are the stoutest that can marshal an element of reality to assist them in protecting against the underlying anxiety. When terrorists and others attack, for example, the USA, I have to ask myself, does this come solely out of envy, or is there something about the way that the USA conducts itself which adds force to their resentment, and if so, what is the origin of the defensive structure of the USA? This thought led me to look at the history of the USA, just as I have tried to look at my own and at other communities' histories, on the model of the reconstruction of the individual story in psychoanalysis, and I focus here on the USA rather than the UK because I think that in this case, the UK is an addendum to the USA story.

The collective myth in the USA seems to run something like this.

After the discovery of the New World by Columbus, North America received attention not alone from the imperial powers of Spain, France, and Britain, but also from adventurers and fugitives from famine and persecution. These different groups struggled with each other and eventually the malign influence of the old imperial powers was seen off and a new progressive nation was founded out of many nations, and now leads the world.

There is little in this story about the fact that many indigenous people already lived in North America. What happened to them? I have followed this story a little way, enough to meet some of these first nation people and hear the terrible history of broken treaties, dishonesty, disregard for the law, and the brutal use of force. An extraordinary number of these people were killed off, not only by disease, but through massacres and atrocities such as the "Trail of Tears", when the Cherokees were driven from their homes in North Carolina and thousands died on the way to Oklahoma. This set me to recalling my own memories of cowboy and Indian films. The cowboys had personalities and stories. They had names and relationships, wishes, personal lives, and children, and they were heroically protected with their own guns and the arrival of the US Cavalry. The Indians were portrayed as brutal, dishonest savages whose lives had little value, and whose destruction and defeat was always a cause of celebration. An examination of the rhetoric of the time, and, indeed, of much later, makes clear that it was not just that their humanity was shut out from thinking as if, under the anxiety of their precarious lives, the colonists had regressed to the stage of the toddlers to which I referred earlier. A much more active mental step was taken. Arguments were constructed that these were not human beings to be considered in the same way as the colonists. This was a process beyond denial; it was dehumanization. It was not just applied to Native Americans, but later also to slaves brought against their will from Africa, and to their descendents. Only with the use of the powerful defence mechanism of dehumanization would it be possible for someone to perceive another person and yet intentionally treat them so ill, while still satisfying the requirements of a superego. "I am not doing harm, for this is not really a human being." Indeed, under the pressure of the superego, the perceived dehumanized person may further become a representation of evil, and, therefore, it is not just permissible to do damage to them, it may even be given a moral imprimatur. Is it possible that some of this historical construction of the personality of the USA has not yet been fully addressed and processed, and that when America spreads its civilizing influence around the world, it does so with an unconscious negative underlying flavour drawn from this history of not so long ago? Is it possible that this is detected and responded to with great negativity? So, paradoxically, US "Cavalry" help is seen as an attack, and the USA embarks on attacks because it believes that this is how to help.

Whatever the truth or otherwise of this speculation, the observation about the sometimes brutal origins of the USA makes it clear that dehumanization is not a mechanism that we can locate only in those people and places where terrorist activity takes place. It is, rather, a protective device which maintains the integrity of the self when the pressures of aggressive demands bring conflict with other aspects of the self. While it may, therefore, protect to some degree the integrity of the self, it removes important restrictions on the permissibility of inhuman behaviour. The profoundly disturbing degree to which this can develop was described in detail in R. J. Lifton's remarkable study, *The Nazi Doctors* (1986). In it, he charts the various psychological elements in the process of dehumanization, from the German experiences of humiliation in the First World War through the process by which powerful feelings of aggression are given expression in a community and the appreciation of reality gradually distorted for a whole body of people, while an increasingly harsh superego comes into the service of instinctual expression and killing becomes the mechanism for healing of the nation.

Three things seem to me to emerge from his work. First, dehumanization may be less a mechanism than a group of mechanisms. Second, it has a profoundly infectious and paradoxical nature. And third, flowing from this, it may even more easily appear in groups than in individuals.

Those who invoke dehumanization in their assault on the other, or in order to make such an assault possible, rapidly find themselves dehumanized, and this dehumanized self can then be used to attack the other. Here, we return to the question of terrorism and, in particular, the form in which it has presented itself in the 9/11 attacks and since then in the suicide bombings in Israel–Palestine. In these terrorist attacks, dehumanization of the self is a prerequisite for the attack. 9/11 was not, of course, the first demonstration of such a mechanism. The Tamil Tigers had used it much earlier, and arguably something of this mechanism was at play in Japanese pilots flying suicide missions in the Second World War. Here, in Northern Ireland, we could observe this mechanism at first hand when it appeared during the Hunger Strike in 1981. The failure of the IRA's terrorist campaign in the 1970s to bring about a withdrawal of British forces led to a strategic rethink by the prisoners, and their struggle with the authorities descended into a cycle of regressive self-abuse and dehumanization. First they refused to wear prison clothes, since these would identify them as criminals rather than prisoners of war. When this resulted in the prisoners being refused leave from their cells for calls of nature, they responded by taking faeces from their slop buckets and smearing themselves and their cell walls. The inhumanity of the circumstances for them and their jailers brought about by this so-called "Dirty Protest" was responded to by the prison authorities with power hosing and disinfection of the cells and, inevitably, physical abuse and fights. The cold, unswerving, and punitive approach taken by the highly symbolic woman Prime Minister, Margaret Thatcher, was reacted to with a decision to go on hunger strike. When the first of these hunger strikes ended with recriminations and accusations by the prisoners of bad faith by her and her officials, the stage was set for a climactic starvation to death of ten men. The tensions heightened when the leader of the hunger strike, Bobby Sands, was elected an MP at Westminster. He continued his fast and was, as he had planned, the first to die. This progressive and profoundly inhuman treatment of themselves brought few obvious short-term benefits, in that they died and the process was abandoned without concessions when their own families, especially their mothers, began to intervene after the later partici-pants in the hunger strike fell unconscious. They successfully requested resuscitative measures to be employed on the uncon-scious hunger strikers—good mothers who cared deeply, in contrast to the symbolic bad mother in 10 Downing Street who allowed her MP colleague, as well as sworn enemy, Bobby Sands, to die.

The result was that the hunger strikers became martyrs, in a remarkable and probably conscious repetition of the executions of the leaders of the 1916 Easter Rising. Theirs was seen as a blood sacrifice and became the basis for the political rise of Sinn Fein. That party has now taken over as the majority representative of the Catholic nationalist community in Northern Ireland and may even emerge later today as the largest political party in the province, but, until the advances of recent years in the Peace Process, leading members were involved in very violent criminal activity even after 9/11, when overt terrorist tactics largely ceased. The dehumaniza-tion involved in their treatment of their own community during the period of the Troubles was very marked, with control of their own people and terrain by the use of punitive attacks on their own young people involving destroying their elbows and knees and breaking other bones by savage beatings and shootings and even killings.

In the Middle East, suicide bombings are also creating a gener-ation of martyrs by conscious, voluntary blood sacrifice. By treating themselves in a less than human fashion, they become glorified. While their enemies in Israel respond with a superficial behavioural fantasy that punishment will stop the bad behaviour, Islamists have grasped the transcendence and paradox on the other side of dehu-manization.

Rene Girard (1977) has written extensively and with consider-able insight about these connections between violence, sacrifice, law, religion, culture, and the scapegoat mechanism. Freud realized that while the evidence of the clinic had led him to valuable insights into the vicissitudes of the libidinal drive, the inescapable tragedies of the First World War required him to re-evaluate his understand-ing of aggression. Girard draws attention to the reference in *Group Psychology and the Analysis of the Ego* (1921c) where Freud points up the inevitable conflict arising from identification in the relationship between the boy and his father. The inevitable emergence of hostility when the boy imitates the desire of his father in relation to his mother leads to the Oedipus complex, but, as Freud notes in the paper, "Identification, in fact, is ambivalent from the very first . . .". Girard's complaint is that Freud does not then follow this insight through to its logical conclusion, which, for him, is the relational and imitative nature of aggression and its outcome in violence. Girard himself goes on to explore the ways in which the mechanism that we call identification and which he refers to as "mimesis" leads inevitably to violence unless the social and political boundaries of religion, law, and culture are able to be respected. The implication of this approach is that, in the case of the current global jihadist terrorism, it is not religion which is the cause of violence, but the breakdown of the boundaries established by religion that results in the release of violence. This argument has some force for those of us who recognize that the breakdown of the horrible but stabilizing boundary of the Cold War has not led to a new and peaceful world order, but, rather, that globalization, with its freedom to trade, travel, and communicate, is perceived as a threat, and the current regression to fundamentalist ways of thinking in the East and West is a flight from, and defence against, this new freedom. The Islamists make this clear when they proclaim that the solution is for the great evil which is America to leave their part of the world; that is to say for a new East–West boundary to be established.

I wonder if it was some recognition of just such problems or limits in Sigmund Freud's theorizing, along with clinical experience, that led Anna Freud to warn about the limits of what can be done analytically (1986, p. 65). She said,

> In analysis we always reassure the patient who is afraid of admitting his id impulses into consciousness by telling him that once they are conscious they are less dangerous and more amenable to control than when they are unconscious. The only situation in which this promise may prove to be illusory is that in which the defence has been undertaken because the patient dreads the strength of his instincts. All that the ego asks for in such a conflict is to be reinforced. Insofar as analysis can strengthen it by bringing the unconscious id contents into consciousness it has a therapeutic effect here also. But insofar as the bringing of the unconscious activities of the ego into consciousness has the effect of disclosing the

defensive processes and rendering them inoperative, the result of analysis is to weaken the ego still further and to advance the pathological process.

Girard would, I think, concur with the implication that aggression is not always reduced by the removal of boundaries and defences; on the contrary, and, of course, although he was looking at the individual, his real focus was on the social and political. In other words, the power of unspeakable rage may not inevitably be weakened by thinking about the unthinkable, which brings us back to Nina Coltart.

In her paper she described her struggle with a male patient who becomes increasingly silent, brooding, and depressed. This state proves refractory to the application of all her analytical skill, insight, and patience. Its origin was clearly in a profoundly inhibited aggression towards his mother and the freedom of the psychoanalytical sessions led to a downward spiral as the power of those aggressive feelings was able to be experienced by him. It was eventually broken, not by a finely toned interpretation by the analyst, not even one which was repeated time and again, but rather by a single outbreak of genuine emotion from her in which she angrily refused to be destroyed by his aggression. Her passionate humanity broke through when she did not allow herself to be held in an inhumane relationship with the patient or in an inhuman straitjacket of analytic dogma. Instead of condemning the patient to continue with his punitive behaviour, she set down a boundary and said, in effect, "Stop it!" Herein is the intellectual, emotional, and therapeutic struggle: when to say, "No!" Where are the boundaries of freedom? We work, as do artists and lawyers, at the boundaries. Where are we, then, without them? Only with boundaries is there the possibility of transcendence of the boundaries. If boundaries are necessary for freedom, is transcendence the ultimate expression of freedom? When Yeats refers in that poem "The Second Coming" to the "ceremony of innocence", it is hard not to be reminded of the religious ritual with which he would have been most familiar, the Eucharist or Mass. In the centrepiece of this is the symbolic representation of a killing which was healing; a scapegoat mechanism, in which one individual was sacrificed for all. This month, as we reflect on the sixty-fifth anniversary of VE Day and the liberation of the Nazi concentration camps, it is clear that we have not yet as a race got beyond the need for the scapegoat mechanism. Certainly, as Rene Girard has suggested, it is hard to be convinced that the strength of the intellect alone can enable us to master the power of our instincts, especially our aggression, without the boundaries, arbitrary and symbolic as they often appear, of religion, culture, and law. Without them, we are vulnerable to the violence and dehumanization which makes evil, cruelty, and murder possible.

Contrariwise, perhaps on this day, when will be hosted at the City Hall by the Lord Mayor of Belfast a young woman of passionate liberal conviction, the fact that she has just won the Westminster election in the east of this city on the platform of a shared future for all the people of this city will allow us to dare to see an alternative to the words of W. B. Yeats with which we started, and hope that here

> The blood-dimmed tide is stemmed, and here and there
> The ceremony of innocence again observed;
> The best full of conviction, overcoming the worst
> With passion and intensity.

References

Freud, A. (1982a). Comments on aggression. In: *Psychoanalytic Psychology of Normal Development* (pp. 151–175). London: Hogarth.

Freud, A. (1982b). A study guide to Freud's writings. In: *Psychoanalytic Psychology of Normal Development* (pp. 209–276). London: Hogarth.

Freud, A. (1986). *The Ego and Mechanisms of Defence* (revised edn). London: Hogarth.

Freud, S. (1921c). *Group Psychology and the Analysis of the Ego. S.E., 18*: 67–147. London: Hogarth.

Gilligan, J. (1996). *Violence—Our Deadly Epidemic and Its Causes.* New York: GP Putnam's Sons.

Girard, R. (1977). *Violence and the Sacred.* Baltimore, MD: Johns Hopkins University Press.

Lifton, R. J. (1986). *The Nazi Doctors.* London: Macmillan.

Yeats, W. B. (1921). The second coming. In: *Michael Robartes and the Dancer* (p. 19) [reprinted Montana, MT: Kessinger Publishing Whitefish, 2003].

Discussion of Lord Alderdice's paper

P *hilip McGarry*: "Thank you, John, for that *tour de force*, everywhere from the Maze Prison to Katmandu to Lima. I'm sure we have plenty of questions."

Question: "You referred to these political acts, the communicable act of a terrorist, but how would you describe the American government's attack on Iraq or Afghanistan, that sort of 'rescuing' countries from violence?"

John Alderdice: "One of the things that's terribly important for us, whether in medicine or psychiatry or psychoanalysis, is to try to be as clear as possible about the language we use. One of the problems about emotionally driven language is that it tends to expand to mean everything and nothing. The term terrorism is a description of a specific triangular tactic where people who don't have the power to confront a power or authorities directly, because they would be destroyed, then attack a victim, but the victim is not the target of the attack. The target of the attack is the powerful government that is responsible for this victim, so it's a triangular process. What an authoritarian government does, whether it is the USA attacking Iraq, or whoever, whatever you like to call it, it's not terrorism because it's a direct attack, the victim is the target, so it's not the same kind of thing. It's done because that authoritarian government or authority figure doesn't feel any great fear that it can't cope with any attack that comes back. So, I think it's important to use the term terrorism not as a moral term, where, by using the very term, you are condemning it and everybody that's involved with it simply by the use of the term. It's emotionally loaded. I don't use it in this way, I use it as a technical term that describes a very specific clear tactic that was developed quite strongly by the anarchists in the nineteenth century and we've seen it continuing on since. It's not a question of whether you like or don't like what they stand for, that's not the issue; it's a specific description of a tactic. The tactics that governments use, whether on their own citizens or on others, of spreading fear and terror, are no less frightening and I'm not setting one against the other in a moral sense, but it is a very different kind of tactic."

Question: "This is not a political question. I just wanted to ask Lord Alderdice about the generation of shame through a conflict between the ego ideal and the ego, and in terms of the group where the ego ideal then becomes the ego ideal of the whole group it becomes very powerful, and what he thinks of the role of the super-ego and where that comes in?"

John Alderdice: "If we take it in a kind of practical sense, and I hope I'm addressing what you're pointing to, we have this curious conundrum whereby most of those in Britain from the immigrant community who get involved in terrorism are not first generation people. It's usually second, third, and fourth generation, and this has been extremely puzzling to people, to sociologists and others who have looked at it, because surely the solution is to get people jobs, integrate them into the community, make sure they are educated, and so on. Yet, most of these young people, when you look at them, *are* educated, they often have university degrees, some of them work in the health service, they are kind to old ladies, they are married, they have families, all this kind of stuff: they are second and third generation. We need to think about that because the normal sociological model doesn't fit. It seems that the story, if you like, goes something like this. Their parents and grandparents come to the country and have still some kind of sense of importance of where they came from. But they weren't coming here because it was a good place to be: they left somewhere that was not good and they came to the UK and there was a degree of gratitude that they had been able to arrive, that they had been able to settle, but they weren't necessarily treated well. So, when a next generation comes along, although they speak out about how they feel alienated and disenchanted, particularly from the politics and foreign policy of the government, actually what doesn't get spoken about is the great antipathy they feel towards their own parents for having failed by leaving their own country, having failed by coming and accepting being discriminated against and abused and so on, and, therefore, feeling very negative against those people who, in other contexts, might be their ideal, or their model, or their roots. So that component of them, their identity, which is their roots, their model, what they grew up with, becomes much criticized by the other part of themselves that is looking at what is right and fair and what is good and so on. But the attack is only partly against the parents; the attack is against the society they are in. So, if we put it in a less theoretical and more practical sense, it seems to me that this kind of dynamic is really important to understand, otherwise you don't get the result that you want by simply socializing people, giving them jobs, saying there is no discrimination now, just forget about the way it used to be. There is a much more difficult process of digestion that has to take place. One of the things that's really worrying about it is that some of the strongest criticisms of current immigration to the UK are not coming from people whose families have been here for ten generations, but are coming from people who have come relatively recently to the UK and are afraid now that the people coming in afterwards are going to make life very difficult for them. I think the kinds of things you are referring to have got to be incorporated into our thinking about what is happening in the group or we just simply won't understand it."

Question: "Thank you for a very interesting and fascinating talk. My question links a bit with the last one, but brings it more to home, and I particularly want to focus on your use of the terms of disrespect, humiliation, dehumanization, and so on. My question relates to England, where we have a lot of young violence, young aggression, family aggression, and so on, and I see that as a social phenomenon more than I see it as a psychiatric phenomenon, but it is getting to the point where it is becoming a mental health problem and is increasing to a degree that is having an impact on those who work in mental health services, who are overrun. So, I suppose my question is, what about the aggression in groups and what is your comment on that without taking it out into the wider world?"

John Alderdice: "I think that over the past few years there has been the beginnings of some understanding that some of the things we're talking about, like respect, people being treated fairly, and so on, that there is something important here, but the truth was it was only the words that got used. People would talk about consulting with people, but they'd already decided beforehand what the outcome of consultation is going to be. People would talk about respect, but they wouldn't actually behave with respect. I'm talking about government, very senior levels of our community. It was very deceitful and dishonest. I think the second thing is that some of these issues have simply not been able to be talked about because another part of the issue is that it wasn't politically all right to talk about certain difficult problems. I think we've got to find a way of talking about some of these problems and doing something about them. For example, some of those of us who have been very positive about the European project because we saw it as Europe's way of making sure we did not go back to war again as we had twice in the first part of the twentieth century, were not sufficiently careful in thinking about what the practical implications were that a rapid expansion of that European Union that did not make cultural changes, but allowed people to pretend they were abiding by rules when they were no longer doing so. Let me give you an example outside of Europe: many of us were involved for quite some time in trying to introduce the notion of free and fair elections in various parts of the world, as though that would produce liberal democracy. In substantial parts of sub-Saharan Africa, constitutions would change to make sure there were elections and we thought "great, that's going to change things for the better". It hasn't, because in most of those countries the underlying culture didn't change, and so what we did was to give tribal chieftains greater technology, power, and security apparatuses and legal structures that made it possible for them to oppress their own people even more. There was no fundamental change in the culture. I remember Neville Symington saying at the beginning of one of his books, "never be deceived when you walk past a clinic room and it says psychotherapy in progress". There may be a therapist and there may be a patient and they may be undertaking a process, but it doesn't mean something is fundamentally changing inside. What you are referring to are the symptoms of the fact that things have not changed for the better inside despite the fact that many of the words that have been used appear to have been reasonable, tolerant, fair, respectful. All these kinds of things have just been words: they haven't really changed things underneath and it's not clear to me that we have yet come to the point that we can do that."

Question: "I'm particularly noticing that you are using the past tense when you started talking about these things and I suppose my concern is that actually it's very much present tense. We're living in a virtual system with virtual services, virtual ideas, and things that are filtering down from above, and I believe this is having a impact on the younger generations hugely because they can't grasp anything, as it's not real."

John Alderdice: "It's absolutely true, and if one were to make a worrying predication, it would be that, having gone through a period of time since the Second World War and then through the period of the breakdown of communism, where things where looking better, there is a real danger that we're sliding back towards more nationalism and xenophobia. Not only will we not have the resources for the services we need to provide, we won't actually have a sense of compassion in the community to deal with the problems that you're describing, and it's not an encouraging position."

Question: "Congratulations on this afternoon's presentation, which was even better than I had expected. I have to say I share the first questioner's concerns about the use of the word terrorism. This is a term with which I've never been happy in clinical situations or in research papers. You certainly have defined a concept; you have pointed out how you perceive how the term should be used, but you have also mentioned that it is ever so often, indeed generally, used in an emotive context. The first time I ever heard the term used was at the time of the Palestinian war in the 1940s and the emphasis put on it seemed a bit of a gimmick. Do you not think now the time has come for the concept that you have been defining to have a completely different name? Maybe it's a tall order."

John Alderdice: "It's an interesting business, naming things. I had a discussion recently with some folk here in Northern Ireland who are very cross about the use of the term "dissident republicans" because they are not really republicans at all. I said, "Fine, give me another name that works and I'll quite happily use it, but it has to convey the meaning you are trying to refer to." I have no emotional attachment to the term terrorism, but I think the truth is when you use the term, people at least know what you are dealing with. If somebody can come up with another term that actually conveys the meaning then that's absolutely fine by me. But be under no illusions: those who actually get involved in using the tactic are absolutely aware of what they are doing and trying to do, they are trying to create terror, that is part of the process."

Response from questioner: "But there is also a risk that if you introduce another term it will soon develop the same connotations that are understood by the vast bulk of the people who use it."

John Alderdice: "Absolutely. I'm reminded of the remarks many years ago about the term 'hysteria', that it is a tough old bird that tends to outlive its obituarists. If only we could come up with a better word that conveyed things it would be good, but we haven't."

Cathal Cassidy: "Thank you, John, for your stimulating talk, but I want to go back to your comment about the place of religion, culture, and the law in defending against aggression and violence in society. We are certainly seeing in our local society, here in Ireland, north and south, a serious humiliation, dismantling, and disrespecting of all of these things, and a great deal of shaming in religion, politics, the law, and culture. I'm wondering if you see that as a constructive thing towards a new beginning or as destructive thing. I'm not so sure about it. I have very mixed feelings about it so I wonder how you see what is happening very visibly on a daily basis in our society."

John Alderdice: "I think it's quite a mixed picture in many ways, because, on the one hand, you could say there is all of this apparent deconstruction of some aspects of the religious structure in Ireland, but it is largely over the past ten years that the structure within the Catholic Church hierarchy has been under attack. Perhaps because there was a degree of confidence that they gave such security to the community that nobody could ask serious questions and, therefore, there wasn't accountability, things went on that otherwise could have been stopped and now you get into a kind of cleansing operation, with terrible damage to the structure and hurt and dismay for many ordinary people. But it's not something that's taken place right across the whole of the community. In fact, what's happening for much of the community beyond this island and elsewhere is actually a strengthening of quite fundamentalist religious views: in the Jewish community, in the Hindu community, and so on. I even met Buddhist fundamentalists in Sri Lanka. I thought that this would be one religious faith that wouldn't have fundamentalists, but I was wrong. In Sri Lanka, they are strongly supportive of physical force. I think there are particular problems for the structure of the Catholic Church and there is obviously a lot of thinking to be done on that, but I don't think it represents a destructuring of religious faith and community throughout the world. In many other parts of religious communities, they're actually becoming fundamentalist, which is not the same as becoming conservative.

"I think there are also important differences between faith and doctrine. Doctrine and belief are, in many ways, the opposite of faith. Doctrine and belief are what you do to create a degree of certainly in the midst of uncertainty. Faith is when you trust, yet know that it is not certain. In this part of the world and most other places I've look at, fundamentalism does not occur due to changes in religious belief, but because of uncertainties in the political situation. In any place where there is political anxiety along with uncertainty, you slide back, just as with an individual who can slide into psychosis. You slide back as a group into fundamentalist ways of thinking, not necessarily religious, which can then be extremely damaging. You open up a huge Pandora's box, but it is very important in the island of Ireland, and particularly in the Catholic communion, not to think that the destructuring that is taking place, which, one hopes, will be repairable in some way, is something that applies to all religious views."

Cathal Cassidy: "I wonder about politics and the law where shaming and humiliation is very evident."

John Alderdice: "Let me be quite clear: I'm not disagreeing with you that there are many aspects of structure which have become shaken over the last few years. That's absolutely true. The issues about hierarchies and respect, all the kinds of things you're talking about, have happened, but I have a thought that what we are likely to slide into is a return to a quite rigid fundamentalist way of thinking. If you look at what is happening in the politics of Europe, every party is talking about immigration as a fearful and worrying thing. Every party is pulling back to a nationalistic, proud of my country, position, and I think that is something that is happening right across Europe. In a way, what is happening is that the uncertainty that you describe has gone further and so we're getting a regression at a group level. People are sliding back in to these ways of thinking to provide them with a sense of security."

Philip McGarry: "One final question."

Carine Minne: "One of the things that has come up at the conference is that we've had many references to people who have been violent and the impact of the parenting, especially the mothering, on them. How on earth do we begin to think of the mothers, for example, of suicide bombers, who are very proud of what their sons and sometimes daughters have achieved? It's not just the mothers, it's also the fathers. How can we get our heads around that? We've been talking a lot about how to understand violent acts, from fantasy to action, but if we go back one step we have to think about the parenting that may have contributed enormously to it as well. Are these parents similar to the kinds of parents who produce our violent mentally disordered patients?"

John Alderdice: "There are two things I would say about it. The first is that for any individual to come to the kind of point you describe requires some degree of dehumanizing, both of themselves and, by connection, of their own children. I think the key to understanding this is to understand that things like terrorism, whether it's suicide terrorism or any other kind of terrorism, is that this is a group phenomenon, so when you start thinking about the parent component, you've got to think about it at a group level. Let me give you an example. If you want to think about Northern Ireland as a community divided against itself in some kind of breakdown within itself and doing violence to itself, and you think about parenting, you need to think about the parents being the British state and the Southern Irish state: those are the parents, not individual people who produce children, but the states that acted as parents that produced this child. Think about Northern Ireland as the kind of child of a rape where the parents are the British state and the Irish state. Think about what it felt like, for example, if you think back to the reaction of Unionists after the Anglo-Irish Agreement, when they felt, and in truth had been, betrayed by the British state. They were not consulted. Not only that, they were told lies, they were told lies right up to the day before the agreement—"There is no discussion going on, there will not be any agreement, nothing is happening". Absolutely untrue, totally untrue, and they felt utterly abused by this parent. When you go to City Hall tonight, every 1st July in Belfast there is a special meeting of Belfast City Council, and that meeting is called for one purpose, and that is to pass a motion remembering all of those who died at the Battle of the Somme in the First World War. Nobody in the House of Commons remembered these sacrifices, but the people here remember them. They still have Somme Associations and the City Council to do these kind of things, but only they do it. The sense of betrayal by the parent is absolutely enormous. Terrorism is a group phenomenon; therefore, the parents you need to think about are the group parents, the other states, the background, the history, where it came from, and so on. When you think about the USA, you need to think about Britain as a parent against which it came to rebel. If you do think about the individual parents, I believe that you need to think about the process of dehumanization. Finally, just to say that one question I asked people in Israel and in the Palestinian area, Hamas,

Hezbollah people, and others was: "Do you want to continue with this process?" The answer from both sides was: "Do you think we are mad? This is an awful way to be, an awful way to live." One woman, a mother whose son is in the IDF (Israel Defence Force) said to me, "My son is a soldier. I desperately hope he doesn't kill a Palestinian." I said, "What do you mean?" She replied, "Well of course it would be bad for the Palestinian, but it will damage my son." I thought to myself that this is a hopeful sign. Some people come to the point of understanding the dehumanizing effect of attacking others, and when they do there is the beginning of some hope."

Philip McGarry: "Thank you, John, including for that very compelling image of Northern Ireland and its antecedents. Thank you all for being such a good audience."

CHAPTER NINE

Plenary session

Chair, Brian Martindale

B rian Martindale: "We have got from 3.15 p.m. until 5.00 p.m. The idea is that the distinguished colleagues on my left and right will speak for some of the time, as this is a time for your questions, comments, etc. The plan is that Rosine Perelberg is going to be available from about 3.45 p.m. If you have questions for Rosine, it would be helpful to have them beforehand, although I would welcome your exchange with her when she comes online. I have a few questions here for four speakers already, but does anyone in the audience want to ask a question or make a comment about anything that has come up? Let's start with a question to James Gilligan from Gabby Marks."

Gabby Marks: "This in response to Professor Gilligan's very interesting talk and the fact that he mentioned that recidivism was completely halted in prison by giving murderers a degree course and that the people who achieved a degree didn't come back to prison. What sort of violence is perpetrated on serious offenders, murderers, by the state in not allowing them to re-educate their minds and their psyches by continuing to offer degree course and also intensive therapy? I'm not sure if that still holds that they took away all the services that were being offered, but what you said was frightening. I thought, in general, there is so little education while people sit in prison and each time I have tried to explain it or have written the odd letter to a newspaper they see you as protecting prisoners, being on the wrong side."

Brian Martindale: "To make you aware of the people on the panel, Marie Zaphiriou Woods and Marianne Parsons, on my right, are psychoanalysts and child psychotherapists and were presenting papers this morning on work, for Marie, with someone younger than an adolescent, and for Marianne, with an adolescent. I hope you will ask questions/make comments and make use of their expertise in child development. James Gilligan is from New York; he is a psychiatrist and psychoanalyst working at national level in the prison services. Franco De Masi is from Italy and has a great deal of psychoanalytic experience working with psychosis, both in public sector and in recent years in private practice."

James Gilligan: "Thank you for your question. What you have touched on is a painful subject that I spent a lot of my time working on in the USA. I don't know how much this is happening in other countries, but I know it is a huge problem in the USA. Once we find a policy or practice that is successful in reducing the rate of crime and violence in our society, some political operative or other, usually from a conservative, republican background, will undo it. Both in Massachusetts and in Indiana and Folsom State Prison in California and many other places, when prisoners get a college degree and are released from prison, they don't return. It's not 100% everywhere but it is certainly statistically very powerful and is one of the most powerful ways of preventing recidivism or future offending. Why does that get cancelled? There are many ways you could try to understand it. One way is to ask, who benefits from having a high rate of crime and violence? There can be political benefits to people who can exploit the fear of crime in society, as this provides incentives for some very conservative political policies. One of our most conservative presidential candidates was a man named Barry Goldwater, back in 1964. His campaign manager said that crime is a free multi-billion dollar gift to the Republican Party. President George Bush Senior's campaign manager, Lee

Atwater, once said, 'Crime is the issue with which we will divide the Democratic Party'. You can divide the Democrats because some people running for political office wouldn't dare do anything that would sound like they were being 'soft on crime', such as providing a free college education for prisoners. We're faced with the paradox that sometimes it is beneficial to certain groups, for political purposes, to introduce the very policies that give us the highest possible rates of crime and violence. This is a hard thing to talk about without sounding like it's a conspiracy theory, and I don't mean it that crudely. I don't think there's a committee that meets to say 'how can we raise the rate of crime and violence in America today?' But I do think there is a conflict of interest between those who benefit from having a society with a lot of crime and a lot of punishment versus a society that would like to minimize both. I want to suggest that the psychology of crime and the psychology of punishment are very much one and the same: that is, the motives that stimulate criminal violence often are the same motives that stimulate legal violence, or what some call laws violence. For example, the states in America that have the highest murder rates also have the highest rates of capital punishment, and I mean by far, twenty times as many capital punishments as the less murderous states. They are called the red states in America, and their execution rate is twenty times as high and so is their murder rate. There are many ways you can interpret a correlation like this, but to me it suggests the psychology of one and the psychology of the other go together."

Question from the floor: "It seems to me that what you are talking about connects with what John Alderdice was talking about in terms of the fundamentalism: there's a threat to us maybe, at the moment, in our western society generally, that uncertainty, the idea that things you could hold fast to aren't necessarily secure, is going to lead to a situation where there is increasing intolerance and that's bad news for all us, in terms of what the outcomes might be."

James Gilligan: "I completely agree".

Brian Martindale: "Thank you. If anyone wants to respond from the panel, please do."

Question from the floor: "It's the same topic, but concerns developmental aspects. I was thinking about linking it to the way children are managed from very young upwards and how their development is effected in terms of punishment and the crimes that they commit, which then lead the parent to punish them. I wonder if the experts on the panel have a view about that. It seems to be a feature of development in our cultures and societies that just becomes more sophisticated as it goes into the criminal system. We try to make it better, so we've got people at the other end of the table who are then doing therapy with the criminals to help them get better again, but it's a kind of circular thing that we do to try and make ourselves feel better. Do the experts who deal with this kind of thing and are more knowledgeable than myself agree with that idea, and is there something we could do with much earlier intervention that would break that cycle?"

Brian Martindale: "I think that's probably what people working with younger age groups are trying to do. To intervene early, nip things in the bud, hopefully help people recover a more healthy developmental trajectory."

Marie Zaphiriou Woods: "I think there is a lot of scope for preventative work, if one can work with parents individually or in groups to help them understand their children better. Not to project on to them, see them as bad, but to give them some understanding of normal development, where aggression is understood as normal and serving a purpose in terms of helping separation and so on, and then the condemnation and punitive attitudes will be softened. Children will then have a better chance to develop positive self esteem and sublimations."

Carine Minne: "I am reminded about something my supervisor said to me once. We were driving to Broadmoor Hospital together the day after the 7 July London terrorist bombings, and I remember saying to him, 'What is to be done with these kind of terrorist atrocities?', and he said quite simply, 'More child guidance clinics.'"

James Gilligan: "I just wanted to mention that there is a lot of research on child rearing, suggesting that the more harshly children are punished the more violent they become, both as children and as adults, and I have seen this in prisons. The more harshly the prisoners are treated, the more violent they would become in the prisons, until they reached the point where they didn't care if they lived or died, so long as they could get back at the people they saw as tormenting them. I think it's important to draw a sharp distinction between punishment meaning the intentional infliction of pain as a form of revenge versus restraint and, say, a two-year-old running in front of traffic who won't respond to language or words, and you then restrain them physically. That doesn't mean that you inflict physical pain on them; you are trying to prevent them inflicting pain on themselves by their behaviour. If we could adapt that attitude to adult criminals, restraint but not punishment, I think we'd be far ahead. Or, as one British criminologist put it, prison *is* punishment, but it's not *for* punishment. Ideally, I would like to replace prisons with locked, secure colleges and universities and mental health therapeutic centres. If we could change the whole meaning and point of them to be forms of restraint while education, psychotherapy, and medical care were going on, I think we would be much more effective in preventing criminal violence."

Marianne Parsons: "There's a related issue concerning prison and punishment where someone who has done something wrong is seen as only bad and nothing else. We see the person as a bad person because of the crime they committed, rather than seeing the child or the adult prisoner as somebody who is a whole person with different aspects of themselves, some of which are valuable. All the patients that I treated at the Portman came feeling they were bad, they were just trouble, they were not wanted; they'd done some pretty terrible things and one of the most important things I needed to do was to help them to rediscover, or even find, some parts of themselves that weren't connected with the crime that they had committed, that they did have something potentially healthy and good inside that they could then value, and that made a big difference."

Brian Martindale: "Rosemary Boucherat, would you like to read your question to Lord Alderdice?"

Rosemary Boucherat: "You portray the behaviour of imperial Europe and the breakaway USA, which became another oppressive culture, both of them as oppressive cultures and perpetrating disrespect and humiliation towards other nations. Why don't western governments own up to and publicize that they now understand this? They surely have advisers who are able to get through to them so that they could then behave like good parents and stop using inflammatory war language and be wise enough to take a more therapeutic approach, using the media to educate the world about these concepts?"

John Alderdice: "Before I got into political life I had a kind on assumption that when cabinet ministers and prime ministers and leading political figures did things that seemed foolish or misguided to me, that was because there was something they knew that I didn't know. Then I got involved in political life and started meeting cabinet ministers and prime ministers and presidents. I remember the first time I met a Secretary of State here in Northern Ireland. I went home and didn't sleep at all that night, which was very unusual for me, because I began to realize that mostly they haven't a clue what they are talking about. And you talk about their advisers; they have no clue what they are talking about. The sorts of things you are describing here are the complete antithesis of working politically, which is one of the reasons why psychotherapists rarely get anywhere politically, as international relations are based on power relations and if you go out to the people and ask them to vote for you they won't vote for you if you say, 'Well of course, I can understand that there are other people who have an understanding of these things, and maybe they understand it better that I do.' Nobody will vote for you so there are really quite fundamental problems about the whole way we operate as human beings and groups. I'm also not saying, in case it should be misunderstood, that what is coming from Europe, or indeed from the USA, is all negative and bad; this is absolutely not the case. There are many hugely good things, hugely civilizing things that have come out of Europe, as well as all sorts of problems. The same is true of the USA or China or any other part of the world. There is a mixture, and I'm focusing on some of the negative things at the moment because they are what produce the negative results. But when you come to the question of how you deal with the past and the way it was, I think you have to be terribly careful. I am extremely sceptical, I have to say, of these apologies that have recently started to become fashionable for what was done at the time of the Irish famine, or what was done to the poor kids who were sent off to Australia, where current political leaders are apologizing for what political leaders in the past did. It doesn't cost anything, it's a complete nonsense and it is dishonest. I don't think it is a real apology at all. I think it is a political game. I think if there is any genuine concern of that kind, then you say, for example, about these kids who were deported to Australia, we are going to sit down with the Australian government and see what kinds of very belated but nevertheless important funding arrangements for counselling facilities, for arranging for those people to be flown back to the UK to meet up with their long lost families, etc., etc. That is an apology, doing something about it, but some fatuous nonsense where you pretend to be sorry about something you had nothing to do with in the first place, is just dishonest, in my view. So I think you have got to be very careful, when we are addressing these things from the past that we are genuinely trying to address them. And I have to say, my experience in political life is that you should not assume anything remotely like the sophistication that you are hoping for; it is much more primitive than that, I'm afraid."

Rosemary Boucheret: "Surely we are at a stage in our civilization where something better could be taught and they could understand the connection between good parenting and what we perpetrate to other nations."

John Alderdice: "That's why I have become involved in political life and why I would very much encourage you, not necessarily to stand for political office, but to be involved in talking, for example, about these kinds of issues. I frankly don't think it is about setting up lots more child guidance clinics, although that is very important. I think it is about sitting down and looking at what we do in our educational system, so that you try to influence the system so that all children who come through the system have a different set of experiences of it than would have been the case before. And don't expect that all parents will welcome that, because it will run counter to some of their short-term expectations about their children doing better than other children. This is a process of trying to move our human family along, and we're part of that process but it takes a while, like therapy does."

Question from the floor: "I work in a very deprived area which is among one of the poorest wards in the country. The children go to school, but the backgrounds they live in are disastrous. It's an ex-mining area, there's poverty, there's social breakdown, substance misuse, crime, and if the children are in school and from a back-ground like this, then the teachers get nowhere, and I think that until the government recognizes the importance of, you might call it social engineering, and actually starts to do something about poverty and the conditions people live in, then the education system is really struggling to do anything at all."

James Gilligan: "In the United States, in Los Angeles, the Rand Corporation conducted an experiment which had dramatic results. They provided prenatal counselling for single mothers living in a poverty-stricken African-American slum where there were high crime rates. They had home visits from nurses and social workers when the baby was born. They provided pre-school, very early educational experiences for the children, and then gave the children an allowance to stay in school. They found that results were so striking: there was so much less child abuse, so much less juvenile delinquency, so much less adult crime, that they figured that this programme, even though it cost money, saved the tax payers about $5 for every $1 spent on the programme because the cost of incar-ceration and adjudication, etc., are far higher once crime starts, or child abuse starts. As a society, we know how to prevent crime and violence. Do we do it? No, except sometimes we do it. When we do it and we find it works, we stop doing it. That's the paradox that I'm talking about."

Brian Martindale: "Carine, a question for yourself from Connie Booth."

Connie Booth: "I wondered about the mother and Miss B, and if you could say a bit more about what was it in that relationship, when she was making progress with you, that allowed her to go back to her mother given all that happened between them?"

Carine Minne: "I think Miss B was the victim of a deeply narcissistic, highly disturbed mother who probably saw Miss B, her child, as nothing but an extension of herself. I don't think she ever had the privilege of being able to separate properly from this narcissistic mother and the progress she made, if you remember, was only able to occur when the patient temporarily cut off actual contact with the mother. I think the proneness to return to the idealized/denigrated, deeply split way of functioning was always there and we weren't surprised. We had always hoped the mother would never make contact again and that we might be able to send the patient from Broadmoor to a medium secure unit away up in the north of England, far away from her original geographical situation, but that wasn't to be. After two years of work with her, literally in two seconds, the relationship was reinstated as it had been before."

Brian Martindale: "What did you think this proneness was about? How would you understand it?"

Carine Minne: "I don't know, I think if we were talking about the enormous capacity for splitting and projecting, I think that she had managed to reduce this in terms of the mental structural changes that I tried to describe. I think that the split had lessened and the degree of projecting had lessened, but it was still very fragile. The getting better of the mind's psychic structure was fragile and it didn't take much for it to regress back to its original deeply pathological format."

Brian Martindale: "Would anybody like to ask a further question of Carine, or comment? Gentleman at the back."

Question from the floor: "I'd like to ask Carine a question about the mother of the suicide bomber. I was thinking of the mother of patient B, and I was thinking about the offering up of the daughter to narcissistic needs and the offering up of the son to narcisstic needs and the splitting and projection involved. I was thinking and comparing the two of them."

Carine Minne: "Connie, did you want say something more; did you have some thoughts yourself, because I don't know the answer, I'm speculating?"

Connie Booth: "I was wondering, Carine, whether in that two years when she was cut off from her mother, at least physically, did you ever communicate the issue directly with her, and if you didn't, what was your reason?"

Carine Minne: "I think in the twice-weekly sessions it was addressed constantly, also transferentially and countertransferentially, because quite often I became this very toxic mother. Sometimes she was able to take it and at other times she didn't want us to even think about this toxic mother any more. I wasn't allowed to—quote—'bad mouth' her mother during those two years, even when the mother was the devil personified for her having done what she had done."

Brian Martindale: "Marianne . . ."

Marianne Parsons: "The mother is always the mother and therefore fundamentally needed, however terrible, isn't that right? The mother is the most important person for every individual and I know from the patients at the Portman who have been abused, left unprotected by their mothers, they wouldn't have a word said against their mothers. So the pull back to the mother is always going to be incredibly strong even if that mother is quite terrible. It can feel like it's primal."

Carine Minne: "Any shift away always felt to her to be a betrayal of her mother."

Brian Martindale: "So primitive fears are of doing terrible harm to the mother, but one also wishes for this."

Carine Minne: "Yes, it's one of the things we discuss at the Portman clinic quite often. I think Don referred to it in his keynote speech yesterday morning—how the more sexually perverse patients have managed to find a way of keeping the mother object through a sexualized perversion."

Brian Martindale: "I remember Hanna Segal saying at some point that when you have got a sadomasochistic relationship, the most likely time for murder is when you see the harm you could do, when you see the horror.

"We haven't made connection with Rosine, so before we do, does anyone have anything further to say? There is another question here for John from Dr Towobola. Would you like to let us have your question?"

Dr Towobola: "Thank you for your very enlightening talk. When you analysed the origins of the problems of sub-Saharan Africa, it got me thinking. Currently, one of the obvious problems is the extreme greed of the leaders. I wondered what your thoughts are on greed as a form of aggression. We do know that are so many problems and a lot of resources are sent from this part of the world to Africa and they end up in the wrong places. Do you have any solution to this?"

John Alderdice: "I think with a number of these problems there is no obvious immediate solution, but starting to talk about the problems and trying to understand them as genuine problems is really important. I remember ten or so years ago an old friend of mine called Fritz Bolkestein, who was the leader of the right of centre liberals in the Netherlands, raised the question of immigration at that time. He said, 'We've got a problem and we're not talking about it and we need to start talking about it because if we don't we're going to end up with a much worse problem further down the line', and he was lambasted as racist. I knew him well and he wasn't racist at all. He saw there was an emerging problem and, of course, what happened is that ten years later Pim Fortuyn was murdered and a massive upset in the politics of the Netherlands ensued which has now resulted in Geert Wilders being the second largest party and politics has moved massively to the right. The Netherlands is a country that in my time of growing up was a beacon of tolerance and liberalism. I think trying to find ways of talking about these problems is very difficult and requires a lot of courage. If we don't talk about them then it will be much the worse for us. The problems of sub-Saharan Africa are not just about post colonial history and not enough aid going in and so on. I don't say that those aren't problems, but there are a whole series of problems that Africans themselves need to own and take responsibility for. Second, some of the things that we have done, really truly believed in, that we thought were going to help solve the problems, like free and fair elections and co-operation on security issues, and so on, have actually made the situation worse because the societies were not ready to import these things, they had to grow into them. In the same kind of way there are certainly patients that we have that to suddenly plunge them into something they can't cope with does not make anything better. It may make things incalculably worse. We're very naïve and simplistic in political life in some ways, and we have the idea that some simple intervention can bring tremendous success when, in fact, sometimes it makes the whole situation much worse. You mentioned greed: in traditional cultures, with relatively limited technology and goods, there was a limit to how much the chief could have because there was only a certain amount there, and whatever was going he could pretty much have the lot. But, if you massively increase the amount there is and you don't change the culture and you don't require accountability, then it simply hypertrophies and gets worse and more corrupted. So talking about it, acknowledging it, not saying, 'Oh goodness, this is not politically correct, I can't speak about this', but finding ways of genuinely and respectfully engaging is hugely important. I don't underestimate the difficulties of doing it, as sometimes raising these things can be really problematic. James and I were talking about a book he hopes to publish quite soon with some fascinating findings about suicide and homicide and politics in the USA. We were talking about how dangerous and potentially incendiary this information will be, and how he needs to be careful because of the potential reaction to it, as the fact that it's not fashionable and politically acceptable is really a serious problem. It is particularly true for people trying to address the problems of sub-Saharan Africa. Sometimes we just have to talk about it here and hope that other people who will be more acceptable can speak about the problems in Africa itself."

Brian Martindale: "I'm struck by the parallels between the different levels that we are talking about. The difficulty of actually getting these discussions going, the difficulty talking about central matters, and in the clinical presentations I think the presenters have made very clear the difficulty in actually engaging in talking about difficult matters. I'm interested in the parallels that we have. It's not enough to say offer psychotherapy, or to offer counselling services. Talking about this at government levels is really the art. John, can I ask you a question to enlarge a bit on something you said about migration to the UK? You said it was interesting that the groups that are often most anxious about migration are those who migrated themselves a generation or so before. Could you enlarge on that, what is the content of their anxieties?"

John Alderdice: "I think there are number of different components to it. One of the components is that often when people come into a community where they are not wholly at home it's anxiety provoking, and they try to protect themselves, not just from anxiety, but from attack, by heavily identifying with the community, taking on its values and mores, and so on. To some extent it was like that before they came, as they had to uproot themselves and come, and they may have had an idealized idea of what it was they were coming to. They come and they are glad to be here, but they also find that it's not perfect and it's not quite what they had hoped for, but instead of becoming disenchanted—going back is not a prospect—then they have to emphasize how they are really becoming a part of things. They realize that they're not completely incorporated, they're not completely welcome, and again that's frightening. They believed that if they came here and settled and were good citizens, worked hard and paid their taxes, they would be accepted by a tolerant country. You find out that you're not really accepted and you begin to become aware that the more people that are coming the more problematic it's going to be, so then you begin to say, 'No don't come, stay away, I know I'm here but you're going to make it worse for all of us.' This kind of stuff is going on and I think at the same time there is a bit of it which is true for all of us. When you join a club or set up a professional organization, you and all your friends get in on the grandfather clause and then you increase the fees, increase the exam criteria to the point where none of you who were in it in the first place could ever have got membership of it. This is the kind of human experience we all do anyway, and I think there is a little bit of that involved. But the more important thing, I think, is the anxiety I was talking about first."

Brian Martindale: "I'm going to anticipate Rosine joining us in few minutes by going over the questions I am going to ask on your behalf and to see if there are any additional areas you might wish to discuss during the time she is available. There are two or three, perhaps connected, questions I have from you: the first question links with what Franco was talking about this morning: 'Are there violent acts that do not convey, are not expressing, meaning?' I think that is something you were suggesting, Franco, so I'm hoping you and Rosine may have some dialogue on this topic. The other two questions are: 'Rosine commented on dehumanized, perverse violent fantasies and actions that occur in severe narcissistic and psychotic conditions. Does her formulation of the two types of aggression fit with this?' Can you say, Paul, what the two types of aggression were?"

Paul Williams: "I imagine everyone remembers this. She was refer-ring to two types of aggression towards the father in males. One was the annihilated, murdered father, and one was the dead father, and she drew a useful distinction in trying to conceptualize the development or lack of development of healthy aggression in males between the type of person who annihilates the father and so can't proceed to a constructive, identificatory pathway and the male who finds a way of addressing his aggression in a relationship in the transference and who can come to mobilize it and use it to do the psychic developmental work of killing the father that creates a dead father, but not a murdered father. The father, of necessity, needs to be killed, and this creates a kind of ownership of a type of aggres-sion that permits mourning. I think what was so interesting about Franco's talk was that he was talking about individuals who have dangerously empty lives, who can fill these lives with perverse delusional constructions which are then acted out in sadomaso-chistic ways, often violently, involving sexual abuse, physical abuse, and so on, which is very different from genuine object related aggression in the form of hate. Hate presupposes an object: we know people we hate. Franco was referring to an escalation of excitement in perverse narcissistic violence that doesn't involve hate. Hateless crimes is a very interesting idea, and there are parallels to be drawn with Rosine's thinking. Franco knows much more about this than I do, so he may like to elaborate."

Brian Martindale: "Franco, while are waiting for Rosine to join us, would you like to share these ideas with the wider audience who weren't with you this morning?"

Franco De Masi: "The purpose of my paper is to distinguish between aggression and destructiveness, because I think that aggression can be defensive or violent against an object who is the object of hate. In destructiveness, there is no hate for the object; there is exultation and triumph, excitation without hate. This is the problem with serial killers. Serial killers don't hate their victims: they have an exultant state of pleasure in which they can dissect, murder, and torture without hating. My proposal is to demonstrate that when there is hate, there is a human relationship, but in a perverse state of mind no human relationship with the object exists. The child who becomes a pervert is in a psychic retreat and is always fantasizing about terrible acts against the other *without* being aggressive. The patient I spoke about was a patient who had the most terrible fantasies. His main fantasy was that he was in a war bunker working as an anatomist, a pathologist who dissects corpses. He also had a fantasy of killing little dogs, but he was quite unable to defend himself or give an aggressive answer to his schoolmates when they attacked and bullied him. There is a great difference between aggression and destructiveness. Hate is a terrible feeling that you want to expel from your mind. When you kill a person or hurt a person the action is finished, albeit with grave consequences. When you take pleasure in fantasy, the pleasure can augment the aggressiveness. Even when the aggressiveness is finished the destructiveness is not at an end, because it is without hate, and so persists."

Brian Martindale: "Would anybody like to take this further, or comment?"

Question from the floor: "It sounds to me as if what you are talking about is what we have long learnt to be the difference between the life and death instincts."

Franco De Masi: "Yes, but according to Freud aggressiveness is a part of the libido. Libido is a vital action, a vital drive for conquering something, but we have to distinguish aggression against a bad object from aggression towards good objects. I am in a perverse, criminal state of mind when I am aggressive against a good object. From a criminal point of view, to be honest is not a good idea as it goes against his aggression towards a good object."

Question from the floor: "The other side, on the other hand, which is equally gratifying, is the death drive: it's not libido, it's exactly the opposite, but is intensely gratifying and has to be recurrently satisfied?"

Franco De Masi: "I think that the death instinct doesn't exist. I think that some people become destructive when they have had some trauma in their infancy. When there are traumas you can develop a violent reaction. You are a borderline patient or psychopath or pervert or psychotic in a secondary way because you have a retreated in your infancy and you are exalted by identifying with a destructive figure or character."

Question from the floor: "This is interesting because I don't believe in the death drive because there is just one drive, which is trying to extinguish itself immediately, so every drive is a kind of sexual and death drive and human sexuality exists because we are condemned to die. If we didn't die we wouldn't have sexuality. So, from the beginning, there is one drive which is furnishing a kind of lust and this lust has to be immediately reduced. The only things we have are education, information, language, and so on. They provide the solution, but there remains always the problem of the good object existing in relation to the bad object, so there is a problem about reducing the bad as there is a risk of reducing the good. Perhaps you cannot reduce aggression because at the same time you reduce libido also."

Brian Martindale: "Thank you for your interesting response. Anybody like to take this further . . . Franco?"

Franco De Masi: "The problem of sexuality is a terribly complicated one in clinical work. I think that there are two kinds of sexuality:

one kind is mixed with love and another kind is excitement. When you are doing therapy with a perverse patient, you can find that these patients were in a sexualized retreat as children and experimented in orgasm, mental orgasm. This is a description by Freud when he spoke about the child being beaten. This kind of patient knew about sexuality and orgasm when they were a child. Normally, we experience orgasm when we are grown up, after adolescence, but these patients have a sexuality, a fantasy subordinated to an act of power over other people, so we have to distinguish normal sexuality from pathological sexuality. If sexuality is linked to an object it is essentially a good sexuality. This is a complex question, but is very important: perhaps the next conference should be on sexuality."

John Alderdice: "I wonder if I might make a brief comment about this, as I know Don mentioned it in his paper at the start and a number of other people have commented on the question of the death instinct in a fairly dismissive way. One observation I would make about psychoanalytic theories is that the theories that people develop are dependent upon the cases that they work with. People develop different kinds of theories depending on whether they work with neurotic patients or psychotic patients or people with disturbed personalities and so on, and they look at the theories that someone developed from a different set of cases and work and they say, 'What a strange idea that was'. I think there is good evidence for Freud's ideas on the death instinct not coming directly from his clinical work, although there were connections with the clinical work. I think it came from the experience of the First World War and trying to make sense of that afterwards. But what happened after the Second World War was that psychoanalysis as a profession largely turned away from the external world because it was so awful. The experience of the vast majority of psychoanalysts was so traumatic and so dreadful that they turned away from trying to understand what had happened in the Second World War and buried themselves in clinical work. This is a very understandable phenomenon. It meant, for example, that when I started looking at the external world from a psychoanalytic perspective, you can go back to the 1930s and find writings which were really relevant. If people focus very much on individual clinical work they may not find so much need for an understanding of a death instinct or some-thing in that realm, as I'm not sure they are looking at what Freud was trying to look at, which was what happens at a group and wider communal level. A concern I would have is that people move away from the external world as though the external world is just something that happens on the basis of the internal world, without any reality of its own. Both are important. What Freud said about the death instinct came from the experience of seeing millions and millions of people dying at the hands of other people, something that nobody in this generation has seen."

Brian Martindale: "Thank you, John, for that interesting social comment on our field. Rosine is on the telephone. Hello, Rosine, it's Brian Martindale."

Rosine Perelberg: "Hello, Brian."

Brian Martindale: "Just to say by way of introduction that there was enormous appreciation and interest in your paper yesterday, Rosine, and as you know we are now having a plenary session with a number of us at the table here who have been contributing to the last two days. We'd like to have you for 20 minutes or so as we have two or three questions we'd like to involve you in, perhaps with some dialogue with one or two members of the panel."

Rosine Perelberg: "Sure. Could I at some point comment on what the last speaker was saying towards the end?"

Brian Martindale: "Why don't you start with that, go ahead and make a response to John?"

Rosine Perelberg: "From what I was hearing, it was the connection between the death instinct and what is going on in the external world, and that Freud was taking this into account. I would agree with that: however, I also think there are dimensions of clinical work that led Freud to have an interest in the death instinct and the two pieces of clinical dimensions that he was interested in most were opposite and negative therapeutic reactions. Even more important was the repetition compulsion. I think that the repetition compulsion tends sometimes to be forgotten when thinking about the death instinct, perhaps because, in the British tradition, the death instinct has been in a way reduced to destructiveness, largely due to the influence of Kleinian theory, and the repetition compulsion itself has been abandoned, while it has gained a lot of importance elsewhere, in France especially. The repetition compulsion is very relevant to today. It denotes something that has not reached representation. It has been developed in many places, including in France in the work of André Green, who relates to the negative. Up until this work, every drive corresponded to representation and to the repetition compulsion. Then there arose the thing that could not be represented before, and I think Green introduces this to the work of psychotherapy, psychoanalysis, in a very special way because this sort of patient who comes to our consulting rooms today is the borderline patient, the perverse patient, the violent patient, who function at the level of acting out. Our work with them is to try to reach representation of meaning that might be connected to their behaviour. The repetition compulsion is, therefore, a very important dimension that Freud brought in when he was discussing the death instinct, but I would make a plea for maintaining an understanding of this dimension of psychic reality as it is so crucial in our contemporary clinical work with patients who are severely disturbed."

Brian Martindale: "That's a very helpful comment; thank you, Rosine. I now move on to the questions in front of me. In your talk, you spent quite a lot of time outlining the meaning of violent acts, and one thing that's been around today, given that Franco DeMasi is here on the panel, is the following question: 'Are there violent acts that don't carry meaning?' Do you want time to think about that, or would you like to hear Franco's point of view to understand how and why this question has come up?"

Rosine Perelberg: "Yes, of course."

Brian Martindale: "Franco?"

Franco De Masi: "I think that destructiveness or violence without meaning occurs when the psychotic part has conquered the sane part, so that the patient is conscious of acting but has no insight into the crime. The aggressive behaviour is without meaning because he is not inside it: the psychotic part of the personality has, with propaganda, conquered his mind. In treating perverse or psychotic patients, I think it is better to have a model from post-Kleinian analysts like Herbert Rosenfeld, Meltzer, or Bion, who describe the patient as splitting in two. The sane part and the psychotic part are two separate parts and they are not in equilibrium. The aim of the psychotic part is to conquer all the mind of the patient."

Brian Martindale: "Franco, would you say the aim of the psychotic one is to destroy any meaning?"

Franco De Masi: "Yes."

Brian Martindale: "Rosine, would you like to come in?"

Rosine Perelberg: "It's very interesting to look at self selection and the way certain kinds of patients reach analysts. I remember an example that Mervin Glasser gave at one of the scientific meetings of The British Psychoanalytic Society of a man who kept going to the Portman once or twice a week to complain that his neighbour was trying to kill him. It was interesting that the man wasn't going to the police, he was going to the Portman, so somewhere he had some kind of sense that the Portman could help him with his problem. When I think about the kind of patients I saw in a young adults' research group, or the kind of patients people see at the Portman, or Carine sees at Broadmoor, I think they are different, with different configurations needing different kinds of work. In terms of the patients who for some reason reach psychoanalysis, and Carl, the violent patient I talked about, it was very important to identify that the violent act contained a narrative that had unconscious meaning and, in a way, it was the unconscious meaning that led to the violent behaviour. I also saw this in twenty-eight patients in the context of a young adults' research group at the Anna Freud Centre over a period of ten years. They were very violent and disturbed patients and part of our task was not only to derive meaning, but, more importantly, to understand the way in which this meaning was what was being repeated in the transference, linking it with the idea of the repetition compulsion. If you believe that meaning is already there in the unconscious, the therapeutic task is to reach that unconscious meaning, but there is a problem with these patients as, more often than not, meaning is something that is reached though a process of construction precisely because there was the absence before. I think this is a profound difference between some of the authors that I think were being mentioned before and the Kleinian tradition, where you think that the unconscious meaning is there and that the analytic task is to reach it, as opposed to some of the work that is present in other traditions, including France. Through the analytic process or through therapy one constructs meaning, so it's something new that is derived from the current work in the context of working with these patients."

Brian Martindale: "Can I just interrupt for moment, as you may not have heard Franco agree with me that actually in this discussion, in the psychotic mind, meaning has been destroyed in that area of the mind so there is either no meaning or, I would think in the case where you say the person is accusing someone of trying to murder them but turns up at the Portman, that actually the attempt to destroy meaning has only been partly successful and traces of the meaning are still there. I think Franco was suggesting that maybe in some patients there is no meaning there."

Franco De Masi: "A good example of Leslie Sohn's was a patient who tried to kill normal people unknown to him, and Sohn asked the patient why he tried to kill an unknown person. The patient was psychotic and was searching for money from an institution. The institution said to him there was no money, so he would have to come back the next week."

Carine Minne: "The benefits office."

Franco De Masi: "Yes, the benefits office. This patient had a figure in his mind, a woman who, when he was frustrated was able to give him many beautiful things, including sexual things, but in this case his fantasy figure did not appear to him in his mind and he was so full of rage against men who, in his view, were indifferent to his fury that he tried to push a man under a train. Apparently this act of violence was not possible to ignore, and the reason why becomes clearer once we take a view of an internal war within the individual and the actions of a psychotic part on the very small, child self part of the personality."

Brian Martindale: "Can I check, Rosine, whether you can hear Franco?"

Rosine Perelberg: "Not fully but the thought that comes to my mind is that there is a very complex narrative, if I understand what he is telling us. I don't fully understand how this can be connected to a lack of meaning: it feels as if there is a lot that is being communicated, which includes confusion between internal and external. Trying to deal with an internal reality through killing something in the external world isn't it. So, if there is meaning, that's one thing. The other thing that comes to my mind is what Freud said about the psychotic phenomenon. It contains bits of things that were hurt and experienced before the psychotic behaviour took place, so it always contains in its narrative a communication about the person's past experiences."

Brian Martindale: " Respond once more, Franco, and then we'll move onto another question."

Franco De Masi: "I think that not everything can transfer in transference. We do need to understand the internal world of the patient before we can say something of meaning to him, but not all could be transferred in transference."

Brian Martindale: "Rosine, I'm going to move on and ask a question that is addressed to John, but I'm going to address it to the whole panel as I think it cuts across all the different topics. It's a general question, but I think it might help to round our discussion up. It's from Brian McKenzie 'Let's say there has been a historical injury. What determines a more adaptive response versus a non adaptive response?' To my mind, this question is really a lot about what this conference has been about. I'm going to ask all the panel members. Rosine, we've got Marianne Parsons and Marie Zaphiriou

Woods here as well, so I think those who work with children will have something to say about what are the factors we think that lead to an adaptive response and what leads to maladaptive response."

John Alderdice: "It seems to me that the kinds of things that can make for a more adaptive response can occur at an individual and group level, and between which are connections. If there has been some previous personal internal experience and/or cultural and social experience that enables people to think and explore with some degree of confidence that a better outcome is possible, rather than feeling that a horrible thing has happened again because it's always horrible things that happen and thus there is no solution, the situation is already much better. If there are ways of exploring these things at a social level—public debate, discussion, disagreement, understanding, etc., in relation to current, established views, or at an individual level, so much the better. If any capacity for review is in some way blocked, this will have negative consequences. If somebody experiences something really difficult and unpleasant, and they are doped up so the chemical culture internally doesn't permit review, or they live in a context where talking about these things is not permitted, this bodes ill. Culturally, it's the same thing: if there are repeated insults or traumas, if there is no capacity for political, intellectual, democratic engagement that allows these things to be processed, then trauma is much less likely to be able to be dealt with. Having said all of that, I don't think we truly know the answer to the question you're asking. Why is it that some people who are abused become abusers and others go on to lead highly constructive lives? There are still things we don't understand, and where this is true at the individual level, it is even truer at the communal and societal level."

Marie Zaphiriou Woods: "Anna Freud said, in observing how children survived the blitz in the Second World War, that the children who stayed in London and who had bombs falling all around them but who had their mother present with them, experienced the relationship as continuing. Feelings could be acknowledged, even terrible fears thought about together, and these children did a lot better than the ones that were sent away to apparent safety, away from the real dangers of bombs falling, but separated from the people whom they knew and who made them feel emotionally safe, instead placed with families of strangers they didn't know."

Brian Martindale: "A very helpful example, I think."

James Gilligan: "This question is so fundamental that it almost involves all of the theory and practice of psychoanalysis really to answer it. It reminds me of the work of E. James Anthony and others on the so-called invulnerable child. Some children grow up in horrendous circumstances with terribly dysfunctional families, yet they turn out pretty healthy and engage in adaptive behaviour patterns as opposed sometimes to their own siblings, for example, or others in a similar dysfunctional family. One answer that these researchers came up with, and this is really just a continuation of Anna Freud's observation that was just mentioned, was that the child who survived well from a traumatic background had been able to find at least one adult in their environment whom they could trust, whom they could relate to, and in some cases this was enough to enable them to internalize a more healthy identification figure and develop better defences. A second thing that I mention in my own work with violent criminals that is an important difference between those who commit acts of serious violence, which I think we can call maladapted behaviour, versus those who don't, even if they may be experiencing some of the same psychological experiences, such as deep humiliation, do not perceive themselves as possessing non-violent means by which to restore their self-esteem. All of us in this room, everybody at one time or another, experiences humiliation, and yet none of us engages in the kind of violence that people do who get sent to prison. One reason for that is obvious: we have lots of other resources available, non-violent resources by means of which to maintain our self-esteem and our sense of personal equilibrium. The people who wind up in prison have almost none of the internal and external resources that we do. But the question would take a whole textbook to answer, because it raises so many fundamental questions about human functioning."

Brian Martindale: "Rosine, can you hear the discussion so far? Would you like to make a comment then Carine?"

Rosine Perelberg: "Yes, I have been very interested in what the last three speakers have been saying and I totally agree. I think one thing that becomes evident to me is how we cannot predict, that our studies and conclusions tend to be retrospective. A couple of examples come to mind. When we started our research with young adults and we had Anna Higgett and Anthony Bateman doing assessments of the various kinds of psychopathologies that our patients presented, which we obviously, as clinicians, only heard about ten years later because we were kept blind to their conclusions for the purposes of the research, they made a few predictions about the patients who would do well, and actually none of their predictions came true in spite of their very careful work. None of it was predictive of outcome, because what became non-predictive but retrospective was that we found out that the patients who did better were the ones with whom the analyst worked more slowly. The single fact that seemed to be most correlated with good outcome was the technique utilized by the analyst. The kinds of interpretations that did well were the ones that were closest to preconscious formulations as opposed to unconscious formulations. The other thing that comes to mind is research done at the Tavistock years ago in relation to thousands of baby observations. When they did a retrospective study, none of the predictions with regard to the likely outcome of the babies came true. I think there is quite a lot of evidence to indicate that we are not very good at predictions. What happens subsequently has such an enormous impact, and this, I think, gives us a lot of room as therapists, so that our work can powerfully influence the outcome of what happens to our patients."

Brian Martindale: "Thank you, Rosine. Carine, would you like to speak?"

Carine Minne: "Just to continue the shopping list of required ingredients for adaptation, I was thinking that maybe we shouldn't forget two factors: one is brain development, which depends on the kind of nurturing or loving that has happened in the first year in particular, and especially the first six months. Professor Gatat Holt, based in Bremn in Germany, has been able to show that the development of the brain in the first six months is flawed if the baby has not been loved adequately. There is a beautiful book on this, entitled *Why Love Matters*, by Sue Gerhardt. The other thing that came to mind was constitutional factors. A wonderful talk took place at the Portman clinic by a man called Stephen Swarme, who has been doing research on rhesus monkeys for decades, with extraordinary results. He was researching monkeys who had psychopathic behaviours and was finally able to trace a genetic predisposition ,so whether it was expressed or not depended on the kind of mothering and nurturing these baby monkeys would have had. Those who had genetic predisposition were then divided into two groups. One group was peer raised, and practically all of them became psychopathic and very disturbed because they didn't have proper adult figures in their lives. Some of them with the genetic predisposition towards psychopathic behaviour were adopted by what were called super mothers, and not only did they not have the psychopathic behaviour, the actual genetic expression altered so that the next generation no longer had the predisposition. It is astonishing work."

Brian Martindale: "We have bit of time for Marianne and Franco. I'm sorry there are a couple of questions that we're not going to have time for, but I think we should stick to our time frame."

Marie Zaphiriou Woods: "Just a quick point to follow on about the importance of the mother. I think that in working with people who are initially too traumatized to think, it may be important to be very patient and to wait until they are able to use you, the analyst, as an object, in a Winnicottian sense. This links to the findings to which Rosine refers, about the value of working slowly."

Brian Martindale: "Thank you."

Franco De Masi: "I think the possibility for a natural growing up depends on the amount of trauma the child receives from the first months of his life. I think that there are many findings from psycho-analysts who do infant research, Beebe and Lachman come to mind, for example, who describe how the pre-verbal interrelationship between mother and baby constitutes a prototype in the uncon-scious. It is very important that the actions of the mother towards the baby are mild, comprising kisses, cuddles, and so on, and a pre-verbal dialogue that is the prototype of the construction of an unconscious. I think that in the very ill patient, this action, this structure, did not take place, and we create a patient without an unconscious. They are able to act but not to think, and this is a very important emotional trauma."

Brian Martindale: "Very interesting. I think I am going to draw the plenary to an end and to thank all of you for all the questions and comments you have made. Thank you very much, Rosine, and all the panellists for their very lively and interesting contributions."

Closing remarks by
Philip McGarry

I would like to close the conference by thanking the speakers, the chairs, and the audience for making this a wonderful occasion. We have had two days of intelligent, sophisticated debate on a very complex and fascinating topic and many of us will carry a lot away from these discussions. As I said before, the proceedings will be published in a book by Karnac, so do look out for this on their website and the Royal College website. On behalf of the Royal College of Psychiatrists, I would like to thank all of our partner organizations who helped to run this conference: the Centre for Psychotherapy in Belfast, the British Psychoanalytic Society, the Northern Ireland Association for the Study of Psychoanalysis, and the Northern Ireland Institute of Human Relations. I would also like to thank some of our supporters: the Department of Health, the Northern Ireland Assembly, Belfast City Council, and Pfizer Pharmaceuticals for their support. I would like to thank the Hilton Hotel, who did a tremendous job in terms of organizing the meeting and excellent hospitality. I would also like to thank Savilles Audio Visual. On Wednesday, we had an anxiety over how we were going to make things work given the threat of the volcanic ash, and I think things worked very well indeed. Please do not forget to fill in your feedback forms. There is still a chance to get to City Hall this evening, and the tour is at 6.45 p.m., meal at 7.30 p.m. Finally, but by no means least, I would like to thank the staff of the office of the Royal College. Nora and Lisa spent many months putting this conference together. We were doing really well until Monday, when the ash cloud reappeared, and it is extraordinary what Nora and Lisa did to make things work as well as they have. For those of you coming to the dinner tonight, I look forward to seeing you, and for those unable to come, this is our second very successful conference and perhaps it will become a tradition every two years. I look forward to seeing you in 2012. Now, tell your friends and colleagues about how wonderful Belfast is. Thank you!"

INDEX

Abram, J., 110, 114
abuse
    child, 31–32, 83, 85, 103, 143, 204,
        206, 219
    physical, 181, 210
    ritual, 102–103
    sexual, 2, 32, 103, 210
    substance, 120
    verbal, 120
addict/addiction, 26, 33, 35–36, 39,
    103, 144, 151, 153
adolescence, 1, 5, 11, 23–24, 32, 55,
    117–120, 122, 125, 127–129, 133,
    139, 154, 213
aggression
    affective, 8, 21, 25
    development of, 109, 111, 117
    function of, 41
    inhibition of, 113
    nature of, 12, 41, 143, 183
    predatory, 8, 21, 25
    primary, 8
    ruthless, 7–11, 14, 20
    sadistic, 8, 14, 20

self-preservative, 8–10
types of, 7, 210
understanding of, xviii, 8, 182
use of, 121, 135, 176
Alderdice, Lord J., 5, 169–170,
    187–196, 199, 201–204, 207–210,
    213–214, 218–219
Alexander, F., 101
Alvarez, A., xii, xvii, 9, 23–24, 29,
    31–32, 37, 39–40, 98
ambivalence, 48, 111–112, 118, 127,
    142, 183
America, 175, 178–180, 183, 187,
    195, 198–199, 202, 208
American Medical Association, 92
American Psychiatric Association,
    26, 37
Americans, 178
    African, 99, 204
    Democrats, 199
    Hispanic, 99
    Native, 179
    Republicans, 105, 198
Anders, G., 147, 162, 168